The Besterman World Bibliographies

The Besterman World Bibliographies

History *and* Geography

A BIBLIOGRAPHY OF BIBLIOGRAPHIES

By Theodore Besterman

VOLUME THREE

TOTOWA, N.J.

Rowman and Littlefield

1972

Published by
Rowman and Littlefield
A Division of
Littlefield, Adams & Co.
81 Adams Drive
Totowa, N. J. 07512

★

Copyright © 1939, 1947, 1965, 1971
by Theodore Besterman
Printed in the United States of America

★

Typography by George Hornby
and Theodore Besterman

ISBN 0-87471-057-X

Contents

Europe

1688–1745

MABEL D[ESBOROUGH] ALLARDYCE, Aberdeen
university library [William M.] MacBean collection. A catalogue of books, pamphlets, broadsides,
portraits, etc. in the Stuart and Jacobite collection.
Aberdeen university studies (no.126): Aberdeen
1949. pp.xxvi.307. [4500.]

1688–1807

THE STUART and jacobite exiles, 1688–1807.
General works. Library of Congress: Washington
1948. ff.13. [80.]*

1700–1715

WILLIAM THOMAS MORGAN [vol.v: and CHLOE
SINER MORGAN], A bibliography of british history
(1700–1715). With special reference to the reign
of queen Anne. Indiana university studies (vols.
xviii &c. = Studies 94 &c.): Bloomington.

    i. 1700–1707. . . . (xviii–xix = 94–95): 1934.
        pp.xvii.524. [5750.]

    ii. 1708–1715. . . . (xxiii–xxiv = 114–118):
        1937. pp.vi.684. [5750.]

    iii. [Source and secondary material]. . . .
        (xxv = 119–122): 1939. pp.viii.705. [5000.]

    iv. [Manuscripts]. . . . (xxvi = 123): 1942.
        pp.381. [large number.]

v. [Supplements, indexes] . . . (xxvi = 124): 1942. pp.xiv.487. [1000.]

1714–1789

STANLEY PARGELLIS and D[UDLEY] J[ULIUS] MEDLEY, *edd.* Bibliography of british history: the eighteenth century, 1714–1789. American historical association *and* Royal historical society: Oxford 1951. pp.xxvi.643. [4558.]

READERS' guide to hanoverian Britain. Library association: County libraries section: [Readers' guide (new series, no.14): 1952]. pp.35. [400.]

1714–1910

HANDLIST of proclamations issued by royal and other constitutional authorities, 1714–1910. Wigan [printed] 1913. pp.iii–xxiii.coll.836. pp. 184. [16,000.]

200 copies privately printed.

1743

GUSTAV STADELMANN, Bibliographie der schlacht bei Dettingen, nebst verzeichnis der vorhandenen abbildungen und pläne. Aschaffenburg [1929]. pp.30. [145.]

1760–1775

JOSEPH REDINGTON [vols.iii–iv: RICHARD AR-

THUR ROBERTS], Calendar of Home office papers of the reign of George III. 1760 (25 Oct.)–1765 [–1775]. 1878–1899. pp.[v].xxvi.808+[v].xl.684 +[v].lxiv.736+[v].xlvii.636. [10,000.]

no more published.

1812

BRIEF list of references on the war of 1812. Library of Congress: Washington 1922. ff.2. [12.]*

1815–1909

RECENT british history. Being the history of the United Kingdom of Great Britain and Ireland from 1815 to 1909. [Historical association]: Leaflet (no.18): 1910. pp.8. [150.]

1815–1948

BENJAMIN SACKS, Teaching bibliography for Great Britain and the British empire since 1815. Albuquerque, N.M. [1949]. pp.[ii].ii.111. [1750.]

1870–1914

[ULRICH BARTHOLD], Bibliographie zur ge-schichte des Britischen reiches 1870–1914. Welt-kriegsbücherei: Bibliographische vierteljahrshefte (no.6): Stuttgart 1935. pp.58. [1200.]

1899–1902

HENRY E. HAFERKORN, The South african war,

1899–1902. A bibliography. U.S. Army engineer school: Washington barracks, D.C. 1924. pp.72. [543.]

J[EAN] G[IDEON] KESTING, The anglo-boer war. . . . Mounting tension, and the outbreak of hostilities as reflected in overseas magazine contributions published January–December 1899. A bibliography. University of Cape Town: School of librarianship: Bibliographical series: [Capetown] 1956. pp.[v].xii.51. [242.]*

1900–

HENRY R[ALPH] WINKLER, Great Britain in the twentieth century. American historical association: Service center for teachers of history: Publication (no.28): Washington [1960]. pp.30. [100.]

an earlier edition appeared in the Journal of modern history (*1960*), *xxxii*.

1914–1918

MAURICE BOURGEOIS, Catalogue méthodique des fonds britannique et nord-américain de la Bibliothèque. Société de l'histoire de la guerre: Publications (1st ser. = Catalogue des 'Bibliothèques et Musée de la guerre').

    i. La crise internationale. 1925. pp.vii.161. [3109.]

Europe

ii. La vie politique, économique et sociale (questions générales). 1926. pp.[iii].120. [2341.]

iii. L'Empire britannique, la Grande-Bretagne et la guerre. 1931. pp.[iii].296. [6222.]

[MAX GUNZENHÄUSER], Bibliographie zur geschichte des Britischen reiches im weltkrieg 1914–1918. 2. . . . . auflage. Weltkriegsbücherei: Bibliographische vierteljahrshefte (no.8/9): Stuttgart 1936. pp.124. [3900.]

1918–1935

[MAX GUNZENHÄUSER], Bibliographie zur geschichte des Britischen reiches in der nachkriegszeit. Weltkriegsbücherei: Bibliographische vierteljahrshefte (no.10): Stuttgart 1936. pp.72. [2000.]

1926–1960

C[HARLES] L[OCH] MOWAT, British history since 1926. A select bibliography. Historical association: Helps for students of history (no.61): 1960. pp.32. [450.]

vi. *Miscellaneous*

J. A. BUCKLEY and W. T. WILLIAMS, A guide to british historical fiction. 1912. pp.182. [656.]
a bibliography of fiction bearing on the history of the British empire.

HISTORY for boys and girls, 10–17. Public libraries: Bromley 1955. pp.18. [200.]*

5. *Topography and local history*

i. *Bibliographies*

ARTHUR L. HUMPHREYS, A handbook to county bibliography, being a bibliography of bibliographies relating to the counties and towns of Great Britain and Ireland. 1917. pp.x.503. [6000.]

ii. *Manuscripts*

[ARTHUR AGARD], The repertorie of records: remaining in the 4. treasuries on the receipt side at Westminster; the two remembrancers of the exchequer. . . . As also, a most exact calender [by Thomas Powell] of all those records of the Tovver: in which, are contayned and comprised whatsoever may give satisfaction to the searcher, for tenure or tytle of any thing. 1631. pp.[viii].217. [100,000.]

EDWARD JONES, Index to records called, the originalia and memoranda on the Lord treasurer's remembrancer's side of the exchequer. 1793–1795. pp.[xviii].xlviii.[360]+[528]. [25,000.]

CALENDARIUM rotulorum patentium in Turri londinensi. [Commissioners on the public records:] 1802. pp.[vii].464. [25,000.]

SIR T[HOMAS] PHILLIPPS, *ed.* Index of leases of manors and lands in England, granted since the reformation, annis 4 and 5 Edw. 6. Edited ... from the original ms. ... in the library of Wm. Wynne. 1832. pp.[v].32. [1750.]

WALTER RYE, Records and record searching. A guide to the genealogist and topographer. 1888. pp.[iii].ii.ii.204. [very large number.]
—— Second edition. 1897. pp.viii.253. [very large number.]

[ALFRED L. HARDY], Lists of manor court rolls in private hands. Manorial society's monographs (nos. 1, 2, 4): 1907–1910. pp.[ii].iv.21+[ii].iv.25+[ii].ii.23. [1500.]
—— Part I. Second edition. 1913. pp.[ii].iv.23. [500.]

[HORACE HEADLAM], List of rentals and surveys and other analogous documents. Public record office: Lists and indexes (no.xxv): 1908. pp.[iii].446. [9000.]

E. MARGARET THOMPSON, A descriptive catalogue of manorial rolls belonging to sir H. F. Burke.

Manorial society's publications (nos.xi–xii): 1922–1923. pp.[ii].20+[ii].58. [827.]

F. TAYLOR, Court rolls, rentals, surveys, and analogous documents in the John Rylands library. Manchester 1948. pp.44. [335.]

iii. *General*

[RICHARD RAWLINSON], The english topographer: or, an historical account, (as far as can be collected from printed books and manuscripts) of all the pieces that have been written relating to the antiquities, natural history, or topographical description of any part of England. . . . By an impartial hand. 1720. pp.[viii].275.[xiii]. [1000.]

JOHN WORRALL, Bibliotheca topographica anglicana: or, a new and compleat catalogue of all the books extant relating to the antiquity, description, and natural history of England. 1736. pp.64. [500.]

[RICHARD GOUGH], Anecdotes of british topography. Or, an historical account of what has been done for illustrating the topographical antiquities of Great Britain and Ireland. 1768. pp.[ii]. xxxvi.740.[xxxiv]. [3000.]

[—] — [Second edition]. British topography [&c.]. 1780. pp.[ii].lii.792.[lix] + [ii].822.[lxi]. [10,000.]

a copy in the Cambridge university library contains cuttings and ms. additions by John Britton.

[BULKELEY BANDINEL], A catalogue of the books, relating to british topography, and saxon and northern literature, bequeathed to the Bodleian library ... by Richard Gough. Oxford 1814. pp. 4.459. [topography: 7000.]

SIR RICHARD COLT HOARE, A catalogue of books relating to the history and topography of England, Wales, Scotland, Ireland. 1815. pp.viii.361. [5000.]
25 copies printed.

WILLIAM UPCOTT, A bibliographical account of the principal works relating to english topography. 1818. pp.[viii].lxiii.642+[iii].581–1068+ [iii].1069–1576. [5000.]

[JOHN BOWYER NICHOLS], Catalogue of the Hoare library at Stourhead, co. Wilts. 1840. pp. xxvi.780. [10,000.]
privately printed.

JOHN CAMDEN HOTTEN, A hand-book to the topography and family history of England and Wales. [1863]. pp.viii.368. [8000.]

JOHN PARKER ANDERSON, The book of british topography. A classified catalogue of the topographical works in the library of the British museum relating to Great Britain and Ireland. 1881. pp.xvi.472. [7500.]
the British museum pressmarks are added in ms. to one of the copies in that library.

A CATALOGUE of the library collected by John Stansfeld, Leeds, comprising a complete series of county histories and local topographies . . . heraldic and genealogical publications. 1882. pp. [iii].228.61. [1000.]
privately printed.

[JOHN] POTTER BRISCOE, British topography and local history. Public libraries: Class list (no.13): Nottingham 1888. pp.34. [1500.]

F[ELIX] LIEBERMANN, Literatur von etwa 1890–1892 zur geschichte Englands . . . mit einem anhange zur bibliographie britischer ortsgeschichte im m.a. Freiburg i. B. 1892. pp.81–208.

CHARLES H. HUNT and WILLIAM T. MONTGOMERY, Where shall I spend my holidays? [Books and maps in the Central public library relating to holiday resorts within the British isles]. Public library: Bootle [1905]. pp.15. [400.]

LIST of works relating to british genealogy and local history. New York 1910. pp.366. [local history: 8500.]

[J. T. SPALDING, A bibliographical account of the works relating to english topography in the library of John Tricks Spalding. Exeter 1912–1913. pp.[viii].464+[v].400+[v].369+[v].459+[v].445. [6500.]
privately printed.

C. G. BEASLEY, Local geography. A guide with sources of information. 1924. pp.24. [150.]

A[LEXANDER] HAMILTON THOMPSON, A short bibliography of local history. Historical association: Leaflet (no.72): 1928. pp.16. [200.]
[—] — Second edition. A short bibliography and list of sources for the study of local history and antiquities. Prepared by the local history committee. Historical association: Special series (S2): 1952. pp.74. [1000.]

BRITAIN and Ireland for the traveller. Prepared by the Travel association. [National book council:] Book list (no.129): 1930. pp.[3]. [125.]

OUR own country. Public libraries: Bristol 1932. pp.48. [1250.]

G. E. FUSSELL, The exploration of England. A

select bibliography of travel and topography: 1570–1815. 1935. pp.56. [353.]

[KATHLEEN CONYNGHAM GREENE], Everyman in the eastern counties. Great books by famous writers of special local interest. Everyman's literary guides to the British Isles (no.7): [1937]. pp.[8]. [50.]

limited to works included in Everyman's library.

THE FACE of England and Wales. Library association: County libraries section: Readers' guide (no.23): 1939. pp.28. [400.]

E. C. WILLIAMS, Britain — land and life. National book council: Book list (no.163): 1940. pp.[4]. [110.]

EDWARD GODFREY COX, A reference guide to the literature of travel, including voyages, geographical descriptions, adventures, shipwrecks and expeditions. Vol.III. Great Britain. University of Washington: Publications in language and literature (vol.xii): Seattle 1949. pp.xiii.732. [5000.]

READERS' guide to the face of England. Library association: County libraries section: [Readers' guide (new series, no.13): 1951]. pp.44. [2000.]

SCENERY of Great Britain and Ireland in aquatint and lithography, 1770–1860, from the library

of J[ohn] R[oland] Abbey. A bibliographical catalogue. 1952. pp.xx.399. [556.]
privately printed.

THE ENGLISH counties, 1558–1953. A coronation month exhibition. Public library: Leamington [1953]. pp.20. [152.]

SUBJECT index to periodicals. Regional lists. Library association: 1954 &c.
brief duplicated lists setting out articles of local interest, county by county.

WINIFRED COTTERILL DONKIN, An outline bibliography of the northern region. University of Durham: King's college [&c.]: Newcastle upon Tyne 1956. pp.40. [354.]

EXPLORING Britain. Surrey county library: Book list (no.21): [Esher 1960]. pp.50. [350.]*

CATALOGUE of an exhibition of borough charters. British records association: [1960]. pp.52. [71.]

EAST ANGLIAN bibliography. A check-list of publications not in the British national bibliography. Library association: Eastern branch: Norwich.*

1–3. 1960. pp.12.12.20. [200.]

 4–7. 1961. pp.12.12.16.11. [200.]
 8–10. 1962. pp.11.16.12. [150.]
 11. 1962–1963. pp.11. [100.]
no more published?

w[ILLIAM] r[AYMOND] POWELL, Local history from blue books. A select list of the sessional papers of the House of commons. Historical association: Helps for students of history (no.64): 1962. pp.43. [750.]

ENGLAND for the foreign visitor. Surrey county library: Book list: [Esher] 1963. pp.[iii].9. [50.]★

THE NORTH MIDLAND bibliography. [Ilkeston].★
 i. 1963. Editor R. A. H. O'Neal. pp.16.33.31. 48. [800.]
in progress.

Greatham.

A[LAN] A[RTHUR] DIBBEN, The Greatham archives. A catalogue. West Sussex county council: Chichester 1962. pp.xviii.22. [138.]

Greece.

ARNOLD [DIETRICH] SCHAEFER, Abriss der quellenkunde der griechischen geschichte bis auf Polybios. Leipzig 1867. pp.[iii].109. [500.]

— — Vierte auflage, besorgt von Heinrıch Nissen. Abrisz der quellenkunde der griechischen und römischen geschichte. . . . Erste abteilung. Griechische geschichte. 1889. pp.vi.118. [500.]

ANTONIOS MELIARAKES, Νεοελληνικη γεωγρα-φικη φιλολογια ἠτοι καταλογος των ἀπο του 1800–1889 γεωγραφηθεντων ὑπο Ἑλλη-νων. Ἀθηναις 1889. pp.Δ'. 128. [1450.]

ADOLF BAUER, Die forschungen zur griechischen geschichte 1888–1898 verzeichnet und besprochen. München 1899. pp.[iv].574. [1000.]
on works relating to the history of ancient Greece published in 1888–1898.

[C. JIREČEK and K. KRUMBACHER], Plan eines corpus der griechischen urkunden des mittel-alters und der neueren zeit. Königliche bayerische akademie der wissenschaften: München 1903. pp. 124. [1500.]
the text actually consists of Paul Marc, Register über das byzantinische und neugriechische urkun-denmaterial.

SELECT list of references on Hellenism and the influence of Greece on civilization. Library of Congress: Washington 1913. ff.4. [35.]*

MAX CARY [MAX OTTO BISMARCK CASPARI], The documentary sources of greek history. Oxford 1927. pp.xi.140. [500.]

E[UGÈNE] BELIN DE BALLU, L'histoire des colonies grecques du littoral nord de la mer Noire. Bibliographie annotée des ouvrages et articles publiés en URSS de 1940 à 1957. Bibliothèque nationale: 1960. pp.vi.165. [656.]*

Grenade.

R. RUMEAU, Inventaire sommaire des archives communales antérieures à 1790. . . . Ville de Grenade. Toulouse &c. 1896. pp.xx.256.68. [10,000.]

Grenoble, city and diocese of.

C[YR] U[LYSSE] J[OSEPH] CHEVALIER, *ed.* Notice analytique sur le cartulaire d'Aimon de Chissé. Documents historiques inédits sur le Dauphiné [vol.iii]: Colmar 1869. pp.96. [157.]

400 copies printed.

[MARIE] A[NTOINE AUGUSTE] PRUDHOMME, Inventaire sommaire des archives communales antérieures à 1790. . . . Ville de Grenoble. Grenoble 1886–1926. pp.[ii].xxiii.47.221 + [iii].456 + [iii].

417+[iii].395+[iii].418. [200,000.]

— — Documents de la période révolutionnaire. 1891. pp.vii.176. [10,000.]

A. PRUDHOMME, Inventaire sommaire des archives historiques de l'hôpital de Grenoble. Grenoble 1892. pp.xxx.432. [6789.]

GABRIEL PÉROUSE, Inventaire sommaire des Archives départementales de la Savoie. . . . Archives ecclésiastiques: Série G. Diocèses de Tarentaise, de Grenoble et de Maurienne: Chambéry 1915. pp.[vi].55. [large number.]

Gronau.

A. PETERS, Inventare der nichtstaatlichen archive der provinz Hannover. Kreis Gronau. Forschungen zur geschichte Niedersachsens (vol.ii, part 4): Hannover 1909. pp.[iv].80. [large number.]

Groningen, province of.

H[ENDRIKUS] O[CTAVIUS] FEITH, Register van het archief van Groningen. Groningen 1853–1877.

J. A. FEITH, Catalogus der inventarissen van de archieven der voormalige zijlvestenijen en dijkrechten in de provincie Groningen. Rijksarchief in de provincie Groningen. Groningen 1901. pp. [xiv].385. [10,000.]

W. J. FORMSMA, Inventaris van de archieven der staten van stad en lande (1594–1798). Rijksarchief in Groningen: 's-Gravenhage 1958. pp.134. [3236.]

S. J. FOCKEMA ANDREAE and F. J. L. BERKENVEL-DER, Groninger plakkatboek 1594–1848. Lijst van uit- en inwendige rechtsvoorschriften de provincie Groningen rakende, van doorlopend of geschiedkundig belang. Groningen 1961. pp.[ii].ix. 125. [1107.]*

Grünberg.

KONRAD WUTKE, Die inventare der nichtstaatlichen archive Schlesiens. I. Die kreise Grünberg und Freystadt. Verein für geschichte Schlesiens: Codex diplomaticus Silesiae (vol.xxiv): Breslau 1908. pp.viii.244. [Grünberg: 5000.]

Guienne.

J. A. BRUTAILS, Inventaire sommaire des archives départementales. . . . Gironde. Série C. Tome III. Chambre de commerce de Guienne. Bordeaux 1893. pp.xlviii.268. [large number.]

MARCEL GOURON, Les chartes de franchises de Guienne et Gascogne. Société d'histoire du droit:

Catalogue des chartes de franchises de la France (vol.ii): 1935. pp.[vii].lix.794. [2075.]

Guildford, diocese of.

[A SURVEY of the ecclesiastical archives of the diocese of Guildford]. Pilgrim trust: Survey of ecclesiastical archives: [1952]. ff.10. [large number.]*

Guillestre.

PAUL [PIERRE MARIE] GUILLAUME, Inventaire sommaire des archives communales antérieures à 1790. . . . Archives de Guillestre. Gap 1906. pp.cxxiv.511. [25,000.]

Guise.

COUNT [MARIE ELISABETH EDMOND] MAXIME DE SARS, Inventaire-sommaire des archives communales de la ville de Guise antérieures à 1800. Laon [printed] 1933. pp.[iii].vii.151. [20,000.]

Haarlem.

A. J. ENSCHEDÉ, Inventaris van het archief der stad Haarlem. Haarlem [1865–]1866. pp.[x].285. [2193.]

c[ornelis] ekama, Catalogus van boeken, pamfletten, enz. over de geschiedenis van Haarlem, van de omstreken, van eenige voorname inwoners en van het huis van Brederode. Haarlem.

    i. 1188–1800. 1874. pp.[viii].136. [705.]

    ii. 1801–1874. 1874. pp.[iv].103. [778.]

    iii. Supplement en register. 1875. pp.[iii]. 19.14. [100.]

Habelschwerdt.

udo lincke, Die inventare der nichtstaatlichen archive Schlesiens. Kreis Habelschwerdt. Verein für geschichte Schlesiens: Codex diplomaticus Silesiae (vol.xxxiv): Breslau 1929. pp.[viii].215. [10,000.]

Hague, The.

[j. h. hingman], Inventaris van het oud archief der gemeente 's Gravenhage. 's Gravenhage 1868. pp.viii.132. [5000.]

a. j. servaas van rooyen, Inventaris van de buurtboeken, buurtbrieven en losse stukken betreffende de buurten, berustende in het oud-archief der gemeente 's-Gravenhage. 's-Gravenhage 1902. pp.81.

H. E. VAN GELDER, Notariëele protocollen van 1597 tot 1811, opgenomen in het archiefdepôt der gemeente 's-Gravenhage. Alfabetische en synchronistische lijsten. 's-Gravenhage 1911. pp.71.

H. E. VAN GELDER, Voorloopige inventaris van de oude rechterlijke archieven van 's-Gravenhage tot 1811. 's-Gravenhage 1912. pp.32.

A[NTHONY] H[ENRIK] MARTENS VAN SEVENHOVEN, Archief van het kapittel von St. Maria op het hof te 's-Gravenhage. Algemeen rijksarchief: 's-Gravenhage 1914. pp.[ii].230. [1054.]

W. MOLL, Catalogus van de historisch-topografische bibliotheek. 's-Gravenhage 1921. pp.944.

F. C. VAN DER MEER VAN KUFFELER, Inventaris van het archief van de weeskamer van 's-Gravenhage, 1482–1852. 's-Gravenhage 1939. pp.153.

G. 'T HART, Inventaris van het oud-archief der gemeente 's-Gravenhage. [The Hague] 1957. pp. 330+[ii].331–722. [large number.]

Haguenau.

[H.] NESSEL [and A. HANAUER], Inventaire-sommaire des archives communales antérieures à 1790. ... Ville de Haguenau. Haguenau 1865–1905. pp. [ii].7.32.24.36.12.22.68.43.38. [50,000.]

Hainault.

A[UGUSTIN FRANÇOIS] LACROIX, Inventaires analytique et chronologique des archives des chambres du clergé, de la noblesse et du tiers état du Hainaut. Mons 1852. pp.[v].xiv.563. [10,000.]

JULES DELECOURT [JULES VICTOR DE LE COURT], Bibliographie de l'histoire du Hainaut. Mons 1864. pp.[iii].151. [1494.]

LÉOPOLD DEVILLERS, Description analytique de cartulaires et de chartriers . . . utiles à l'histoire du Hainaut. Mons 1865–1878. pp.[iv].296.lxx+[iii].276 + [iii].299 + 236.xxxiv + [iii].252 + [iii].473 +[iii].215+[iii].350. [25,000.]

[LÉOPOLD DEVILLERS], Inventaire des cartes et plans, manuscrits et gravés, qui sont conservés au dépôt provincial des archives de l'état à Mons. Mons 1870. pp.viii.238. [750.]
— — Supplément. 1896. pp.[vii].123. [513.]

THÉODORE BERNIER, Dictionnaire géographique, historique . . . & bibliographique du Hainaut. Mons 1879. pp.xxvii.640. [2500.]

LÉOPOLD DEVILLERS, Inventaire analytique des archives des états de Hainaut. Archives de l'état: Mons 1884–1906. pp.ccvii.309+[vii].471+vii.552. [50,000.]

INVENTAIRES sommaires des petites archives du Hainaut. Tome I. [Fascicule I]. Mons 1910. pp. [iii].88. [1000.]

no more published.

CH[ARLES] HODEVAERE, Inventaire sommaire des greffes scabinaux de la province de Hainaut. Archives de l'état, à Mons: [Brussels *c.*1910]. pp. 85. [large number.]

LÉO VERRIEST, Inventaire du fonds de la Cour des mortemains de Hainaut. Inventaire des archives de la Belgique: Bruxelles 1915. pp.89. [484.]

ANDRÉE SCUFFLAIRE, Inventaire des archives du grand baillage de Hainaut. Archives de l'état à Mons: Bruxelles 1957. pp.24. [2000.]

Halluin.

[C. DEHAISNES], Inventaire sommaire des archives communales antérieures à 1790. . . . Ville d'Halluin. Lille 1900. pp.[iii].xx.41. [5000.]

Halton.

WILLIAM BEAMONT, An account of the rolls of the honour of Halton. Warrington 1879. pp.60. [335.]

Hamburg.

JOHANN PAUL FINKE [FINCKE], Index diplomatvm civitatis et ecclesiæ hambvrgensis chronologicvs. Hambvrgi 1751. pp.[x].3–28. [250.]

A[LLEN] B[ANKS] HINDS, Descriptive list of state papers, foreign: Hamburg and Hanse towns (S.P. 82), [1588[–1659. Public record office: 1936. ff.i.31. [600.]*

BÜCHERKUNDE zur hamburgischen geschichte. Verein für hamburgische geschichte: Hamburg.
    1900–1937. Herausgegeben von Kurt Detlev Möller und Annelise [Marie] Tecke. 1939. pp.xv.492. [7187.]
    1938–1954. Herausgegeben von A. Tecke. 1956. pp.xii.215. [2510.]
    the first volume was reproduced in facsimile in 1957.

Hampshire.

EXHIBITION of records relating to Hampshire, shown to the Hampshire field club. Public record office: [1948.]*

Hannover.

[BARON] FRIEDRICH VON OMPTEDA, Neue vaterländische literatur. Eine fortsetzung älterer histo-

risch-statistischer bibliotheken der hannoverschen
lande. Hannover [1810]. pp.xvi.708. [4000.]

MAX BÄR, Übersicht über die bestände des
K. staatsarchivs zu Hannover. Mittheilungen der
K. preussischen archivverwaltung (no.3): Leipzig
1900. pp.viii.130. [50,000.]

Hanseatic league.

INVENTARE hansischer archive des sechzehnten
jahrhunderts. Verein für hansische geschichte:
Leipzig [vol.iii: München] 1896 &c.
in progress.

A[LLEN] B[ANKS] HINDS, Descriptive list of state
papers, foreign: Hamburg and hanse towns
(S.P. 82), [1588]–1659. Public record office: 1936.
ff.i.31. [600.]*

Harderwijk.

P. BERENDS, Het oud-archief der gemeente
Harderwijk. Harderwijk 1935.

Harfleur.

PAUL LE CACHEUX, Répertoire numérique des
archives communales antérieures à 1790. Ville

Europe

d'Harfleur. Archives départementales de la Seine-inférieure: Rouen 1947. pp.62. [large number.]

Harwich.

[L. J. REDSTONE], Calendar of muniments in the possession of the borough of Harwich. Harwich 1932. pp.126. [2500.]

Hasselt.

P. J. TEDING VAN BERKHOUT, Register op het oud-archief van Hasselt. Vereeniging tot beoefening van overijsselsch regt en geschiedenis: Zwolle 1883. pp.[vii].447. [5000.]

W[IEBE] J[ANNES] FORMSMA, De oude archieven der gemeente Hasselt. Van Gorcum's archief der archieven (vol.3): Assen 1959. pp.[ix].371. [25,000.]

Hattem.

P. NIJHOFF, Tijdrekenkundig register van oorkonden, berustende in het oud archief der gemeente Hattem. Arnhem 1854. pp.104.

Haubourdin.

[P.] DE CLEENE and J. VERMAERE, Inventaires sommaires des archives communales et hospita-

lières. . . . Ville d'Haubourdin. Lille 1906. pp.[iii].
xxxiv.117. [25,000.]

Haverford.

HENRY OWEN, A calendar of the public records
relating to Pembrokeshire. Vol.I. The lordship,
castle, and town of Haverford. Honourable society
of Cymmrodorion: Cymmrodorion record series
(no.7): 1911. pp.xii.172. [500.]

Havre.

PH. BARREY and L. PRÉTEUX, Inventaire sommaire
des archives municipales antérieures à 1790. Ville
du Havre. Le Havre 1928. pp.xii.526. [large
number.]

— — Période révolutionnaire. 1930. pp.xv.175.
[large number.]

Hawarden.

FRANCIS GREEN, The Hawarden deeds. National
library of Wales: Calendar of deeds & documents
(vol.iii): Aberystwyth &c. 1931. pp.[viii].478.
[1915.]

Hazebrouck.

[P. DE CLEENE], Inventaire sommaire des archi-

ves communales antérieures à 1790. . . . Ville
d'Hazebrouck. Lille 1886. pp.[iii].xxvii.75.
[25,000.]

Heemstede.

P. N. VAN DOORNINCK, Inventaris van het archief
van de heerlijkheid Heemstede. Haarlem 1911.
pp.viii.175. [1000.]

Heesbeen.

C. C. D. EBELL, Inventaris van de oude archieven
dagteekenende van vóór 1814 der gemeente
Heesbeen, Eethe en Genderen, in . . . het rijksarchief te 's-Hertogenbosch. 's-Hertogenbosch
[c.1910]. pp.14.

Heeze.

W. MEINDERSMA, Inventaris van het archief op
het kasteel to Heere. [s.l.1911]. pp.43.

Heidelberg castle.

MARC ROSENBERG, Quellen zur geschichte des
Heidelberger schlosses. Heidelberg 1882. pp.viii.
264. [250.]

Helmond.

J. J. M. HEEREN and J[OSEPH] P[ETER] W[ILLEM]

A[NTOON] SMIT, Inventaris het huis-archief van Helmond. Helmond 1926. pp.318.

Hendon.

HENDON antiquities. A catalogue of deeds, surveys, maps . . . relating to the manor of Hendon. Mill Hill historical society: 1931. pp.16. [100.]

Hérault.

INVENTAIRE sommaire des archives départementales . . . Hérault. Montpellier. [very large number.]

Série A. Par Joseph Berthelé. 1918. pp.283.
Série B. [Par Maurice Oudot de Dainville]. [c.1860]–1945. pp.72 + 251 + 253–547 + 346.
Série C. Par Eugène Thomas [L. de Lacour de La Pijardière; J. Berthelé]. 1865–1906. pp.xviii.456+480+438+438.
Série D. Par J. Berthelé. 1925. pp.154.
in progress.

Hereford, city, county and diocese of.

WILLIAM DUNN MACRAY, Catalogue of and index to ms. papers, proclamations, and other documents, selected from the municipal archives of the city of Hereford. Hereford 1894. ff.40. [750.]

[A SURVEY of the ecclesiastical archives of the diocese of Hereford]. Pilgrim trust: Survey of ecclesiastical archives: [1952]. ff.19. [large number.]*

Hertfordshire.

HERTFORDSHIRE county records. Hertfordshire county council: Hertford.

  i. Notes and extracts from the sessions rolls, 1581 to 1698. . . . By W[illiam] J[ohn] Hardy. 1905. pp.[iv].xxxviii.494. [2500.]

  ii. — 1699 to 1850 and addenda 1701 to 1824. 1905. pp.[ii].516. [2500.]

  iii. — 1851 to 1894 and addenda 1630 to 1880. 1910. pp.[iii].vi.286. [1500.]

  iv. Notes and extracts from the sessions records of the liberty of St. Alban division, 1770 to 1840, with addenda, 1758 to 1798 . . . by William Le Hardy. 1923. pp.[iii].xxxviii.355. [2000.]

  v. Calendar to the sessions books and sessions minute books and other sessions records . . . 1619 to 1657 . . . by William Le Hardy. 1928. pp.xxix.570. [3500.]

  vi. — 1658 to 1700. 1930. pp.xxxvi.639. [5000.]

vii. — 1700 to 1752. 1931. pp.xxxvi.653.
[7500.]

viii. — 1752 to 1799. 1935. pp.xli.732. [7500.]

ix. — 1799 to 1833 ... by W. Le Hardy [and]
Geoffrey Ll. Reckitt. 1939. pp.xxxii.808.
[7500.]

in progress?

[SIR] HERBERT GEORGE FORDHAM, Hertfordshire
maps: a descriptive catalogue of the maps of the
county, 1579–1900. Hertford [1907.] pp.164. [500.]

50 copies privately printed.

— — Supplement, 1579–1900. 1914. pp.vii.42.
[50.]

70 copies privately printed.

H. R. WILTON HALL, Records of the old arch-
deaconry of St. Alban's. A calendar of papers
A.D. 1575 to A.D. 1637. St. Alban's & Hertfordshire architectural & archæological society:
St. Alban's 1908. pp.[iv].156.xxi. [600.]

BRITISH records association, 1932–1957. Catalogue of an exhibition of records, maps, etc. relating to Hertfordshire. [County record office:
Hertford 1957. pp.24. [150.]

Hertogenbosch, 's.

J. F. HANSSE, Analytische opgave der secreta-

riele en notariele protocollen van 's-Hertogenbosch. 's-Hertogenbosch 1846. pp.48.

R. A. VAN ZUIJLEN, Inventaris van het groot
archief der gemeente 's Hertogenbosch. 1860.
pp.[vii].108.vii. [5000.]

R. A. VAN ZUIJLEN, Inventaris der archieven van
de stad 's-Hertogenbosch,. . . van 1399–1568
[–1800]. 's Hertogenbosch 1863–1879. pp.[iv].
xxvii.794+[iv].795–1592+1593–2150. [20,000.]

CAROLINE M. E. INGEN-HOUSZ, Literatuurlijst
van het beleg van 's Hertogenbosch in 1629.
's Hertogenbosch 1930. pp.60.

W. J. FORMSMA, De archieven van de raad en
rentmeester-generaal der domeinen en der leenen
tolkamer in stad en meierij van 's-Hertogenbosch.
Rijksarchief in Noordbrabant: 's-Gravenhage
1949. pp.117. [931.]

F. A. BREKELMANS, W[IEBE] J[ANNES] FORMSMA
and J[OSEPH] P[ETER] W[ILLEM] A[NTOON] SMIT, De
archieven van het gereformeerd burgerweeshuis
te 's-Hertogenbosch. Rijksarchief in Noordbrabant [Hertogenbosch]: 's-Gravenhage 1952.
pp.145. [large number.]

Hesse. [*see also* **Cassel.**]

HEINRICH EDUARD SCRIBA, Regesten der bis jetzt
gedruckten urkunden zur landes- und ortsgeschichte des grossherzogthums Hessen. Darmstadt 1847–1854. pp.[vi].248+[iv].276+[iv].360
+[vii].33+[ii].112+[ii].73. [14,364.]

FRIEDRICH KÜCH, Politisches archiv des land-
grafen Philipp des grossmütigen von Hessen.
Inventar der bestände. Königliches preussisches
staatsarchiv: Publikationen (vols.lxxviii, lxxxv):
Leipzig 1904–1910. pp.lv.886+xii.872. [2361.]

J. R. DIETERICH, Wegweiser durch das schrifttum
des Historischen Vereins für Hessen. Darmstadt
1934. pp.viii.128. [1500.]

Heusden.

C[ORNELIUS] C[ATHARINUS] N[ICOLAAS] KROM,
Inventaris van het oud-archief der gemeente
Heusden. 's-Hertogenbosch 1885. pp.48.
reprinted in 1915.

Hilvarenbeek.

M. VAN DER BURG and H. VAN DER SANDE, Archief-
inventaris gemeente Hilvarenbeek. 1939. pp.150.

Hindeloopen.

M. P. VAN BUIJTENEN, Inventaris van het oud en nieuw archief der gemeente Hindeloopen. Dokkum 1941. pp.113. [large number.]

Holker.

R[EGINALD] SHARPE FRANCE, The Holker muniments. Penrith [printed] 1950. pp.56. [3000.]
the muniments are now in the Lancashire record office.

Holland.

CATALOGUS van kaarten, enz., betrekking hebbende op de oudere en tegenwoordige gesteldheid van Holland's noordeskwartier, aanwezig op de tentoonstelling in het stedelijk museum te Amsterdam. Nederlandsch aardijkskundig genootschap [Amsterdam]: Leiden [1918]. pp.xi.126.55. [627.]

CATALOGUS van kaarten, enz., betrekking hebbende op de oudere en tegenwoordige gesteldheid van Holland tusschen Maas en IJ, aanwezig op de tentoonstelling in het stedelijk museum te Amsterdam. Koninklijk nederlandsch aardijkskundig genootschap [Amsterdam]: Leiden [1921]. pp.xii. 263. [1920.]

Holthees.

P. M. F. RIETER, Inventaris van . . . het oudarchief van Maashees en Holthees. [*s.l.*] 1917. pp.42.

Hondschoote.

[P. DE CLEENE], Inventaire sommaire des archives communales antérieures à 1790. . . . Ville d'Hondschoote. Lille 1876. pp.[ii].iv.8.4.14.4.3.13.11.4.3. 19. [15,000.]

Honfleur.

CHARLES BRÉARD, Les archives de la ville de Honfleur. [Half-title: Première partie]. Notes historiques et analyses de documents. 1885. pp.lxiv. 423. [large number.]
limited to the pre-revolutionary period.

A. VINTRAS, Répertoire numérique des archives municipales de Honfleur. Caen 1923. pp.[ii].lxxi. 124. [7500.]

Hoorn.

C. J. GONNET and R. D. BAART DE LA FAILLE, Inventaris van het archief der stad Hoorn. Haarlem 1918. pp.552.

Hördt.

GEORG BIUNDO, Regesten der ehem. Augustiner-propstei Hördt. Pfälzische gesellschaft zur förderung der wissenschaften: Veröffentlichungen (vol. xxxii): [Speier] 1954. pp.xii.158. [405.]

Houplin-lez-Seclin.

THÉODORE [HENRI JOSEPH] LEURIDAN, Inventaire sommaire des archives communales antérieures à 1790. . . . Houplin-lez-Seclin. Roubaix 1896. pp. 42. [5000.]

Houplines.

JULES FINOT and [J.] VERMAERE, Inventaire sommaire des archives communales antérieures à 1790. . . . Ville d'Houplines. Lille 1891. pp.[iii].xlv.50. [7500.]

Höxter.

WOLFGANG LEESCH, Inventar des archives der stadt Höxter. Inventare der nichtstaatlichen archive Westfalens (n.s. vol.i): Munster [1961]. pp.xii.592. [large number.]

Hungary.

    1. Cartography, 839.

Europe

2. Foreign relations, 839.
3. History, 840.
4. Topography, 845.

1. Cartography

LAJOS GLASER, A karlsruhei gyűjtemények magyarvonatkozású térképanyaga. Térképészeti közlöny: Különfüzete (no.6): Budapest 1933. pp. 136. [670.]

JULIA NAGY, Térképek, 1936–1940. Országos Széchényi könyvtár: Budapest 1942. pp.xvi.203. [2000.]

KÁLMÁN EPERJESSY, Kézirati térképek Magyarországról a Bésci levéltárakban. Army map service: Washington 1948. ff.23.
reproduced from Föld és ember (*1928*), *viii.42–60.*

FERENC FODOR, A magyarországi kéziratos vízrajzi térképek katológusa 1867-ig. Budapesti műszaki egyetem: Központi könyvtár: Tudományos műszaki bibliográfiák (vols.1, 3, 5): Budapest [1954–1956]. pp.145+156+220. [2072.]

2. Foreign relations

OLASZ–MAGYAR kapcsolatok. Fővárosi könyvtár: Aktuális kérdések irodalma (no.38): [Budapest 1927]. pp.8. [250.]

KATALOG wystawy rękopisów i druków polsko-węgierskich xv i xvi wieku. Bibljoteka jagiellońska: Kraków 1928. pp.59. [121.]

500 copies printed.

L[ÁSZLÓ] RÁSONYI, Ungarische bibliographie der Turkologie und der orientalisch-ungarischen beziehungen. Kőrösi Csoma archivum (no.1): Budapest 1935. pp.68. [750.]

EUGENE [JENÖ] HORVÁTH, The hungarian question. A bibliography on Hungary and central Europe. Budapest 1938. pp.20. [250.]

ENDRE HORVÁTH. Magyar-görög bibliografia. Budapest 1940. pp.96. [153.]

3. *History*

HEINRICH [HENRIK] MARCZALI, Ungarns geschichtsquellen im zeitalter der Árpáden. Berlin 1882. pp.x.164. [500.]

ACTON collection. Class 34: Germany, Austria, and Hungary (general political history). Cambridge university library: Bulletin (extra series): Cambridge 1908. pp.viii.445. [2500.]

BIBLIOGRAPHIA Hungariae. 1. Historica. Verzeichniss der 1861–1921 erschienenen, Ungarn betreffenden schriften in nichtungarischer sprache.

Europe

[Edited by Robert Gragger]. Universität Berlin: Ungarisches institut: Ungarische bibliothek (3rd ser., voli): Berlin&c. 1923. pp.xiii.coll.318. [5000.]

MARIE OPOČENSKÁ, Slovenika uherských listin v domácím, dvorním a státním archivu ve Vídni v období let 1243–1490. Publikace Archivu ministerstva zahraničních věcí (2nd ser., vol.ii): Praze 1927. pp.64. [125.]

JÓZSEF HERZOG, Az országos levéltárban őrzött nádori levéltár 1554–1781 [1790–1848], évi viatainak jegyzéke. Budapest 1928–1930. pp.26+ 17. [very large number.]

EMMA BARTONIEK, Magyar történeti forrás-kiadványok. A Magyar történettudomány kézikönyve (ser.1, vol.3b): Budapest 1929. pp.203. [3109.]

KÁROLY SZLADITS, Hetven év magánjogi iro-dalma. A magyar magánjog bibliográfiája, 1861–1930. Budapest 1930. pp.xix.572.

EMERIC [IMRE] LUKINICH, Les éditions des sources de l'histoire hongroise, 1854–1930. [Magyar tudo-mányos akadémia]: Budapest 1931. pp.169. [500.]

ALBINUS FRANCISCUS [ALBIN FERENCZ] GOMBOS, Catalogus fontium historiae hungaricae aevo ducum et regum ex stirpe Arpad descendentium

841

ab anno Christi DCCC usque ad annum MCCCL.
Academia litterarum de sancto Stephano [Szent
István akadémia]: Budapestini 1937–1938. pp.xi.
811+[iii].813–1715+[iii].1717–2671. [5210.]

BIBLIOGRAPHIA pannonica. A rómaikori Magyarország és a népvándorlás kutatásának. Pécs
[Budapest].

   i. 1932–1933. Összeállította Alföldi András.
   ii. 1934–1935. Pannonia-könyvtár (vol.xxx):
     1936. pp.31.
   iii. 1936.
   iv. 1937.
   v. 1938–1939. Dissertationes pannonicae
     (1st ser., no.10): 1940. pp.72.
   vi. 1940–1941. Dissertationes pannonicae
     (2nd ser., no.17): 1941. pp.213–278.

ILONA HUBAY, Magyar és magyar vonatkozásu
röplapok, ujságlapok, röpiratok az Országos
Széchényi könyvtárban, 1480–1718. Az Országos
Széchényi konyvtár kiadványai (vol.xxviii):
Budapest 1948. pp.xxvii.308. [1226.]

G. TORRO, Bibliografia sugli avvenimenti unghe-
resi del 1848–1849. Accademia di Ungheria:
Roma 1948. pp.48.

BÉLA KŐHALMI, 1848–1849 a kisnyomtatványok
tükrében. A Fővarosi Szabó Ervin könyvtár

"Budapest" gyűjyemények bibliográfiai munkálatai (no.6): Budapest [1948]. pp.40. [328.]

LÁSZLÓ GERÉB, Bibliográfia a hazai parasztlázadások verses és elbeszélő irodalmához, XV–XVIII század. Fővárosi Szahó Ervin könyvtár: Tanulmányok (no.23): Budapest 1949. pp.32. [150.]

ZOLTÁN I. TOTH [iv: G. GÁBOR KEMÉNY and LÁSZLÓ KATUS], Magyar történeti bibliográfia 1825–1867. Keleteurópai tudományos intézet: Történettudományi intézet: Budapest 1950. pp. 119+260+407+xxxv.676. [80,000.]

DOMOKOS KOSÁRY, Bevezetés a magyar történelem forrásaiba és irodalmába. Magyar tudományos akadémia történet tudományi intézete: Budapest 1951–1958. pp.480+638+400. [20,000.] *limited to the period 970–1825.*

MIT olvassunk hazánk történetéről? Válogatott művek bibliográfiája. Fővarosi Szabó Ervin könyvtár: Budapest 1952–1953. pp.288+117. [500.]

MAGYARORSZÁG huszadik szazádi történelmének tanulmányozáskhoz szükséges bibliográfiák és segédkönyvek válogatott bibliográfiája. Tudományegyetem: Könyvtár: Bibliográfiák az egyetemi oktatás számára (no.2): Budapest [1954]. pp.33. [163.]*

GYÖRGY VÉRTES, A Magyar tanácsköztársaság kiadványai és az első kommunista kiedványok. Országgyűlés: Könyvtár: Budapest 1958. pp.496. [4500.]*

THOMAS SCHREIBER, La Hongrie de 1918 à 1958. Fondation nationale des sciences politiques: Centre d'étude des relations internationales: États des travaux (ser. B, no.14): 1958. pp.43. [300.]

[PIROSKA MUNKÁCSI *and others*], A Magyar Tanácsköztársaság plakátjai az Országos Széchényi könyvtárban. Leiró katalogus. Budapest 1959. pp.260. [716.]*

[ANDOR TISZAY, *ed.*], A magyar tanácsköztársaság röplapjai. Bibliográfia és dokumentumgyüjtemény. Fővarosi Szabó Ervin könyvtár és az Országos Széchényi könyvtár: Budapest 1959. pp. 302. [754.]*

[BÉLA KŐHALMI *and others*], A Magyar tanácsköztársaság dokumentumai szegeden. Bibliográfia. Szeged 1959. pp.160. [690.]

ZOLTAN SZTARAY, Books on the hungarian revolution. A bibliography. Imre Nagy institute for political research: Carnets (no.2): Brussels 1960. pp.14. [200.]

Europe

1. L. HALASZ DE BEKY, A bibliography of the hungarian revolution, 1956. Canadian institute of international affairs: [Toronto 1963]. pp.[xiv].179. [2137.]*

4. Topography

REZSŐ HAVASS, Magyar földrajzi könyvtár. A magyar birodalomról bármely nyelven, valamint magyar szerzőktől bármely földrajzi tárgyról és bármely nyelven megjelent irodalmi művek könyvészete. Budapest 1893. pp.xxvii.532. [5000.]

BIBLIOGRAPHIA Hungariae. II. Geographica. Politico-oeconomica. Verzeichniss der 1861-1921 erschienenen, Ungarn betreffenden schriften in nichtungarischer šprache. [Edited by Robert Gragger]. Universität Berlin: Ungarisches institut: Ungarische bibliothek (3rd ser., vol.ii): Berlin &c. 1926. pp.xi-xlix.coll.319-710. [6000.]

LORÁND BENKŐ and LAJOS LŐRINCZE, Magyar nyelvjárási bibliográfia 1817-1949. Budapest 1951. pp.259. [12,5000.]

Huntingdonshire.

G. J. TURNER, A calendar of the feet of fines relating to the county of Huntingdon levied in

the King's court ... 1194–1603. Cambridge antiquarian society: Publications (octavo series, no.
xxxvii): Cambridge 1913. pp.clxiv.300. [1500.]

CATALOGUE of the local history collection.
Huntingdonshire county library: Huntingdon
1950. pp.39. [450.]
— Second edition. 1958. pp.60. [750.]

G[EORGE] H[UGO] FINDLAY, Guide to the Huntingdonshire record office. Huntingdonshire
county council: [Huntingdon] 1958. pp.viii.33.
[large number.]

Hvar.

INVENTAR jovnih erkvenih i privatnih archiva
Otoka Hvara. Split 1955. pp.40. [large number.]

Hyon.

ANDRÉE SCUFFLAIRE, Inventaire des archives de
la commune d'Hyon, 1792–1930. Archives de
l'état à Mons: Bruxelles 1951. pp.51. [1386.]

Idaarderadeel.

M. P. VAN BUIJTENEN, Inventaris van het oud

en nieuw archief der gemeente Idaarderadeel.
[Leeuwarden 1948]. pp.99. [very large number.]

Iglau.

P[ETER] VON CHLUMECKÝ, Die regesten oder die
chronologischen verzeichnisse der urkunden in
den archiven zu Iglau, Trebitsch, Triesch. Die
regesten des archivs im markgrafthume Mähren
(vol. I. B.): Brünn 1856. pp.xli.222+333. [1000.]

Ijselstein.

R. FRUIN, Inventaris van het archief der gemeente Ijselstein. [1892]. pp.127.

Ile-de-France.

H[ENRI] OMONT, Manuscrits relatifs à l'histoire
de Paris et de l'Ile-de-France conservés à Cheltenham dans la bibliothèque de sir Thomas Phillipps.
1889. pp.15. [100.]

Ille-et-Vilaine.

INVENTAIRE-sommaire des archives départementales. . . . Ille-et-Vilaine. Rennes. [very large
number.]

Série C. Par É[douard Quesnet *and others*].
1878–1934. pp.536+[ii].482+xxiv.466.

Série F. Tables. Par ... Yvonne Marceil. 1952.
pp.88.

Série K. 1946. pp.10.

in progress.

Série V. Par René Gandilhon. 1936. pp.142.

LÉON VIGNOLS, Inventaire cartographique des
archives d'Ille-et-Vilaine, du Musée archéologique de Rennes et de la bibliothèque de m. de
Palys pour les époques antérieures à 1790. 1895.
pp.40. [76.]

Indre.

INVENTAIRE-sommaire des archives départementales. . . . Indre. Paris [*afterwards:* Château-
roux]. [very large number.]

Série A. Par Eugène [P. G. A. J. B.] Hubert.
1901. pp.lxvii.coll.568. pp.40.

Série E. Par A. Desplanque et Théodore
[Jean Baptiste] Hubert [J. Massiet Du
Biest]. 1876–1955. coll.326.pp.6+[xi].291.

Série G. Par Th. et E. Hubert. 1893. pp.xviii.
coll.728. pp.6.29.

Série H. Par Th. Hubert. 1876. coll.622 pp.3.
in progress.

EUGÈNE [P. G. A. J. B.] HUBERT, Les sources de l'histoire du Bas-Berry aux Archives nationales. Répertoire des documents concernant le département de l'Indre (XIe–XVIIIe siècles). 1893. pp.vi.31. [large number.]

EUGÈNE [P. G. A. J. B.] HUBERT, Répertoire numérique de la série Q (biens nationaux). Archives départementales de l'Indre: Châteauroux 1914. pp.viii.124. [large number.]

Indre-et-Loire.

INVENTAIRE-sommaire des archives départementales. . . . Indre-et-Loire. Paris [*afterwards:* Tours]. [very large number.]

> Séries A–E. Par Charles Loizeau de Grandmaison. 1867. pp.xx.2.58.164.6.112.
> Série E, supplément. Par L. Loizeau de Grandmaison. 1906. pp.xxxix.462.
> Série G. 1882. pp.ix.316.
> Série H. 1891. pp.xxiii.333.
> Série L. 1933. pp.[iii].xx.71.
> Série Q. 1914. pp.viii.124.

J[ACQUES] M[ARIE] ROUGE, Les livres de l'Indre-et-Loire. Blois [*c.*1938]. ff.3. [60.]

Inverness.

P[ETER] J[OHN] ANDERSON, A concise bibliography of the printed & ms. material on the history, topography & institutions of the burgh, parish and shire of Inverness. University of Aberdeen: Studies (no.73): Aberdeen 1917. pp. 264. [3000.]

Ireland.

1. *Cartography*

CATALOGUE of the maps and plans and other publications of the Ordnance survey of Ireland. 1862. pp.20. [500.]

— [another edition]. Catalogue of the maps and other publications of the Ordnance survey of Saorstát Éireann. Oifig na suirbhéireachta ordonáis, páirc an f hionnuisge áth cliath: Dublin 1933. pp.44. [2000.]

with duplicated supplements.

JOHN [HARWOOD] ANDREWS, Ireland in maps. ...
With a catalogue of an exhibition mounted ... by
the Geographical society of Ireland in conjunction
with the Ordnance survey of Ireland. Dublin 1961.
pp.36. [120.]

2. *History*

WILLIAM [NICHOLSON], The irish historical
library. Pointing at most of the authors and records
in print or manuscript, which may be serviceable
to the compilers of a general history of Ireland.
By William, lord bishop of Derry. Dublin 1724.
pp.xxxix.246.[x]. [400.]

subsequent editions form part of Nicholson's The
english, scotch and irish historical libraries, *which
is entered under Great Britain, 7.v, above.*

A CATALOGUE of political pamphlets, written
in defence of the principles and proceedings of
the patriots of Ireland, and, mostly, published ...
in the memorable years 1751, 2, 3, 4, and 5. [*s.l.
c.*1755]. pp.4. [50.]

CALENDAR of the state papers relating to Ireland
... preserved in .... her majesty's [*afterwards:* the]
Public record office.

    1509–1573. By Hans Claude Hamilton. 1860.
      pp.[v].xlvi.620. [6000.]

1574–1585. 1867. pp.cxliv.719. [7000.]

1586–1588. 1877. pp.xlvi.663. [1000.]

1588–1592. 1885. pp.xlv.660. [4000.]

1592–1596. 1890. pp.xxvii.602. [4000.]

1596–1597. By Ernest George Atkinson 1893. pp.lxviii.595. [2500.]

1598–1599. 1895. pp.lxxxi.676. [1500.]

1599–1600. 1899. pp.lxxxix.633. [500.]

1600. 1903. pp.[iii].lv.673. [500.]

1600–1601. 1905. pp.lxvii.572. [450.]

1601–1603, with addenda, 1565–1654, and [calendar] of the Hanmer papers. By Robert Pentland Mahaffy. 1912. pp.lxxxiii.757. [500.]

1603–1606. By C[harles] W[illiam] Russell and John P[atrick] Prendergast. 1872. pp.cxviii.660. [892.]

1606–1608. 1874. pp.cxxii.792. [1250.]

1608–1610. 1874. pp.cix.706. [966.]

1611–1614. 1877. pp.lxxii.694. [983.]

1615–1625. 1880. pp.xxxvi.716. [1425.]

1625–1632. By R. P. Mahaffy. 1900. pp.xliii.760. [2235.]

1633–1647. 1901. pp.lvii.871. [4000.]

1647–1660. 1903. pp.xxxviii.975. [2500.]

1660–1662. 1905. pp.lviii.766. [2500.]

1663–1665. 1907. pp.lx.768. [2500.]

1666–1669. 1908. pp.lxxii.866. [2000.]

1669–1670, with addenda, 1625–1670. 1910. pp.xxxv.765. [2000.]

the papers for later years are included in the Domestic series of state papers, which are here entered under Great Britain: History.

— Adventurers for land, 1642–1659. By R. P. Mahaffy. 1903. pp.xliv.445. [4000.]

EUGENE O'CURRY, Lectures on the manuscript materials of ancient irish history. Dublin 1861. pp.xxviii.722. [500.]

JAMES MORRIN, Calendar of the patent and close rolls of chancery in Ireland. Dublin 1861–1863. pp.xliv.616+lxxix.688+[ii].700. [10,000.]

covers the periods 1514–1602 and 1625–1633.

C[HARLES] W[ILLIAM] RUSSELL and J[OHN] P[ATRICK] PRENDERGAST, The Carte manuscripts in the Bodleian library, Oxford. A report presented to the right honourable lord Romilly, master of the rolls. 1871. pp.[ii].236. [100,000.]

[EVELYN PHILIP SHIRLEY], Catalogue of the library at Lough Fea, in illustration of the history and antiquities of Ireland, 1872. pp.vii.386. [3500.]

CALENDAR of documents relating to Ireland, preserved in her majesty's Public record office, London.

1171–1251. Edited by H[enry] S[avage] Sweetman. 1875. pp.lxx.588. [3215.]

1252–1284. 1877. pp.liv.736. [2367.]

1285–1292. 1879. pp.lxii.672. [1189.]

1293–1301. 1881. pp.xlvii.482. [851.]

1302–1307. Edited by H. S. Sweetman and Gustavus Frederick Handcock. 1886. pp. xxi.424. [729.]

[RICHARD BARRY O'BRIEN], The best hundred irish books. . . . By 'Historicus'. [Freeman's journal reprints (no.vii): Dublin 1886]. pp.60. [100.]

[SIR JOHN THOMAS GILBERT], The manuscripts of Charles Haliday. . . . Acts of the Privy council in Ireland, 1556–1571. Fifteenth report of the Royal commission on historical manuscripts (appendix iii): 1897. pp.xii.339. [271.]

JOHN RIBTON GARSTIN, Descriptive catalogue of a collection of manuscripts formerly belonging to . . . William Reeves . . . and now deposited in the Diocesan library. Belfast 1899. pp.15. [250.]

CONSTANTIA [ELIZABETH] MAXWELL, A brief bibliography of irish history. Historical association: Leaflet (no.23): 1911. pp.16. [300.]
reissued in Dublin 1911.

—— A short bibliography [&c.]. Revised 1921. pp.32. [525.]

HERBERT WOOD, A guide to the records deposited in the Public record office of Ireland. Dublin 1919. pp.xvi.334. [very large number.]

ROBERT H. MURRAY, A short guide to the principal classes of documents preserved in the Public record office, Dublin. Helps for students of history (no.7): 1919. pp.64. [very large number.]

ROBERT H. MURRAY, Ireland, 1494–1603. Helps for students of history (no.33): 1920. pp.32. [300.]
— — 1603–1714.... (no.34): 1920. pp.48. [200.]
— — 1714–1829.... (no.35): 1920. pp.47. [200.]

ANALECTA hibernica. Including the reports of the Irish manuscripts commission. Coimisiúu láimhscríbhinní na hÉireann: Dublin.

- i. [Report on manuscripts in the Bodleian library, Oxford; &c.]. 1930. pp.xv.232. [500.]
- ii. [Report on manuscripts in the Bodleian library, Oxford; manuscripts of irish interest in the British museum]. 1931. pp.[ii].x. 340. [100.]
- iii. [various texts]. 1931. pp.viii.228.
- iv. [Fitzwilliam manuscripts at Milton, England; and texts]. 1932. pp.vii.326. [71.]
- v. Index to nos.I–IV. Compiled by Newport B. White. 1934. pp.vii.177.

vi. [various texts]. 1934. pp.ix.450.

vii. A guide to irish geological collections. By Séamas Pender. [1935]. pp.167. [2500.]

viii. [List of documents of irish interest from the Ellesmere collection in the Henry E. Huntington library; and texts]. 1938. pp. vii.447. [100.]

ix. Index to nos. VI [1934] and VIII [1938]. Compiled by N. B. White. 1940. pp.vii. 142.

x. [Guide to english financial records for irish history, 1461–1558; and texts]. 1941. pp.vii.286. [large number.]

xi. Two diaries of the french expedition, 1798. 1941. pp.174.

xii. [Miscellaneous]. pp.vi.187.

xiii. Index to no.10 (1941) and no.12 (1943). Compiled by N. B. White. 1944. pp.79.

xiv. Report on documents relating to the wardenship of Galway. Edited by Edward MacLysaght. 1944. pp.[ii].250. [500.]

xv. Survey of documents in private keeping. First series. By Edward MacLysaght. 1944. pp.iii–x.459. [1500.]

xvi–xvii. [Miscellaneous] pp.vii.389+vii. 353.

xviii. The O'Clery book of genealogies.

Edited by Séamus Pender. 1951. pp.xxxv. 200.

xix. Index to no.16, by B. MacGiolla Choille, and to Proceedings of the Dublin society of united Irishmen (no.17). 1957. pp.117.

xx. Survey of documents in private keeping. Second series. By John F. Hinsworth and Edward MacLysaght. 1958. pp.[ii].xvii. 393. [2000.]

xxi. Franco-irish correspondence, December 1688–August 1691. Edited by Lilian Tate. 1959. pp.240. [307.]

xxii. [Miscellaneous]. 1960.

in progress.

P[ATRICK] S[ARSFIELD] O'HEGARTY, [Bibliographies of 1916 and the irish revolution]. Dublin 1931 &c.

in progress?; 25–30 copies privately printed.

EDMUND CURTIS, Calendar of Ormond deeds, 1172–1350. Coimisiún láimhscríbhinní na hÉireann: Dublin.

[i]. 1172–1350. 1932. pp.lxiii.424. [863.]
ii. 1350–1413. 1934. pp.xli.403. [442.]
iii. 1413–1509. 1935. pp.xxxi.432. [356.]
iv. 1509–1547. 1937. pp.xxxiv.432. [361.]
v. 1547–1584. 1941. pp.xliii.396. [372.]
vi. 1584–1603. 1943. pp.[ii].xix.240. [145.]

F. S. BOURKE, The rebellion of 1803. An essay in bibliography. Bibliographical society of Ireland (vol.v, no.1): Dublin 1933. pp.16. [150.]

CATALOGUE of publications issued and in preparation, 1928–1938. Irish manuscripts commission: Dublin [1938]. pp.41.

JAMES CARTY, Bibliography of irish history. National library of Ireland: Dublin.
1870–1911. 1940. pp.xviii.321. [2800.]
1912–1921. 1936. pp.xxxix.177. [1400.]
in progress?

R[OBERT] HERBERT, Catalogue of the Museum and Reference library. Public library: Limerick 1940. pp.16. [200.]

CATALOGUE of publications issued and in preparation, 1928–1957. Irish manuscripts commission: Dublin [1957]. pp.72. [100.]

CATHALDUS GIBLIN, Catalogue of material of irish interest in the collection *Nunziatura di Fiandra,* Vatican archives. Collectanea hibernica (nos.1, 3, 4): Dublin 1958–1962. pp.136+144+139. [2000.]

3. *Topography*
BRITAIN and Ireland for the traveller. Prepared

by the Travel association. [National book council:] Book list (no.129): 1930. pp.[3]. [Ireland: 10.]

IRELAND for the traveller. A selected list of books, now in print, compiled by the Dublin branch of the Associated booksellers of Great Britain and Ireland. [National book council:] Book list (no.150): 1937. pp.[2]. [100.]

— Second edition. Compiled by the Dublin and Northern Ireland branches [&c.]. 1939. pp.[4]. [150.]

READERS' guide to the face of Ireland. Library association: County libraries section: [Readers' guide (new series, no.10): 1951]. pp.16. [150.]

THOMAS P. O'NEILL, Sources of irish local history. Library association of Ireland: Dublin 1958. pp.38. [100.]

4. *Northern Ireland*

M. A. COSTELLO, De annatis Hiberniae. A calendar of the first fruits' fees levied on papal appointments to benefices in Ireland, A.D. 1400 to 1535. . . . Volume I: Ulster. St. Patrick's college: [Catholic] Record society: Maynooth 1912. pp. xxxi.324. [500.]

no more published.

Europe

Irún.

SERAPIO [DE] MÚGICA [Y ZUFIRIA], Índice de los documentos del archivo del excmo. Ayuntamiento de la ... villa de Irún. Irún 1898. pp.ix.282. [3000.]

Isère.

INVENTAIRE sommaire des archives départementales. . . . Isère. Grenoble. [very large number.]
 Séries A–B. Par [Jean Joseph Antoine] Pilot-Dethorey. 1864. pp.29.4.424.
 Série B. Par [J. A. J.] Pilot-Dethorey et [Marie] A[ntoine Auguste] Prudhomme. 1884–1919. pp.310+416+422.
 Série H. Par Robert Avezov. 1951. pp.108.
 Série L. Par A. Prudhomme. 1900–1908. pp. 516+lxxviii.390.
 Série M. Par Gustave Finet. 1949. pp.viii.103.
 Série S. 1948. pp.71.
in progress.

[MARIE] A[NTOINE AUGUSTE] PRUDHOMME, Les archives de l'Isère, 1790–1899. Grenoble 1899. pp.[iii].375. [5000.]

G. ETONNELIER, Répertoire des minutes de notaires conservées aux archives de l'Isère. Grenoble 1930. pp.196. [large number.]

860

Europe

Italy.

1. *Cartography*

CATALOGO delle carte e dei libri vendibili dall'Istituto geografico militare. Firenze 1883. pp.18. [83.]

there are numerous intermediate editions, with varying titles, the latest being:

Catalogo delle pubblicazioni. 1962–1963. pp. 3–31. [4000.]

GIOVANNI MARINELLI, Saggio di cartografia italiana. Programma dell'opera. Schema e esemplari. Firenze 1894. pp.29. [11.]
a specimen only.

PAOLO ARRIGONI and ACHILLE BERTARELLI, Le carte geografiche dell'Italia conservate nella raccolta delle stampe e dei disegni. Catalogo descrittivo. Comune di Milano: Istituti di storia e d'arte: [Milan] 1930. pp.xv.424. [3286.]

this is a catalogue of the maps preserved in the Castello Sforzesco.

CATALOGO ragionato delle carte esistenti nella cartoteca dell'Istituto geografico militare. Parte II. Carte d'Italia e delle colonie italiane. Firenze 1934. pp.xxxi.587. [1500.]

2. *Foreign relations*

SEBASTIANO CIAMPI, Bibliografia critica delle antiche reciproche corrispondenze politiche, ecclesiastiche, scientifiche, letterarie, artistiche dell'Italia colla Russia, colla Polonia ecc. Firenze 1834–1842. pp.[vi].v.366 + xii.326 + [vi].137. [2500.]

[PIERRE] JULES THIEURY, Bibliographie italico-normande, contenant 1° Un essai historique . . .; 2° Une bibliothèque des ouvrages relatifs aux relations des deux pays; 3° Une bibliothèque des ouvrages relatifs à l'Italie composés par des auteurs normands. 1864. pp.80. [100.]

ISIDORO CARINI, Gli archivi e le biblioteche di Spagna in rapporto alla storia d'Italia in generale e di Sicilia in particolare. Sovraintendenzia agli archivi siciliani: Relazione, documenti ed allegati: Palermo 1884-[1897]. pp.viii.547.civ+[iii].607. [large number.]

GIOVAMBATISTA ADRIANI, Sopra alcuni documenti e codici manoscritti di cose subalpine ed italiane conservati negli archivi e nelle publiche biblioteche della Francia meridionale. Torino 1885. pp.78.

CH[ARLES] DEJOB, Madame de Staël et l'Italie, avec une bibliographie de l'influence française en Italie, de 1796 à 1814. 1890. pp.[iii].267. [400.]
—— Supplément à un essai de bibliographie pour servir à l'histoire de l'influence française en Italie de 1796 à 1814. [1893]. pp.35. [250.]

ELENCO di documenti diplomatici (libro verde) presentati al Parlamento italiano dal 27 giugno 1861 al 7 giugno 1890. Roma 1890. pp.8. [71.]

CARL RUSSELL FISH, Guide to the materials for american history in roman and other italian archives. Carnegie institution: Publication (no. 128): Washington 1911. pp.ix.289. [large number.]

OLASZ–MAGYAR kapcsolatok. Fővárosi könyvtár: Aktuális kérdések irodalma (no.38): [Buda-
pest 1927]. pp.8. [250.]

ELENCO degli atti internazionali conchiusi dal
regno d'Italia e da quello di Sardegna in vigore
al 1°. luglio 1890. Ministero degli affari esteri:
Roma 1890. pp.162. [1000.]

WOJCIECH MEISSELS, Italja a powstanie styczniowe. Bibliografja. Kraków 1926. pp.31. [230.]
205 copies printed.

A[LLEN] B[ANKS] HINDS, Descriptive list of state
papers, Foreign: Italian states (S.P. 85). Public
record office: 1933. ff.i.34. [750.]*
covers the period 1544–1664.

DANIEL C[ARL] HASKELL, Ethiopia, and the italo–
ethiopian conflict, 1928–1936. A selected list of
references. Public library: New York 1936. pp.13.
[325.]

RICARDO MAGDALENO REDONDO, Papeles de
estado de la correspondencia y negociación de
Nápoles. Consejo superior de investigaciones
científicas [&c.]: Archivo general de Simancas:
Catálogo (no.xvi): Valladolid 1942. pp.xv.413.
[large number.]

PIH SHUT'ANG [SHU-T'ANG PI], Catalogo di opere in cinese tradotte dall'italiano o riguardanti l'Italia. Centro culturale italiano: Saggio di bibliografia (no.1): [Pekin] 1942. pp.[ii].79. [202.]

PETĂR JORDANOV [IORDANOV], La Bulgaria in Italia. Bibliografia delle pubblicazioni italiane sulla Bulgaria (1870–1942). Associazione italo-bulgara: Bibliotechina bulgara (no.7): Roma 1943. pp.86. [1250.]

[JAN VIGGO BERTRAND] TÖNNES KLEBERG, Italien i svensk litteratur. Bibliografisk förteckning. Acta Bibliothecae gotoburgensis (vol.ii): Göteborg 1944. pp.xviii.252. [2953.]

REIDAR [ADOLF PETER KARL] ØKSNEVAD, Italia i norsk litteratur. En bibliografi. Oslo 1947. pp.66. [1000.]

MARIA and MARINA BERSANO BEGEY, La Polonia in Italia. Saggio bibliografico, 1799–1948. Università di Torino: Istituto di cultura polonica: Pubblicazioni (vol.ii): Torino 1949. pp.295. [3375.]

J[ORMA VÄINÖ] VALLINKOSKI, Italia Suomen kirjallisuudessa 1640–1953. Helsingin yliopiston kirjaston: Julkaisuja (vol.25): Helsinki 1955. pp. 340. [5997.]

ARTURO CRONIA, La conoscenza del mondo slavo in Italia. Bilancio storico-bibliografico di un millennio. Istituto di studi adriatici [Venezia]: Padova [printed] 1958. pp.[vi].793. [3500.]

BIBLIOGRAPHIE italo-française, 1948–1958.
> i. 1948–1954. [By Guido Marinelli, Glauco Natoli and Claude Margueron]. [1962]. pp.[x].295. [2700.]

in progress.

3. *History*

i. *Bibliographies*

EMILIO CALVI, Biblioteca di bibliografia storica italiana. Catalogo tripartito delle bibliografie finora pubblicate sulla storia generale e particolare d'Italia. Roma [1903]. pp.iv.39. [522.]
—— [second edition]. 1907. pp.17.

ii. *General*

[JACOPO MORELLI], Catalogo di storie generali e particolari d'Italia. Venezia 1782. pp.xii.293. [1500.]
> *a catalogue of the collection of T. G. Farsetti.*

SIR RICHARD COLT HOARE, A catalogue of books relating to the history and topography of Italy. 1812. pp.vii.102. [1733.]
> *12 copies printed; the copy in the British museum,*

*to which the collection was presented, contains à ms.
list of additions.*

GIUSEPPE MOLINI, Notizia dei manoscritti italiani
o che si riferiscono all'Italia esistenti nella Libreria
dell'Arsenale in Parigi. Firenze 1836. pp.[iv].25.
[47.]

ALFREDO [ALFRED VON] REUMONT, Bibliografia
dei lavori pubblicati in Germania sulla storia
d'Italia. Berlino 1863. pp.xi.468. [1250.]

CARLO LOZZI, Biblioteca istorica della antica e
nuova Italia. Saggio di bibliografia analitico,
comparato e critico. Compilata sulla propria collezione. Imola 1886–1887. pp.[iii].493+[iii].505.
[6508.]

GIUSEPPE MAZZATINTI [vols.v–ix: GIUSTINIANO
DEGLI AZZI], Gli archivi della storia d'Italia. Rocca
S. Casciano 1897–1915. pp.423+461+408+401
+ xviii.403 + xii.357 + [iv].viii.475 + [iv].301 +
[iv].xxiv.272. [200,000.]
vols.vi–ix also form serie II, vols.i–iv.

ANNUARIO bibliografico della storia d'Italia dal
sec. IV dell'e.v. ai giorni nostri. Supplemento . . .
degli Studi storici. Pisa [vol.viii: Pavia].
    [i]. 1902. [Edited by A. Crivellucci, Giovanni
        Monticolo and Fortunato Pintor]. 1903.
        pp.lxvii.515. [6227.]

[ii].1903. 1904–1905. pp.lxxix.566. [6876.]
iii. 1904. 1906. pp.lxxxiii.607. [7144.]
iv. 1905. 1907. pp.lxxxiii.585. [6486.]
v. 1906. 1908. pp.lxxxiv.500. [6137.]
vi. 1907. 1908. pp.lxxxviii.530. [6086.]
vii. 1908. 1909. pp.xiv.574. [6335.]
viii. 1909. Edited by A. Crivellucci, F. Pintor and G. Coggiola. 1910. pp.cvii.367. [3928.]

ANGELO PESCE, Notizie sugli archivi di stato. Roma 1906. pp.159. [very large number.]

MARIA PASOLINI PONTI, Sommario della storia d'Italia con guida bibliografica. Torino &c. 1928. pp.v.160. [1000.]

EUGENIO CASANOVA, L'Archivio di stato in Roma e l'Archivio del regno d'Italia. Indice generale storico, descrittivo ed analitico. Bibliothèque des 'Annales institutorum' (vol.ii): Roma 1932. pp.3–253. [very large number.]
200 copies printed.

[FEDERICO CURATO *and others*], Studi storici, militari; etnografia popolare. Istituto nazionale per le relazioni culturali con l'estero: Bibliografie del ventennio: Roma 1941. pp.214. [history: 1000.]

BIBLIOGRAFIA storica nazionale. Giunta centrale per gli studi storici: Roma.

    i. 1939. [Edited by Eugenio Dupré-Theseider]. 1942. pp.iii–xxxi.355. [5306.]

    ii. 1940. [Edited by Ersilia Liguori Barbieri *and others*], 1945. pp.iii–xxxiii.475. [7264.]

    iii. 1941. [Edited by Raffaello Morghen]. 1947. pp.iii–xxxii.324. [6475.]

    iv. 1942. 1948. pp.iii–xxvii.147. [2631.]

    v–viii. 1943–1946. 1949. pp.iii–xxvii.221. [4104.]

    ix–x. 1947–1948. 1950. pp.xxiii.188. [3356.]

    xi. 1949. 1951. pp.xxiv.152. [2626.]

    xii. 1950. 1952. pp.xxv.149. [2683.]

    xiii. 1951. 1953. pp.xxiv.148. [2509.]

    xiv. 1952. 1954. pp.iii–xxiv.153. [2693.]

    xv. 1953. 1955. pp.iii–xxiii.175. [2819.]

    xvi. 1954. 1956. pp.xxiii.191. [3159.]

    xvii. 1955. 1957. pp.iii–xxvii.195. [3399.]

    xviii. 1956. 1958. pp.iii–xxviii.201. [3327.]

    xix. 1957. 1959. pp.iii–xxviii.197. [3342.]

    xx. 1958. 1960. pp.xxvii.259. [3697.]

    xxi. 1959. 1961. pp.iii–xxvii.259. [3551.]

    xxii. 1960. 1962. pp.xxviii.282. [4037.]

    xxiii. 1961. 1963. pp.xxvii.293. [4180.]

in progress; almost wholly limited to italian history and writings in italian.

PIER FAUSTO PALUMBO. Gli studi di storia medievale e moderna in Italia. Roma 1959. pp.276. [1000.]

GLI ARCHIVI di stato italiani. Ufficio degli archivi di stato: Bologna 1944. pp.x.606. [many million.]

ARCHIVI privati. Inventario sommario. Pubblicazioni degli archivi di stato (vols.xi, xiv &c.): Roma 1953 &c.

in progress.

iii. *Ancient history*

[PIETER BURMAN], Catalogvs rarissimorvm & praestantissimorvm librorvm, qui in Thesavris romano, graeco, italico, & sicvlo [of Graevius and Gronovius] continentur. Leidae 1725. pp.[vii].88. [650.]

[PIETER BURMAN], Catalogvs omnium · . librorvm, qui in Thesavro antiqvitatvm & historiarvm Italiae, Neapolis, Siciliae, Sardiniae, Corsicae, Melitae, &c., &c., Joannis Georgii Graevii ... reperiuntur. Lvgdvni Batavorvm 1725. pp.[ii].17. [300.]

[ULYSSE GUIDI], Catalogi quatuor quorum duo ad Gronovii, Graevii, Sallengre, Poleni, et Burmanni thesauros antiquitatum graecarum, romanarum, et italicarum; duo ad collectionem scrip-

torum rerum italicarum Muratorii, Tartinii, et
Mittarelli. Bononiæ 1853. pp.[iv].161. [3500.]

GIOVANNI FRANCESCO GAMURRINI, Bibliografia
dell'Italia antica. . . . Volume I. Arezzo 1905. pp.
xv.454. [8000.]
no more published.

iv. *Medieval history*

[GIOVANNI MICHAELE BATTAGLINO and JOSEPH
CALLIGARIS], Indices chronologici ad Antiquitates
italicas medii ævi et ad opera minora Ludovici
Antonii Muratorii. [Operis moderamen sibi
susceperunt Carolus Cipolla et Antonius Manno].
Augustae Taurinorum [1889–] 1896. pp.xii.460.
[8500.]
*on the cover of the first part Battaglino's second
forename appears as Maria.*

C[ARLO] MERKEL, Documenti di storia medievale italiana. Bibliografia degli anni 1885–1891.
Istituto storico italiano: Bollettino (no.12): Roma
1892. pp.164. [3000.]

PUBBLICAZIONI sulla storia medioevale italiana.
Appendice al Nuovo archivio veneto. [R. Deputazione veneta di storia patria:] Venezia.

   1896. [By] Carlo Cipolla 1899. pp.308.
   [1000.]

1897. 1900. pp.208. [1000.]
1898. 1901. pp.149. [750.]
1899. 1902. pp.140. [1000.]
1900. 1903. pp.133. [1000.]
1901. 1904. pp.183. [1500.]
1902. 1906. pp.152. [1500.]
1903. 1907. pp.140. [1500.]
1904. 1909. pp.156. [1500.]
1905. 1910. pp.173. [1500.]
1906–1910. 1914. pp.379.

issues for 1890–1895 form part of the Archivio
veneto.

A. COLOMBO, Le fonti storiche della repubblica
Ambrosiana. (Saggio critico-bibliografico). Vige-
rano 1911. pp.48. [200.]

ESTER PASTORELLO, Indici per nome d'autore e
per materia delle pubblicazioni sulla storia
medioevale italiana (1899–1910). R. deputazione
veneta di storia patria: Venezia 1916. pp.619.
[15,000.]

PIETRO EGIDI, La storia medioevale. Guide
bibliografiche: Roma 1922. pp.[ii].219. [2000.]

GUIDO PARAZZOLI, Cenni sulle fonti della storia
medioevale. Milano [1956]. pp.[i].144. [700.]

v. *Modern history*

OTTO MÜHLBRECHT, Die literatur des deutschen und italienischen krieges im jahre 1866. Prag 1867. pp.xxviii.68. [1750.]

RELAZIONE sugli archivi di stato italiani (1874–1882). Ministero dell'interno: Roma 1883. pp.410. [very large number.]

AUTOGRAFI ed altri documenti relativi al risorgimento italiano esistenti nelle collezioni di Amilcare Ancona. Milano 1884. pp.51. [1000.]

CATALOGO delle opere che trovansi nella raccolta storica del dott. A. Norlenghi, specialmente relativa alle cose italiane del periodo 1815–1870. Torino 1884. pp.51. [850.]

[GIOVANNI] BATTISTA MONTAROLO, Bibliografia del risorgimento italiano. Opere anonime e pseudonime. Roma 1884. pp.38. [250.]
250 copies printed.

[LUIGI ARRIGONI], Documenti storici ed autografi relativi alla storia del risorgimento italiano. Milano [1884]. pp.vi.66. [253.]

[FEDELE LAMPERTICO], Catalogo della Raccolta Fantoni nel Museo civico di Vicenza per la storia del 1848 in particolare e del risorgimento nazionale in generale. Vicenza 1893. pp.viii.444.xxiii. [5000.]

CATALOGO della Mostra storica del risorgimento italiano ordinata nella Biblioteca nazionale Vittorio Emanuele in occasione del venticinquesimo anniversario dell'unione di Roma al regno d'Italia. Roma 1895. pp.vii.93. [800.]

LISTE de pièces imprimées pour la plupart à Venise en 1797 pendant l'occupation française. Bibliothèque nationale: 1897. pp.26. [300.]
— N[ikolai] P[etrovich] Likhachev, По поводу изданія "Liste [&c.]" C.-Петербург 1898. pp.25. [49.]
200 copies printed.

ANTONIO VISMARA, Bibliografia storica delle cinque giornate e degli avvenimenti politico-militari in Lombardia nel 1848. Municipio di Milano: Milano 1898. pp.xi.275. [3750.]

LIST of references on the unification of Germany and Italy. Library of Congress: Washington 1905. ff.4. [18.]*

ERNESTO MASI, La storia del risorgimento nei libri. Bibliografia ragionata. Bologna 1911. pp.v. 194. [600.]

CATALOGUE of Panizzi pamphlets. Reform club: 1920. pp.59. [250.]

[EDWARD BULLOUGH], Italy in the nineteenth century. Chronological tables with a list of works recommended for study. Cambridge 1920. pp.[8]. [200.]

LIST of books on the history of Italy (1850–1920). Library of Congress: Washington 1921. ff.3. [30.]*

GUIDO ZADEI, Saggio d'una bibliografia dei compromessi bresciani nei processi del 1821–23. Brescia 1923. pp.12. [25.]

ACHILLE BERTARELLI, Inventario della raccolta donata da Achille Bertarelli al comune di Milano. Risorgimento italiano. Società nazionale per la storia del risorgimento italiano: Bergamo 1925. pp.[ix].677+481+202. [22,222.]

FRANCESCO LEMMI, Il risorgimento. Guide bibliografiche: Roma 1926. pp.320. [3000.]

ALBANO SORBELLI, Opuscoli stampe alla macchia e fogli volanti riflettenti il pensiero politico italiano (1830–1835). Saggio di bibliografia storica. Biblioteca di bibliografia italiana (vol.viii): Firenze 1927. pp.iii–lxxxviii.273. [964.]

RINALDO CADDEO, Le edizioni di Capolago, storia e critica. Bibliografia ragionata. Nuovi studi sulla topografia elvetica, il risorgimento italiano e il canton Ticino. Milano 1934. pp.475. [493.]

500 copies printed.

CONTRIBUTO alla bibliografia dell'interventismo italiano. Fondazione Gualtiero Castellini: Milano 1935. pp.xi.221. [3500.]

a bibliography of the irredentist and nationalist movements and of the colonial wars.

BIBLIOGRAPHIE zur geschichte Italiens in der vor-kriegszeit und im weltkrieg. Weltkriegsbücherei: Bibliographische vierteljahrshefte (no.17–18): Stuttgart 1938. pp.97. [2800.]

BIBLIOGRAPHIE zur geschichte Italiens in der nachkriegszeit. Weltkriegsbücherei: Bibliographische vierteljahrshefte (no.19): Stuttgart 1938. pp.69. [2000.]

IL RISORGIMENTO italiano. Enciclopedia bio-grafica e bibliografica 'italiana' (ser.xlii): Milano [Roma].

  i. I martiri. Di Francesco Ercole. [1939]. pp. 5–429. [7500.]

  [ii–iv]. Gli uomini politici. Di F. Ercole. 1941–1942. pp.[ii].v.13–428+5–396+v–381. [10,000.]

v. I combattenti. Di Almerico Ribera. [1943].
pp.5–395. [4000.]

GIUSEPPE BASSI, Dal risorgimento al fascismo.
Raccolta di opera interessanti la storia civile,
politica, militare e sociale d'Italia dal 1796 ai
giorni nostri. Imola 1941. pp.64.

LEOPOLDO MARCHETTI, Il 1848. Fonti bibliografiche e documentarie esistenti presso l'Istituto [per
la storia del risorgimento italiano]. Raccolte storiche del comune di Milano: Milano 1948. pp.3–
219. [5926.]

SANDRO PIANTANIDA, LAMBERTO DIOTALLEVI and
GIANCARLO LIVRAGHI, Autori italiani del seicento.
Catalogo bibliografico. 1. Costumi e storia del
secolo. Milano 1948. pp.xxii.238. [1078.]

L'ATTIVITÀ dell'Istituto e della scuola di storia
moderna e contemporanea. Roma 1955. pp.8.
[29.]

ALFONSO BARTOLINI, GIULIO MAZZON and LAM-
BERTO MERCURI, Resistenza. Panorama bibliografico. Biblioteca di sintesi storica: [Roma 1957].
pp.344. [2800.]
covers the period from 1923.

[STEFANO CANZIO and VINCENZO BENNIGARTNER],
L'unità d'Italia (luglio 1858–marzo 1861). Fonti

bibliografiche e documentarie esistenti presso l'istituto. Museo del resorgimento: Milano 1959. pp.iii–xi.657. [9877.]

UGO FEDELI, Un decennio di storia italiana, 1914–1924. La nascita del fascismo. Bibliografia. Centro colturale Olivetti: Quaderni: Ivrea 1959. pp.[vi].136. [1000.]*

GLI ARCHIVI dei governi provvisori e straordinari 1859–1861.... Inventario. Pubblicazioni degli archivi di stato (vols.xlv, xlvi &c.): Roma 1961 &c. *in progress.*

SALVATORE CARBONE, Fonti per la storia del risorgimento italiano negli archivi nazionali di Parigi. I rifugiati italiani 1815–1830. Istituto per la storia del risorgimento italiano: Biblioteca scientifica (ser.II, vol.xliii): Roma 1962. pp.xxiii.203. [large number.]

4. *Topography and local history*

[GIOVANNI ANTONIO COLETI], Catalogo delle storie particolari, civile ed ecclesiastiche delle città e de' luoghi d'Italia. Vinegia 1779. pp.xii.328. [3000.]

CARLO CIOCCHI, Lettera scritta all'eruditissimo signor canonico Domenico Moreni. Modena 1803. pp.29. [64.]

SIR RICHARD COLT HOARE, A Catalogue of books relating to the history and topography of Italy. 1812. pp.vii.102. [1733.]

12 copies printed; the copy in the British museum, to which the collection was presented, contains a ms. list of additions.

PIETRO LICHTENTHAL, Manuale bibliografico del viaggiatore in Italia. Collezione di manuali componenti una enciclopedia: Milano 1830. pp.vii. 258. [2500.]

—— Terza edizione. Biblioteca scelta di opere italiane (vol.cdlxxvii): 1844. pp.xx.388. [4000.]

STUDJ bibliografici e biografici sulla storia della geografia in Italia. Società geografica italiana: Roma 1875. pp.iii–xvii.a–j.510. [2000.]

LUIGI MANZONI, Bibliografia statutaria e storica italiana. Bologna.

 ii. Bibliografica storica municipale. . . .
  Volume 1°. A–E. 1892. pp.xxxi.563.
  [4000.]

vol.i is entered under Law, above; no more published.

[BARON FERDINAND VON PLATNER], Katalog der Bibliotheca platneriana, enthaltend municipalstatuten und staedtegeschichten Italiens, vom freiherrn F. von Platner dem Kaiserlichen deutschen archaeologischen institut geschenkt. Rom 1886. pp.491. [5000.]

—— Supplemento. 1894. pp.78. [500.]

ACHILLE BERTARELLI, Inventario della raccolta formata de Achille Bertarelli. Volume I. Italia geografica. Istituto italiano d'arti grafiche: Bergamo 1914. pp.xv.418. [3379.]
200 copies privately printed; no more published.

JEAN [LÉON] BÉRARD, Bibliographie topographique des principales cités grecques de l'Italie méridionale et de la Sicile dans l'antiquité. 1941. pp.116. [2000.]

ITALIAN municipal elections in 1946: a selected list of references to preliminary statistics. Library of Congress: Washington 1947. ff.29. [82.]*

[JAN VIGGO BERTRAND] TÖNNES KLEBERG, Svenskar i Italien. Bibliografisk förteckning över litteraturen om Svenskars resor i Italien. Acta Bibliothecae gotoburgensis (vol.iii): Göteborg 1949. pp.xv.102. [986.]

ANTONIO PESCARZOLI, I libri di viaggio e le guide della raccolta Luigi Vittorio Fossati Bellani. Catalogo descrittivo. Sussidi eruditi (vols.9–11): Roma

1957. pp.v–lxviii.641+3–647+3–663. [5189.]

[ADRIO CASATI, *ed.*], Catalogo della mostra delle pubblicazioni edite dagli enti locali italiani. Milano 1961. pp.92. [1169.]

GIAN CARLO MENICHELLI, Viaggiatori francesi reali o immaginari nell'Italia dell'ottocento. Primo saggio bibliografico. Fondazione Primoli: Quaderni di cultura francese (no.4): Roma 1962. pp. xx.183. [1900.]

Jaarsveld.

M. C. G. DIEMONT, Het archief van het huis te Jaarsveld, 1455–1890. 1937. pp.118.*

Jauer.

ERICH GRABER, Die inventare der nichtstaatlichen archive Schlesiens. Kreis Jauer. Verein für geschichte Schlesiens: Codex diplomaticus Silesiae (vol.xxxv): Breslau 1930. pp.[viii].350. [10,000.]

Jemappes.

ARMAND LOUANT and RENÉE DOEHAERD, Inventaire des archives de la commune de Jemappes (1335–1914). Archives de l'état à Mons: Gombloux 1942. pp.24. [large number.]

Jura.

INVENTAIRE sommaire des archives départementales. . . . Département du Jura. Paris [*afterwards:*
Lons-le-Saulnier]. [very large number.]

Série A. [By Jules Finot]. 1872. pp.112.

Série B. 1868. pp.120.

Séries C–F. Par [ ] Rousset, E. Junca et J.
Finot. 1870. pp.170.22.134.[iii].

Série G. Par Bernard Prost, A. Vayssière et
H. Libois. 1892. pp.iii.443.

in progress.

Kampen.

REGISTER van charters en bescheiden in het oude
archief van Kampen. . . . Van 1251 [tot 1620].
1862–1887. pp.[iii].iv.332+viii.280+[iii].iv.304
+xi.259+7.310+xi.368. [7500.]

vols.iv–vi are by J. Nanninga Uitterdijk.

J. NANNINGA UITTERDIJK, Register van charters
en bescheiden in het oude archief van Kampen
(archief der Armenkamer). Kampen 1902. pp.
xviii.222. [633.]

Kent.

HERBERT W. KNOCKER, Kentish manorial inci-
dents. Manorial society's publications (no.7): 1912.
pp.12. [300.]

IRENE JOSEPHINE CHURCHILL, A handbook to Kent records, containing a summary account of the principal classes of historical documents relating to the county, and a guide to their chief places of deposit. Kent archæological society: Kent records (vol.ii): 1914. pp.xii.186. [100,000.]

IRENE JOSEPHINE CHURCHILL, East Kent records. A calendar of some unpublished deeds and court rolls in the library of Lambeth palace, with appendices referring especially to the manors of Knowlton, Sandown, South Court, and North Court. Kent archæological society: Kent records (vol.vii): 1922. pp.l.224. [152.]

C. EVELEIGH WOODRUFF, Calendar of institutions by the chapter of Canterbury sede vacante. Kent archæological society: Kent records (vol.viii): Canterbury 1924. pp.xviii.182. [1000.]

CATALOGUE of books on local history. Kent county library: Maidstone 1932. pp.67. [1250.]

FELIX HULL, Guide to the Kent county archives office. Kent county council: Maidstone 1958. pp. iii–xvi.290. [large number.]

KENT and the civil war. Catalogue of an exhibition of documents. Kent archives office: [Maidstone 1960]. pp.[ii].7. [51.]*

Kincardineshire.

JAMES FOWLER KELLAS JOHNSTONE, A concise bibliography of the history, topography, and institutions of the shires of Aberdeen, Banff, and Kincardine. Aberdeen university studies (no.66): Aberdeen 1914. pp.193. [4000.]

INDEX to secretary's and particular registers of sasines, sheriffdom of Kincardine, 1600–1608, 1617–1657. Registers and records of Scotland: Indexes (no.16): Edinburgh 1929. pp.[ii].168. [5500.]

King's Lynn.

H[ENRY] HARROD, Report on the deeds & records of the borough of King's Lynn. King's Lynn 1874. pp.[vi].153. [large number.]

[JOHN CORDY JEAFFRESON], The manuscripts of the corporations of Southampton and King's Lynn. Eleventh report of the Royal commission on historical manuscripts (appendix iii): 1887. pp.xv.292. [King's Lynn: 1000.]

Kircudbright.

INDEX to particular register of sasines for sheriff-dom of Dumfries and stewartries of Kircudbright

and Annandale. Registers and records of Scotland:
Indexes (no.21 &c.): Edinburgh.

   i. 1617–1671 . . . (no.21): 1931. pp.[iii].380.
    [11,000.]

   ii. 1672–1702 . . . (no.25): 1933. pp.[iii].375.
    [11,000.]

   iii. 1703–1732 . . . (no.27): 1934. pp.[iii].378.
    [11,000.]

Kloosterrade, abbey of.

G. D. FRANQUINET, Beredeneerde inventaris der
oorkonden en bescheiden van de abdij Kloosterrade. Beredeneerde inventaris der oorkonden en
bescheiden berustende op't Provinciaal archief
van Limburg (vol.i): Maastricht 1869. pp.viii.311.
[353.]

Kralingen.

R. BIJLSMA, De archieven der gemeenten Kralingen, Charlois en Katendrecht. Rotterdam 1909.
pp.76.

Kreuzlingen.

J[EAN] A[DAM] PUPIKOFER, Die regesten des stif-
tes Kreuzlingen im canton Thurgau. Die regesten

Europe

der archive in der Schweizerischen eidgenossenschaft (vol.iii): Chur 1853. pp.40. [440.]

*the index to this calendar is published with that
devoted to Disentis, q.v.*

Kurland.

[KARL EDUARD NAPIERSKY], Index corporis
historico–diplomatici Livoniae, Esthoniae, Curoniae. Verbundene ritterschaften Liv-, Esth- und
Kurland's: Riga &c.

> i. 1198–1449. 1833. pp.xvi.375. [1815.]
> ii. 1450–1631. 1835. pp.[iii].414. [1899.]

JULIUS PAUCKER, Die literatur der geschichte
Liv-, Esth- und Curlands aus den jahren 1836 bis
1847. Dorpat 1848. pp.vi.242. [1250.]

EDUARD WINKELMANN, Bibliotheca Livoniæ
historica. Systematisches verzeichniss der quellen
und hülfsmittel zur geschichte Estlands, Livlands
und Kurlands. St. Petersburg [1869–] 1870. pp.
[ii].x.404. [9060.]

—— Zweite... ausgabe. Berlin 1878. pp.xviii.
608. [11,756.]

F[RIEDRICH] G[EORG] V[ON] BUNGE, Liv, est- und
curländische urkunden-regesten bis zum jahre
1300. Leipzig 1881. pp.x.119. [1882.]

886

герцогскій архивъ въ Митавѣ. Митава [printed] 1903. pp.[iv].101. [2500.]

La Bassée.

[P. DE CLEENE], Inventaire sommaire des archives communales antérieures à 1790. Ville de La Bassée. Lille 1880. pp.[iii].v.3.5.32.11.5.10.14. 3.2.9.2.3. [10,000.]

La Bresse.

L[ÉOPOLD] DUHAMEL, Inventaire-sommaire des archives communales antérieures à 1780. . . .Ville de La Bresse. Épinal 1870. pp.[iii].13.9.5.7.17.10. 3.13. [5000.]

La Gorgue.

[P. DE CLEENE], Inventaire sommaire des archives communales antérieures à 1790. . . . Ville de La Gorgue. Lille 1885. pp.[iii].xvii.99. [30,000.]

La Mothe.

[HENRI LEPAGE, *ed.*], Inventaire des titres enlevés de La Mothe. Recueil de documents sur l'histoire de Lorraine (vol.iii): Nancy 1857 [on cover: 1858]. pp.266. [2500.]

125 copies printed.

Lancashire.

WALFORD D[AKING] SELBY, Lancashire and Cheshire records preserved in the Public record office. Record society for the publication of original documents relating to Lancashire and Cheshire (vols.vii–viii): 1882–1883. pp.xliv.222+ vi.223–626. [25,000.]

CAROLINE FISHWICK, A calendar of Lancashire and Cheshire exchequer depositions by commission from 1558 to 1702. Record society for the publication of original documents relating to Lancashire and Cheshire (vol.xi): Manchester [printed] 1885. pp.xxvi.216. [Lancashire: 500.]

[M. S. GIUSEPPI], List of the records of the duchy of Lancaster. Public record office: Lists and indexes (no.xiv): 1901. pp.viii.142. [20,000.]

JOHN [WILLIAM ROBINSON] PARKER, A calendar of the Lancashire assize rolls preserved in the Public record office. Record society for the publication of original documents relating to Lancashire and Cheshire (vols.xlvii, xlix): 1904–1905. pp.xxix.175+176*.176–439. [2000.]

LIST of records of the palatinates of Chester, Durham & Lancaster, the honour of Peveril, and the principality of Wales. Public record office:

Lists and indexes (no.xl): 1914. pp.xiv.183. [Lancaster: 50,000.]

JOHN R. NUTTALL, A calendar of charters and records belonging to the corporation of Lancaster. [Lancaster] 1929. pp.45. [25,000.]

HAROLD WHITAKER, A descriptive list of the printed maps of Lancashire, 1577–1900. Chetham society: Remains historical and literary (n.s. vol.ci): Manchester 1938. pp.xvi.247. [696.]

REGINALD SHARPE FRANCE, Guide to the Lancashire record office. Second edition. Preston 1962. pp.xii.353. [very large number.]

Landes.

H. TARTIÈRE, Inventaire-sommaire des archives départementales. Landes. [large number.]
    Séries A–H. 1868–1869. pp.xxvii.5.6.17.93. 10.35.8.4. ff.3.61.
    Série K. Par Marcel Gouron. 1928. pp.10.
    Série L. Par J. Mangin. 1946. pp.38.
    Série Q. Par Paul Aimès. 1931. pp.28.
    Série S. 1927. pp.36.
    Série U. 1935. pp.16.

É[MILE MARIE] TAILLEBOIS and H[ENRY] POY-DENOT, Bibliographie pour le congrès archéologique de Dax et Bayonne. Caen 1888. pp.20. [200.]

Langres

JULIEN DE LA BOULLAYE, Inventaire-sommaire des archives communales de Langres antérieures à 1790. Troyes 1882. pp.xiv.238. [75,000.]

[ALPHONSE] ROSEROT [*and others*], Inventaire sommaire des archives départementales. . . . Haute-Marne. Série G. Tome i. Évêché de Langres. Chaumont 1909. pp.481. [large number.]

Languedoc.

EUGÈNE THOMAS [vol.ii: L. DE LA COUR DE LA PIJARDIÈRE, iii: L. DE LA COUR DE PIJARDIÈRE and JOSEPH BERTHELÉ; iv: J. BERTHELÉ], Inventaire sommaire des archives départementales. . . . Hérault. Série C. Intendance de Languedoc. Montpellier 1865–1906. pp.xviii.456+480+438 +438. [large number.]

A[UGUST MARIE LOUIS ÉMILE] MOLINIER, Catalogue des actes de Simon et d'Amauri de Montfort. 1874. pp.[ii].109. [225.]

CATALOGUE des travaux manuscrits ou imprimés, cartes, ouvrages et documents divers . . . qui ont figuré à l'exposition organisée par la Société

languedocienne. Montpellier 1880. pp.xxxiv.
[275.]

ÉMILE BONNET, Collections de la Société archéologique de Montpellier. Catalogue des manuscrits.
Montpellier [printed] 1897. pp.[i].44. [106.]

J[EAN JOSEPH] TISSIER, Les sources de l'histoire
de Languedoc d'après les inventaires des archives
narbonnaises. Narbonne 1911. pp.69. [large number.]

M[AURICE OUDOT] DE DAINVILLE, Inventaire
sommaire des archives départementales. . . .
Hérault. Série B. Cour des comptes, aides et
finances de Languedoc. Montpellier 1931–1938.
pp.251+253–547+[iii].iv.coll.638. [large number.]

Laon.

[   ] LEFEBVRE, État sommaire des offices et
pratiques des notaires dont les minutes existent,
de 1518 au 1ᵉʳ août 1881, dans l'arrondissement de
Laon. Laon 1881. pp.47. [large number.]

AUGUSTE MATTON and VICTOR DESSEIN, Inventaire sommaire des archives communales antérieures à 1790. . . . Ville de Laon. Laon 1885.
pp.21.23.24.122.8.8.18.98.21.4.132. [75,000.]

Largentière.

ÉDOUARD ANDRÉ, Inventaire sommaire des archives communales antérieures à 1790. . . . Ville de Largentière. Le Puy 1914. pp.[v].142. [20,000.]

La Roche-sur-Yon.

EUG[ÈNE] LOUIS BITTON and A[LEXANDRE] BITTON, Catalogue des archives historiques de la ville de La Roche-sur-Yon. . . . Revues . . . par Victor Boudaud. Roche-sur-Yon 1908. pp.56. [large number.]

La Rochelle.

LÉOPOLD [GABRIEL] DELAYANT, Bibliographie rochelaise. La Rochelle 1882. pp.xv.439. [1377.]

[LOUIS MARIE DE MESCHINET] DE RICHEMOND, Inventaire sommaire des archives départementales antérieures à 1790. Département de la Charente-Inférieure. Série E. . . .Ville de La Rochelle. 1892 [*on cover:* 1893]. pp.515. [10,000.]

Lathum.

W. WIJNAENDTS VAN RESANDT and J. S. VAN VEEN, Register op de leenen der bannerheerlijkheid Baer . . . en der heerlijkheid Lathum. Gelre, vereeniging tot beoefening van geldersche geschiedenis, oudheidkunde en recht: Arnhem 1926. pp.iii–xvi.98. [200.]

the Lathum calendar is by J. S. van Veen only.

Lauderdale.

INDEX to particular register of sasines for shire of Berwick and bailiary of Lauderdale, 1617–1780. Record office, Scotland: Indexes (nos.12–13): Edinburgh 1928. pp.[ii].588 + [ii].470. [32,500.]

Lauingen.

REINHARD H[ERMANN] SEITZ, Stadtarchiv Lauingen. Bayerische archivinventare (no.14): München 1960. pp.xiii.283. [4500.]

Lavernat.

F[ORTUNÉ] LEGEAY, Inventaire-sommaire des registres de l'état civil antérieurs à 1790 des paroisses d'Aubigné, Coulongé, Lavernat, Sarcé, Vaas et Verneil-le-Chétif. Le Mans 1883. pp.23. [125.]

La Vid.

ÍNDICE de los documentos procedentes de los monasterios y conventos suprimidos que se conservan en el archivo de la Real academia de la historia. . . . Sección primera. Castilla y León. Tomo I. (Monasterios de Nuestra señora de la Vid y San Millan de la Cogolla). Madrid 1861. pp.vii. 453. [La Vid: 225.]

Léau.

[GUILLAUME JOSEPH CHARLES PIOT], Inventaire des chartes, cartulaires et comptes en rouleau de la ville de Léau. Inventaires des archives de la Belgique. Inventaires divers: Bruxelles 1879. pp.[ii]. iii.80. [203.]

Lede.

H. COPPEJANS-DESMEDT, Inventaris van het archief van de parochie en van het markizaat van Lede. Rijksarchief te Gent: Brussel 1960. pp.vii.21. [large number.]

Leeds.

KENNETH J[OHN] BONSER and HAROLD NICHOLS, Printed maps and plans of Leeds, 1711–1900. Thoresby society: Publications (vol.xlvii): Leeds 1960. pp.xxiv.148. [374.]

Leeuwarden.

G. J. VOORDA, Register van de archiven, stukken

en documenten, liggende in de stadsarchivekas te Leeuwarden. Leeuwarden 1803. pp.xxiv.91. [large number.]

[WOPKE EEKHOFF], Inventaris van het archief der stad Leeuwarden (vóórhist. tijdvak–1810). Leeuwarden 1880. pp.320. [large number.]

J. C. SINGELS, Inventaris van het oud-archief der stad Leeuwarden (van 1299–1814). Leeuwarden 1893. pp.341. [large number.]

W. JAARSMA, Inventaris van het archief der gemeente Leeuwarderadeel. Leeuwarden 1903. pp.84.

Leicester, city, county and diocese of.

JOHN CORDY JEAFFRESON, An index to the ancient manuscripts of the borough of Leicester. Westminster [1878]. pp.[iv].95. [2500.]

W. G. DIMOCK FLETCHER, Notes on Leicestershire mss. in the Public record office and our national libraries. Leicester 1882. pp.20. [1000.]
privately printed.

A. HAMILTON THOMPSON, A calendar of charters and other documents belonging to the hospital of William Wyggeston at Leicester. Leicester 1933. pp.[ii].xlvi.660. [1175.]

BASIL L. GIMSON and PERCY RUSSELL, Leicestershire maps. A brief survey. Leicester 1947. pp.vii. 40. [43.]

[A SURVEY of the ecclesiastical archives of the diocese of Leicester]. Pilgrim trust: Survey of ecclesiastical archives: [1952]. ff.9. [large number.]*

THE RECORDS of the corporation of Leicester. Museums and art gallery: Department of archives: Leicester 1956. pp.59. [large number.]

J. M. LEE, Leicestershire history. A handlist to printed sources in the libraries of Leicester. University of Leicester: Vaughan college papers (no.4): [Leicester] 1958. pp.viii.64. [500.]*
— — Corrections and additions. 1959. pp.4. [50.]*

Leipzig.

SIEGFRIED MOLTKE, Katalog der von der Handelskammer zu Leipzig aufbewahrten alten archive kaufmännischer körperschaften und ihres archivs zur wirtschaftsgeschichte Leipzigs. Handelskammer: Leipzig 1913. pp.[iii].126. [2000.]

Leith.

JOHN GRAHAM DALYELL, A brief analysis of the

chartularies of the abbey of Cambuskenneth, — chapel royal of Stirling, — preceptory of St. Anthony at Leith. Edinburgh 1828. pp.xi.93. [100.]

Lenzburg.

WALTHER MERZ, Inventar des stadtarchivs Lenzburg. Aarau 1916. pp.14. [2500.]

León, cathedral of.

RODOLFO [RUDOLF] BEER and J. ELOIS DIAZ JIMENEZ, Noticias bibliográficas y catálogo de los códices de la santa iglesia catedral de León. León 1888. pp.xxxv.44. [40.]

ZACARIAS GARCÍA VILLADA, Catálogo de los códices y documentos de la catedral de León. Madrid 1919. pp.263. [11,000.]

Le Puy.

[FRANCISQUE MANDET], Inventaire des principales pièces qui se trouvent déposées dans les archives des hospices du Puy. [s.l. 1862]. pp.4. [25.]

R. JOUANNE, Inventaire sommaire des archives hospitalières. Archives de l'hôtel-dieu du Puy. Le Puy 1931. pp.137. [large number.]

Europe

Lesquin.

THÉODORE [HENRI JOSEPH] LEURIDAN, Inventaire-sommaire des archives communales de Lesquin antérieures à 1790. Lille [printed] 1889. pp.25. [2500.]

25 copies privately printed.

Levant.

ANDRÉ LEVAL, Voyages en Levant pendant les XVIᵉ, XVIIᵉ et XVIIIᵉ siècles. Essai de bibliographie. Budapest 1897. pp.30. [125.]

ERMANNO ARMAO, Catalogo ragionato della mia biblioteca. Opere di consultazione, Venezia, Albania, oriente mediterraneo. Firenze 1953. pp. xiii.316. [800.]

Leyden.

W. J. C. RAMMELMAN ELSEVIER, Inventaris van het archief der gemeente Leyden, bevattende hare charters en privilegiën, alsmede die van den burg, van de kerken, gasthuizen en voormalige kloosters, 1240–1644. Leyden [1863]. pp.xiv.301 +viii.189. [2500.]

L. G. LE POOLE, Catalogus van de stukken en boeken in het archief van het Heilige geest- of

Europe

Arme wees- en kinderhuis te Leiden. Leiden 1902. pp.xl.89.

J[ACOB] C[ORNELIS] OVERVOORDE, Gemeente-archief Leiden. Archieven van de gasthuizen. Inventarissen en regestenlijsten. Leiden 1913. pp. xv.709. [3814.]

J. C. OVERVOORDE, Archieven van de stads-heerlijkheden en van de vroonwateren van Leiden. Inventarissen en regestenlijsten. Leiden 1914. pp.177.

J. C. OVERVOORDE, Gemeente-archief Leiden. Archieven van de kerken. Leiden 1915.
  i. Inventarissen en regesten van de s. Pieters-en van de O. l. v.-kerk. pp.xliii.334. [2093.]
  ii. Regesten uit de archieven van de sint Pancraskerk. pp.502. [1855.]

J. C. OVERVOORDE, Archieven van de gilden, de beurzen en van de rederijkerskamers van Leiden. Leiden [1921]. pp.207.

J. C. OVERVOORDE, Archieven van den Leidsche hallen. Leiden 1928. pp.79.

J. C. OVERVOORDE and J. W. VERBURGT, Archief der secretarie van de stad Leiden, 1253–1575.

Inventaris en regesten. Leiden 1937. pp.xxiv.683. [4000.]

Libourne.

J. A. BRUTAILS, GASTON DUCAUNNÈS-DUVAL and O. BIGOT, Inventaire sommaire des archives municipales antérieures à 1790. Ville de Libourne. Bordeaux 1903. pp.188. [large number.]

Lichfield, diocese of.

J. CHARLES COX, Catalogue of the muniments and manuscript books pertaining to the dean and chapter of Lichfield. Analysis of the Magnum

[A SURVEY of the ecclesiastical archives of the diocese of Lichfield]. Pilgrim trust: Survey of ecclesiastical archives: [1952]. ff.17. [large number.]*

Lichtenfels.

HEINRICH MEYER, Stadtarchiv Lichtenfels. Bayerische archivinventare (no.12): München 1958. pp.[iv].215. [2697.]

Licques, abbey of.

D[ANIEL] HAIGNERÉ, Les chartes de l'abbaye de Notre-Dame de Licques, ordre de Prémontré,

1078–1311. Mémoires de la Société académique de l'arrondissement de Boulogne-sur-Mer (vol. xv): Boulogne [1890]. pp.xvi.175. [104.]

Liége, bishopric, city, and principality of.

A. DEJARDIN, Recherches sur les cartes de la principauté de Liége et sur les plans de la ville. Liége 1860. pp.87. [200.]

—— Supplément. 1862. pp.22. [50.]

J. G. SCHOONBROODT, Inventaire analytique et chronologique des chartes du chapitre de Saint-Lambert à Liége. Liége 1863. pp.xii.446. [1294.]

STANISLAS BORMANS, Note sur les matériaux destinés à former un recueil de chroniques liégeoises. Bruxellès [c.1865]. pp.50. [300.]

X[AVIER MARIE GEORGES THÉODORE] DE THEUX [CHEVALIER DE MONTJARDIN], Bibliographie liégeoise. Contenant 1º Les livres imprimés à Liége. . . . 2º Les ouvrages . . . concernant l'histoire de l'ancienne principauté de Liége et de la province du même nom. Bruxelles 1867. pp.vii.359+[iii]. 361–713.ix–xv. [6500.]

—— Deuxième édition. Bruges 1885. pp.[iii]. coll.viii.1713. [15,000.]

S[TANISLAS] BORMANS, Répertoire chronologique des conclusions capitulaires au chapitre cathédral de Saint-Lambert à Liége. . . . Tome I. 1427–1650. Liége 1869–1875. pp.546. [6300.] *no more published.*

STANISLAS BORMANS, Inventaire chronologique des paweilhars conservés dans les dépôts publics et les bibliothèques privées de la province de Liége. [*s.l. c.*1870]. pp.125. [850.]

J. G. SCHOONBROODT, Inventaire analytique et chronologique des chartes du chapitre de Saint-Martin à Liége. Liége 1871. pp.vi.304. [855.]

STANISLAS BORMANS, Notice des cartulaires de la collégiale Saint-Denis, à Liége. Bruxelles [printed] 1872. pp.170. [251.]

STANISLAS BORMANS, Notice d'un cartulaire du clergé secondaire de Liége. Bruxelles [printed] 1873. pp.56. [83.]

J. G. SCHOONBROODT, Inventaire analytique et chronologique des archives de l'abbaye du Val-Saint-Lambert. Liége 1875. pp.xi.547. [1327.]

EUGÈNE BACHA, Catalogue des actes de Jean de Bavière. Liége 1899. pp.57. [202.]

ALPH. DELESCLUSE and DD. [DIEUDONNÉ] BROU-WERS, Catalogue des actes de Henri de Gueldre, prince-évêque de Liége. Bibliothèque de la Faculté

de philosophie et lettres de l'université de Liége
(vol.v): Bruxelles 1900. pp.xvi.467. [423.]

ÉDOUARD PONCELET, Inventaire analytique des
chartes de la collégiale de Saint-Pierre à Liége.
Commission royale d'histoire: Bruxelles 1906.
pp.xcv.540. [1254.]

ÉDOUARD PONCELET, Inventaire analytique des
chartes de la collégiale de Sainte-Croix à Liége.
Commission royale d'histoire: Bruxelles 1911
[-1922]. pp.clxxxviii.524+[iii].552. [2864.]

L[ÉON] LAHAYE, Analyses des actes contenus
dans les registres du Scel des grâces. Société des
bibliophiles liégeois: I iége 1921–1931. pp.iii–xii.
260+[iii].431. [5000.]
covers the period 1702–1794.

L[ÉON] LAHAYE, Inventaire analytique des chartes
de la collégiale de Saint-Jean l'évangéliste à Liége.
Commission royale d'histoire: Bruxelles 1921–
1933. pp.[iii].cxix.450+505. [1939.]

LOUIS JADIN, Les actes de la Congrégation
consistoriale concernant les Pays-Bas, la principauté de Liége et la Franche-Comté, 1593–1677.
Institut historique belge de Rome: Bulletin
(fasc.xvi): Rome 1935. pp.622. [2500.]

J. YERNAUX, Inventaire sommaire des archives des greffes scabinaux, communautés, seigneuries et paroisses conservées au Dépôt des Archives de l'état à Liége. Archives de l'état à Liége: Tongres 1937. pp.108. [very large number.]

ÉMILE FAIRON, Inventaire des archives de la Chambre des comptes. Archives de l'état à Liége: Tongres 1937. pp.87. [very large number.]

GUIL[LAUME] HENNEN, Inventaire des protocoles de notaires conservés aux Archives de l'état à Liége. Archives de l'état à Liége: Tongres [printed] 1938. pp.67. [large number.]

MÉMORIAL des archives détruites en 1944. Institut archéologique liégeois: Liége.
   i. Inventaire des dépêches du Conseil privé de Liége. Épiscopat d'Ernest de Bavière. 1945. pp.vii.156. [1500.]
   ii. — Épiscopats . . . 1763 . . . –1801. 1947. pp.vii.156. [1500.]

L. E. HALKIN and J. HOYOUX, Bulletin bibliographique d'histoire liégeoise. Travaux publiés de 1949 à 1952. Commission belge de bibliographie: Bibliographia belgica (no.7): Bruxelles 1954. pp. 120. [808.]

a bibliography for 1944–1948 appeared in the Annuaire d'histoire liégeoise (*1948*), *iv.51–168.*

RAOUL VAN DER MADE, Inventaire analytique et chronologique du chartrier des Guillemins de Liége (1317–1669). Académie royale de Belgique: Commission royale d'histoire: Bruxelles 1955. pp.302. [334.]

INVENTAIRE analytique de documents relatifs à l'histoire du diocèse de Liège sous le régime des nonces de Cologne (1584–1606). Institut historique belge de Rome: Analecta vaticano-belgica (2nd ser., section B, no.2 &c.): Bruxelles &c.

  2. 1584–1606. Par Henry Dessart, Léon E. Halkin, Jean Hoyoux. 1957. pp.253. [596.]
  3. 1606–1634. Par Georges Hansotte, Richard Forgeur. 1958. pp.315. [974.]
  4. 1680–1687. Par Jean Hoyoux. 1962. pp.70. [222.]

JEAN HOYOUX, Bulletin bibliographique d'histoire liégeoise. Bibliographia belgica (no.36 &c.): Bruxelles 1958 &c.

in progress; the first two numbers form part of the Annuaire d'histoire liégeoise.

Liesse.

J[OSEPH] SOUCHON, Inventaire sommaire des archives hospitalières antérieures à 1790. . . . Ville de Liesse. Laon 1902. pp.52. [10,000.]

Lille.

A[NDRÉ JOSEPH GHISLAIN] LE GLAY and A. DES-
PLANQUE, Inventaire sommaire des archives départementales. . . . Nord. Série B. Chambre des
comptes de Lille. Tome I. Lille 1863. pp.v.xxii.447.
[large number.]

no more published.

—— [another edition]. Par [Chrétien] De-
haisnes [*and others*]. [1872–]1899–1931. pp.xxiv.
421 + v.561 + [iii].276 + 420 + 465.2.3 + 385.
6.2+384.2.6.3+348+cxii.391+xliii.453. [large
number.]

in progress?

[CHARLES EDMOND HENRI DE COUSSEMAKER],
Inventaire analytique et chronologique des
archives de la Chambre des comptes, à Lille.
Société impériale des sciences, de l'agriculture et
des arts de Lille: 1865. pp.xii.954. [2000.]

250 copies printed; covers the archives of 706–1270.

CH[ARLES] PAEILE, Notice sur les archives communales de Lille, antérieures à 1790. Lille 1868.
pp.41. [large number.]

[CHRÉTIEN DEHAISNES], Inventaire analytique et
chronologique [vol.ii: sommaire] des archives
hospitalières de la ville de Lille [vol.ii: antérieures

à 1790]. Lille 1871–1898. pp.[xvi].466+[iv].555. [50,000.]

L[OUIS FRANÇOIS] QUARRÉ-REYBOURBON, Essai bibliographique et catalogue de plans et gravures concernant le bombardement de Lille en 1792. Lille 1887. pp.xi.121. [200.]

L[OUIS FRANÇOIS] QUARRÉ-REYBOURBON, Plans anciens et modernes de la ville de Lille, suivis des cartes de la châtellenie de Lille. 1901. pp.82. [390.]

HUBERT NÉLIS, Chambre des comptes de Lille. Catalogue des chartes du Sceau de l'audience. Tome premier. Inventaire des archives de Belgique: Bruxelles 1915. pp.xciii.iii.464. [2011.]
no more published.

MAX BRUCHET, Inventaire sommaire des archives municipales de Lille antérieures à 1790. Lille 1926. pp.lxxviii.191. [50,000.]
limited to series AA; the introduction includes a historic bibliography of the town; in progress?

Limburg.

INVENTARISSEN van het oud-provinciaal archief in Limburg. Maastricht 1885. pp.26.

A[UGUSTE] J[EAN] FLAMENT, Inventaris der atlassen en van de kaarten zoo gedruckte, als geteekende, die op het hertogdom Limburg betrekking hebben, zich bevindend op het Rijksarchief in Limburg. Maastricht 1888. pp.85.

supplements by A. J. A. Flament and J. M. van de Venne appear in the Verslagen omtrent 's rijks oude archieven *(1915–1921), xxxviii–xliv.*

HENRI VAN NEUSS, Dépôt de Hasselt. Inventaires sommaires des archives de l'état en Belgique: Bruxelles 1901. pp.66. [10,000.]

ALPHONSE VERKOOREN, Inventaire des chartes et cartulaires des duchés de Brabant et de Limbourg et des pays d'outre-mer. Première partie. . . . Tome 1er [&c.]. Inventaire des archives de la Belgique: Bruxelles 1910 &c.

in progress.

A[LFRED] HANSAY, Inventaire des archives notariales conservées au dépôt des Archives de l'état à Hasselt. [Brussels *c.*1910]. pp.69. [large number.]

BIBLIOGRAFIE van Limburg. Limburgs geschieden oudheidkundig genootschap: Maastricht 1947. pp.6.

H[ERMAN] HARDENBERG, Inventaris van de archieven der rechtscolleges, alleensprekende rechters en rechterlijke ambtenaren, van 1794 tot 1841 gefungeerd hebbende op het grondgebied van de tegenwoordige nederlandsche provincie Limburg. Ministerie van onderwijs, kunsten en wetenschapen: 's-Gravenhage 1949. pp.167. [2461.]

Limerick.

ROISIN DE NAIS, A bibliography of Limerick history and antiquities. Limerick county library: [Limerick 1962]. pp.[v].61. [581.]

Limoges.

CHARLES NICOLAS ALLOU, Sur les manuscrits conservés au séminaire et à l'hôtel de ville de Limoges. Paris 1836. pp.18. [210.]

[ANDRÉ] ANTOINE THOMAS, Inventaire-sommaire des archives communales de Limoges antérieures à 1790. Limoges 1882. pp.[ii].16.5.4.7.3.2.2.67.2.2. 29.4.5. [25,000.]

[AUGUSTE] ALFRED LEROUX, Inventaire sommaire des archives hospitalières antérieures à 1790. . . . Ville de Limoges. Limoges 1884–1887. pp.xxxviii. [502]. [large number.]

LOUIS GUIBERT, Documents, analyses de pièces, extraits & notes relatifs à l'histoire municipale des deux villes de Limoges. Société des archives historiques du Limousin (1st ser., vols.vii–viii): Limoges 1897–1902. pp.xiii.379+vi.432. [1100.]

[AUGUSTE] ANTOINE LEROUX and C. RIVAIN, Inventaire sommaire des archives départementales. . . . Haute-Vienne. Série G. Évêché de Limoges. Limoges 1908. pp.xxix.316. [large number.]

Limousin.

[AUGUSTE] ALFRED LEROUX, Chroniqueurs et historiens de la Marche et du Limousin avant la révolution. Limoges 1886. pp.59. [193.]

[AUGUSTE] ALFRED LEROUX, Les sources de l'histoire du Limousin. Société archéologique et historique du Limousin: Bulletin (vol.xliv): Limoges 1895. pp.viii.260. [5000.]

also issued as vol.i of the Bibliothèque historique du Limousin.

Limoux.

L. A. BUZAIRIES, Libertés et coutumes de la ville de Limoux, avec le catalogue des chartes et des documents historiques déposés dans les archives de l'hôtel de ville. Limoux 1851. pp.144. [250.]

Lincoln, city, county and diocese of.

ERNEST L. GRANGE, A list of civil war tracts and

broadsides relating to the county of Lincoln. Horncastle 1889. pp.[iii].20. [77.]

75 copies privately printed.

[w. BOYD and w. O. MASSINGBERD], Lincolnshire records. Abstracts of final concords, temp. Richard I, John, and Henry III. Vol.I. 1896. pp. vii.176+[ii].177–394. [1250.]

privately printed.

— — Volume II. Final concords of the county of Lincoln from the feet of fines preserved in the Public record office, A.D. 1244–1272, with additions from various sources, A.D. 1176–1250. . . . By C. W. Foster. Lincoln record society: Publications (vol.xvii): 1920. pp.[iii].lxxxi.448. [1000.]

C. W. FOSTER, Institutions to benefices in the diocese of Lincoln, 1540–1670: calendar no.1. [*s.l.* 1903]. pp.32. [300.]

WALTER DE GRAY BIRCH, Catalogue of the royal charters and other documents belonging to the corporation of Lincoln. [Lincoln] 1906. pp.88. [1000.]

C. W. FOSTER, Lincoln episcopal records in the time of Thomas Cooper. Lincoln record society: Publications (vol.ii): 1912. pp.xxiv.447. [3000.]

[WILLIAM JOHN HARDY], The rt. hon. lord Boston's muniments at Hedsor relating to south Lincolnshire. Horncastle 1914. pp.75. [207.]

C. W. FOSTER, Calendars of administrations in the Consistory court of Lincoln, A.D. 1540–1659. Lincoln record society: Publications (vol.xvi): Horncastle 1921. pp.xi.410. [20,000.]

[A SURVEY of the ecclesiastical archives of the diocese of Lincoln]. Pilgrim trust: Survey of ecclesiastical archives: [1952]. ff.22. [large number.]*

KATHLEEN MAJOR, A handlist of the records of the bishop of Lincoln and of the archdeacons of Lincoln and Stow. 1953. pp.xv.122. [2500.]

Lindau.

JOSEPH WÜRDINGER, Urkunden-auszüge zur geschichte der stadt Lindau, ihrer klöster, stiftungen und besitzungen, vom jahr 1240 bis zum jahr 1621. Verein für geschichte des Bodensee's und seiner umgebung: Lindau 1872. pp.88. [600.]

Linselles.

TH[ÉODORE DÉSIRÉ JOSEPH] LEURIDAN, Inventaire sommaire des archives communales antérieures à

1790. . . . Commune de Linselles. Lille 1881. pp. [iii].xiii.11.5.31.4.4.9.19.3.4.3.9.6. [15,000.]

Lisieux, diocese of.

[LÉOPOLD FERDINAND DÉSIRÉ] PIEL, Inventaire historique des actes transcrits aux insinuations ecclésiastiques de l'ancien diocèse de Lisieux, ou documents officiels analysés pour servir à l'histoire du personnel de l'évêché, de la cathédrale, des collégiales, des abbayes . . . ainsi que de toutes les familles notables de ce diocèse (1692–1790). Lisieux 1891–1895. pp.[v].lxxx.887+791+965+ 907+969. [25,000.]

Lithuania.

ISTORIJOS archyvas.

    i. XVI amžiaus Lietuvos inventoriai. Surinko K[onstantinas] Jablonskis. 1934. pp.xii.coll. 680. pp.131. [7500.]

Liverpool, city and diocese of.

R. D. RADCLIFFE, Schedule of deeds and documents, the property of colonel Thomas Richard Grosse . . . at Shaw hill, Chorley. Liverpool [printed] 1895. pp.83. [250.]

[A SURVEY of the ecclesiastical archives of the diocese of Liverpool]. Pilgrim trust: Survey of ecclesiastical archives: [1952]. ff.4. [large number.]*

Livonia.

[K. E. NAPIERSKY], Index corporis historico-diplomatici Livoniae, Esthoniae, Curoniae. Verbundene ritterschaften Liv-, Esth- und Kurland's: Riga &c.

    i. 1198–1449. 1833. pp.xvi.375. [1815.]
    ii. 1450–1631. 1835. pp.[iii].414. [1899.]

JULIUS PAUCKER, Die literatur der geschichte Liv-, Esth- und Curlands aus den jahren 1836 bis 1847. Dorpat 1848. pp.vi.242. [1250.]

— — [supplement]. Verzeichniss der neu erschienenen schriften zur geschichte [&c.]. Riga 1857. pp.43. [250.]

EDUARD WINKELMANN, Bibliotheca Livoniæ historica. Systematisches verzeichniss der quellen und hülfsmittel zur geschichte Estlands, Livlands und Kurlands. St. Petersburg [1869–]1870. pp.[ii].x.404. [9060.]

— — Zweite . . . ausgabe. Berlin 1878. pp. xviii.608. [11,756.]

C[ARL CHRISTIAN GERHARD] SCHIRREN, Verzeichniss livländischer geschichts-quellen in schwedischen archiven und bibliotheken. Dorpat 1861-1868. pp.[vi].232. [6000.]

— — Zweite . . . ausgabe. Berlin 1878. pp. xviii.608. [11,756.]

F[RIEDRICH] G[EORG] V[ON] BUNGE, Liv-, est- und curländische urkunden-regesten bis zum jahre 1300. Leipzig 1881. pp.x.119. [1882.]

DIE LIVLÄNDISCHE geschichtsliteratur [1902– 1913: Gesellschaft für geschichte und altertums- kunde der Ostseeprovinzen Russlands:] Riga.

   1883. Von . . . Arthur Poelchau. pp.87. [202.]
   1884. pp.95. [282.]
   1885. pp.108. [299.]
   1886. pp.102. [300.]
   1887. pp.84. [350.]
   1888. pp.100. [361.]
   1889. pp.103. [362.]
   1890. pp.108. [331.]
   1891. pp.[iii].96. [378.]
   1892. pp.92. [354.]
   1893. pp.111. [379.]
   1894. pp.90. [400.]
   1895. pp.[iii].76. [400.]
   1896. pp.[iv].139. [600.]
   1897. pp.[iii].59. [400.]
   1898. pp.[iii].94. [750.]
   1899. pp.[iii].71. [400.]
   1900–1901. pp.[iii].124. [600.]

1902. Herausgegeben . . . durch Arnold Feuereisen. 1904. pp.vi.99. [756.]

1903. 1905. pp.[v].83. [835.]

1904. 1907. pp.[v].72. [600.]

1905. 1908. pp.[iv].76. [620.]

1906. 1909. pp.[iv].74. [557.]

1907. 1910. pp.[v].77. [561.]

1908. Herausgegeben . . durch P[aul von der] Osten-Sacken. 1911. pp.[viii].75. [630.]

1909. Herausgegeben . . . durch Woldemar Wulffius. 1912. pp.[vi].65. [537.]

1910. Herausgegeben . . . durch Leonid Arbusow. 1912. pp.[vi].90. [657.]

1911. Herausgegeben . . . durch W.Wulffius. 1913. pp.[iv].67. [563.]

1912. 1913. pp.[v].70. [547.]

1913. 1923. pp.[vi].80. [696.]

no more published.

Loir-et-Cher.

INVENTAIRE sommaire des archives départementales. . . . Loir-et-Cher. Blois [very large number.]

Séries C–E. Par [Louis Georges] A[lfred] de Martonne [*and others*]. 1887. pp.x.7.3.208. 211.

Série G. Par Fernand Bournon [*and others*]. 1894–1913. pp.335+431.

Série H. Par G. Trouillard. 1936–   . pp.
[iii].441+   .
in progress.

Loire.

INVENTAIRE-sommaire des archives départe-
mentales. . . . Loire. Paris [*afterwards:* Saint-
Etienne] 1865. [very large number.]
Séries A–B. Par Auguste Chaverondier. 1870.
pp.32.432.
Série B. Par A. Chaverondier [J. de Frémin-
ville]. 1888–1905. pp.384+356.
Série C. [1862]. pp.13.
Série E. Par J. Augagneur. [1867]. pp.72.
Série E, supplément. Par A. Chaverondier et
J. de Fréminville. 1899. pp.57.547.
Série H, supplément. Par J. de Fréminville,
1926. pp.140.
in progress.

LOUIS BIERNAWSKI, Répertoire critique des anciens inventaires conservés aux archives départementales de la Loire. Montbrison [printed] 1932.
pp.[iii].47. [150.]

Loire, Haute-.

INVENTAIRE-sommaire des archives départe-

mentales. . . . Département de la Haute-Loire.
Le Puy. [very large number.]

Série B. Par A. Aymard. 1865. pp.116.

Série G. Par A. Jacotin. 1903. pp.287.

Série G, supplément. Par Étienne Delcambe.
1948. pp.[iii].136.

Série H, supplément. Par René Jouanne . . .
Pierre Fournier et Etienne Delcambre.
1931. pp.137.

in progress.

Loire–Inférieure.

INVENTAIRE-sommaire des archives départementales. . . . Loire-Inférieure. Paris [*afterwards:*
Nantes]. [very large number.]

Série B–D. Par L. Maître [et É. Gabory].
[1898–]1902–1930. pp.478 + 253 + xviii.
210.

Série C. Par S. Canal et E. Brouillard. 1948.
pp.69.

Série E. 1879. pp.vi.473.

Série E, supplément. 1892–1930. pp.xii.438
+336.

Séries G–H. 1884. pp.xxiv.304.

Série K. Par B. Pocquet du Haut-Jussé, [   ]
Chevrel et [   ] Gabory. 1920. pp.11.

Série L. 1909. pp.x.422.

Série Q. Par Léon Maitre. 1911. pp.32.
Série T. 1941. pp.20.
Série V. 1913. pp.15.
in progress.

Loiret.

INVENTAIRE-sommaire des archives départementales. . . . Loiret. Paris [*afterwards:* Orléans].
[very large number.]

> Série A. Par F. Maupré et J. Doinel. 1878.
> pp.383.
> Séries A–B. Mar J. Doinel. 1886. pp.18.382.
> Série B. Par C. Bloch. 1900. pp.45.372.
> Série C. Par C. Bloch et Jacques Soyer. 1927.
> pp.xi.280.
> Série D. 1917. pp.viii.260.
> Série E. Par Jacques Soyer. 1934. pp.15.
> Série F. 1933. pp.29.
> Série I. 1935. pp.15.
> Série K. 1912. pp.15.
> *in progress.*

[JACQUES SOYER], Répertoire bibliographique
sommaire de l'histoire du département du Loiret.
[Société archéologique: Bulletin (nos.208–209,
219–224: Supplément): Orléans 1915–1925]. pp.
lxxxiv.100. [2750.]

JACQUES SOYER, Répertoire des cartes et plans conservés dans les archives départementales du Loiret. Orléans 1925. pp.39. [5000.]

Lokeren.

ROBERT SCHOORMAN, Inventaire sommaire des archives seigneuriales et communales de Lokeren. [Brussels *c.*1910]. pp.8. [5000.]

Lombardy.

ISAIA GHIRON, Bibliografia lombarda. Catalogo dei manoscritti intorno alla storia della Lombardia esistenti nella Biblioteca nazionale di Brera. Milano 1884. pp.152. [800.]

ANTONIO VISMARA, Bibliografia storica delle cinque giornate e degli avvenimenti politico-militari in Lombardia nel 1848. Municipio di Milano. Milano 1898. pp.xi.275. [3750.]

Lombez.

VICTOR MARSEILHAN, Inventaire sommaire des archives hospitalières antérieures à 1790. . . . Hospice de Lombez. Auch 1878. pp.[iii].7.9.4.5.7. [1000.]

London, city, county and diocese of.

[W. H. and H. C. OVERALL], Analytical indexes

to volumes II. and VIII. of the series of records known as remembrancia, preserved among the archives of the city of London . . . Vol.II.1593–1609, Vol.III. 1613–1640. 1870. pp.xv.172. [750.]

[W. H. and H. C. OVERALL], Analytical index to the series of records known as the remembrancia, preserved among the archives of the city of London. A.D. 1579–1665. 1878. pp.[ii].xvii.624. [2500.]

JOHN GREGORY CRACE, A catalogue of maps, plans, and views of London, Westminster & Southwark collected . . . by Frederick Crace. 1878. pp.xxii.696. [1000.]
the collection is now in the British museum.

CATALOGUE of the maps, plans, and views of London and Westminster collected by the late mr. Frederick Crace. Lent for exhibition in the South Kensington museum. Science and art department: 1879. pp.viii.152. [1000.]

REGINALD R. SHARPE, Calendar of letters from the mayor and corporation of the city of London, circa A.D. 1350–1370, enrolled and preserved among the archives of the corporation. 1885. pp. xxx.186. [353.]

W[ILLIAM] P[HILLIMORE] W[ATTS] PHILLIMORE, A calendar of inquisitiones post mortem for Middlesex and London returned into the Court of chancery 1 Henry VII to 20 Charles I., 1485–1645. 1890. pp.54. [2250.]

CHARLES WELCH, The bibliography of the livery companies of the city of London. 1890. pp.7. [50.]

LONDON. British museum: Catalogue of printed books. 1891. coll.444. [7500.]

W[ILLIAM] J[OHN] HARDY and W[ILLIAM] PAGE, A calendar to the feet of fines for London & Middlesex . . . Richard I. to Richard III [to 11 and 12 Elizabeth]. 1892–1893. pp.[iv].240.lxiii+[iii]. 159.xxxv. [5000.]

AN EXHIBITION of the records of the city of London, held . . . in connection with the Anglo-american conference of professors of history. 1921. pp.8. [100.]

A[RTHUR] H[ERMANN] THOMAS, Calendar of early mayor's court rolls preserved among the archives of the corporation of the city of London at the Guildhall, a. d. 1298–1307. Cambridge 1924. pp. xlv.304. [400.]

A[RTHUR] H[ERMANN] THOMAS, Calendar of plea and memoranda rolls preserved among the archives of the corporation of London. Cambridge.

    1323–1364. 1926. pp.xxxvi.334. [1250.]
    1364–1381. 1929. pp.lxiv.360. [1250.]
    1381–1412. 1932. pp.xli.369. [500.]
    1413–1437. 1943. pp.xli.370. [1000.]
the title varies; in progress?

CHARLES W. F. GOSS, The London directories, 1677–1855. 1932. pp.xi.147. [300.]

PHILIP E[DMUND] JONES and RAYMOND SMITH, A guide to the records in the corporation of London records office and the Guildhall library muniment room. 1951. pp.203. [very large number.]

[A SURVEY of the ecclesiastical archives of the diocese of London]. Pilgrim trust: Survey of ecclesiastical archives: [1952]. ff.26. [large number.]★

PHILIP E[DMUND] JONES, Calendar of plea and memoranda rolls preserved among the archives of the corporation of the city of London at the Guildhall, A.D. 1437–1457. Cambridge 1954. pp. xxviii.229. [500.]

VESTRY minutes of parishes within the city of London: A handlist. Guildhall library: 1958. pp. [i].27. [500.]

CHURCHWARDENS accounts of parishes within the city of London. A handlist. Guildhall library: 1960. pp.[ii].28. [large number.]

WILLIAM F. KAHL, The development of London livery companies: an historical essay and a select bibliography. Harvard graduate school of business administration: Kress library of business and economics: Publications (no.15): Boston [1960]. pp. viii.104. [2000.]

PHILIP E[DMOND] JONES, Calendar of plea and memoranda rolls preserved among the archives of the corporation of the city of London at the Guildhall a. d. 1458–1482. Cambridge 1961. pp. xxi.217. [500.]

Loo, abbey of.

P[HILIPPE] DE STOOP, Notice sur l'abbaye de Loo et inventaire de ses archives. Société d'émulation de Bruges: Recueil de chroniques, chartes et autres documents concernant l'histoire et les antiquités de la Flandre (vol.i): Bruges 1843. pp.58. [430.]

Lorraine. [*see also* **Alsace-Lorraine.**]

[JEAN NICOLAS BEAUPRÉ], Notices analytiques de quelques écrits à consulter pour l'histoire de

Lorraine au XVIe et au XVIIe siècle. Saint-Nicolas-de-Port [printed] 1846. pp.24. [8.]

25 copies privately printed.

[FRANÇOIS JEAN BAPTISTE NOËL], Catalogue raisonné des collections lorraines . . . de m. Noël . . . contenant la table de la deuxième édition de l'Histoire de Lorraine de d. Calmet et celle des titres diplomatiques qui se trouvent dans la première édition et qui ne sont pas reproduits dans la seconde, avec mention de ceux de ces titres qui ont été supprimés par la censure. Nancy 1850–1851. pp.xxviii.450+[iii].451–807. [7000.]

[JEAN NICOLAS] BEAUPRÉ, Nouvelles recherches de bibliographie lorraine, 1500–1700. Nancy &c. [1853–]1856. pp.32+84+116+64+4. [50.]

RECUEIL de documents sur l'histoire de Lorraine. Société d'archéologie Lorraine: Nancy 1857. pp. 266. [2000.]

125 copies printed.

[   ] CLERCX, Catalogue des manuscrits relatifs à l'histoire de Metz et de la Lorraine. Bibliothèque de la ville: Metz 1856. pp.[iii].238. [2000.]

AUG[USTE] PROST, Tables . . . des morceaux accessoires, documents et titres contenus dans les deux éditions de l'Histoire de Lorraine par dom Calmet. 1877. pp.56. [1000.]

ÉDOUARD SAUER, Département de la Lorraine. Inventaire-sommaire des archives départementales antérieures à 1790: Metz 1879–1895. pp.[x]. 7.49.127.12.124+[v].284+[v].v.455. [100,000.]

J[USTIN] FAVIER, Catalogue des manuscrits de la Société d'archéologie lorraine. Nancy 1887. pp.86. [1000.]

PAUL MARICHAL, Catalogue des manuscrits conservés à la Bibliothèque nationale sous les n°s 1 à 725 de la Collection de Lorraine. Société d'archéologie lorraine: Nancy 1896. pp.xlv.480. [5000.]

150 copies printed.

CATALOGUE des collections manuscrites et imprimées relatives à l'histoire de Metz et de la Lorraine léguées par m. Auguste Prost. Bibliothèque nationale: 1897. pp.114. [2500.]

ÉMILE DUVERNOY, Catalogue des actes des ducs de Lorraine de 1048 à 1139 et de 1176 à 1220. Nancy 1915. pp.[ii].264. [382.]

HENRI [AUGUSTE] OMONT, Collections Emmery et Clouët-Buvignier sur l'histoire de Metz et de la Lorraine conservées à la Bibliothèque nationale.

Inventaire. Société nationale des antiquaires de la France: Mettensia (vol.vii): 1919. pp.[vii].156. [20,000.]

P. D'ARBOIS DE JUBAINVILLE, Fonds de la présidence de Lorraine, 1870–1918. Répertoire numérique. Archives départementales de la Moselle: Metz 1920 &c.

in progress.

Lot.

INVENTAIRE-sommaire des archives départementales. . . . Lot. Cahors. [very large number.]
Séries A–B. Par Louis Combarieu. 1883. pp. 11.448.
Séries B–C. 1887. pp.10.270.
Séries D–H. 1900. pp.7.263.
Série L. 1947. pp.70.
Série V. Par V. Fourastié. 1913. pp.5.
in progress.

RENÉ PRAT, Étude de m^e Herbecq, notaire à Cahors, étude actuelle de m^e Rieucau. Archives du département du Lot: Minutier des notaires du Lot: Répertoires numériques des archives déposées par les notaires du Lot: Cahors 1943. pp.12.

Lot-et-Garonne.

[ERNEST CROZET], Catalogue indicatif des documents intéressant le Département de Lot-et-Garonne conservés aux Archives de l'empire et aux Archives du département de la Gironde. [Agen 1861]. pp.15. [100.]

INVENTAIRE-sommaire des archives départementales. . . . Lot-et-Garonne. Agen. [very large number.]

> Séries A–E, G–H. Par [Ernest] Crozet, J. B. A. Bosvieux et G[eorges Eustache] Tholin. Agen 1863–1878. pp.xxi.297.12.1. 11.93.3.4.
>
> Série E, supplément. Par G. Tholin [et René Bonnat]. 1885–1932. pp.xv.351.
>
> Série K. Par Louis Desgraves. 1946. pp.13.
>
> Série L. Par R. Bonnat. 1908–1925. pp.xx: 398+xi.402.
>
> — Tables dressées par [G. E.] Tholin. 1883. pp.189.

in progress.

G[EORGES EUSTACHE] THOLIN, Catalogue du fonds de Bellecombe légué et conservé aux archives départementales de Lot-et-Garonne. Auch 1902. pp.xxxvii.309. [125.]

Loudun.

N. CHAUVINEAU, Inventaire-sommaire des ar-

chives communales antérieures à 1790 de Loudun.
Loudun 1869. pp.[iii].vii.5.16.13.4.4.6.31.3.
[20,000.]

Louny.

BOŘIVOJ LŮŽEK, Okresní archiv v Lounech.
Průvodce po fondech a sbírkách. Archivní správa
ministerstva vnitra: Praha 1956. pp.119. [large
number.]

Lourdes.

E. DUVIAU, Inventaire sommaire des archives
communales antérieures à 1790. . . . Lourdes.
Lourdes 1913. pp.307. [large number.]

MIGUEL HERRERO GARCÍA, Bibliografía española
de Lourdes, 1858–1958. Libros azules (no.ii): Madrid 1958. pp.23. [80.]

Louth.

[R.] W. GOULDING, The court rolls of the manor
of Louth. [*s.l.* 1901]. pp.[12]. [50.]

Louvain.

MARCEL BOURGUIGNON, Inventaire des archives
de l'assistance publique de la ville de Louvain.

Archives générales du royaume: Tongres 1933. pp.cxxxv.701. [100,000.]

—— Table onomastique. 1934. pp.87.

Lozère.

INVENTAIRE-sommaire des archives départementales. . . . Lozère. Mende. [very large number.]

Série B. Par Raymond Daucet. [*c.*1934]. pp.50.

Série C. Par F[erdinand] André. 1876. pp. 386.

Série E. Par Ch. Porée [*and others*]. 1926. pp.xxxix.296.

Série G. Par F. André. 1882–1890. pp.7.328 +334.

Séries G–H. Par F. André [*and others*]. 1904. pp.xxiii.54.300.6.66.

Série N. Par R. Rohmer. 1916. pp.6.

Séries O–P. Par Cl. Brunel. 1911. pp.12.

Séries U–V. 1913. pp.7.

in progress.

Lübeck.

JOHANN PAUL FINCKE, Conspectus bibliothecae historicae saxoniae inferioris cvivs specimen exhibet scriptores lvbecenses. Hambvrgi [1744]. pp.31. [100.]

Lucca.

[SALVATORE BONGI], Inventario del R. archivio di stato in Lucca. Documenti degli archivi toscani: Luca 1872–1888. pp.xxxii.408+[v].426+xi.460+viii.558. [25,000.]

[LUIGI FUMI, MARQUIS GIUSTINIANO VITELLESCHI DEGLI AZZI and E. LAZZARESCHI], Regesti. R. archivio di stato in Lucca: Lucca, Pescia 1903 &c.
in progress.

[CESARE SARDI], Comune di Lucca. Inventario dall'archivio. Lucca 1913. pp.124. [10,000.]

Lucerne, abbey of.

P. LE CACHEUX, Inventaire sommaire des archives départementales. . . . Manche. Série H. Tome IV. Abbaye de la Lucerne. Saint-Lô 1914. pp.[iii].66. [3000.]

Lüdinghausen.

ERNST MÜLLER and REINHARD LÜDICKE, Inventare der nichtstaatlichen archive des kreises Lüdinghausen. Historische kommission der provinz Westfalen: Inventare der nichtstaatlichen archive (vol.ii, no.3): Münster 1917. pp.[ix].115. [2500.]

Lunéville.

CHARLES DENIS, Inventaire des registres de l'état

931

civil de Lunéville (1562–1792). Nancy [printed] 1899. pp.x.371. [5000.]

280 copies printed.

É[MILE] DUVERNOY, Inventaire sommaire des archives départementales.... Meurthe–et–Moselle. Tome VIII. Série E, supplément. Tome II. Arrondissement de Lunéville. Nancy 1900. pp.415. [large number.]

Lunigiana.

GIOVANNI SFORZA, Bibliografia storica della città di Luni e suoi dintorni. Torino 1910. pp.[iii].178. [557.]

Lusatia.

RUDOLF LEHMANN, Bibliographie zur geschichte der Niederlausitz. Historische kommission für die provinz Brandenburg und die reichshauptstadt Berlin: Veröffentlichungen (vol.ii = Brandenburgische bibliographien, vol.iii): Berlin 1928. pp.xii.226. [2867.]

Luxemburg.

ALPHONSE VERKOOREN, Inventaire des chartes & cartulaires du Luxembourg. Inventaire des archives de la Belgique: Bruxelles 1902–1922. pp.[vi]. xl.320+479+375+575+543. [2352.]

—— Tome 1. [Second edition]. 1914. pp.[vi]. xxxix.563. [500.]

—— Introduction. By Marcel Bourguignon. 1931. pp.58.

H. MICHAËLIS, Inventaire sommaire des anciens greffes scabinaux de la province de Luxembourg. [Brussels *c.*1910]. pp.16. [large number.]

H. MICHAËLIS, Inventaire sommaire des archives domaniales du duché de Luxembourg et comté de Chiny conservées au dépôt des archives de l'état, à Arlon. [Brussels *c.*1910]. pp.7. [5000.]

H. MICHAËLIS, Inventaire sommaire des archives du Conseil provincial et souverain du duché de Luxembourg et comté de Chiny conservées au dépôt des archives de l'état, à Arlon. [Brussels *c.*1910]. pp.6. [5000.]

H. MICHAËLIS, Inventaire sommaire des tabelles cadastrales de la province du Luxembourg, 1766. [Brussels *c.*1910]. pp.11. [500.]

H. MICHAËLIS, Inventaire sommaire des archives des seigneuries, prévôtés et voueries du duché de Luxembourg conservées au dépôt des archives de l'état, à Arlon. [Brussels *c.*1910]. pp.5. [300.]

P[IERRE] FRIEDEN and M[AX] GOERGEN, Historiographie luxembourgeoise. [Luxembourg 1948]. pp.20. [300.]

Lyons.

P[IERRE] M[ARIE] GONON, Bibliographie historique de la ville de Lyon. Lyon 1844. pp.548. [3044.]

INVENTAIRE sommaire des archives communales. . . . Ville de Lyon. Paris [*afterwards:* Lyon] 1865. [very large number.]
> i. Séries AA–BB. Par F[ortuné] Rolle. 1865.
> pp.18.52.372.
> ii–iii. Série CC. Par F. Rolle [*and others*].
> 1875–1887. pp.281+406.
> Série I. Par Alice Joly. 1955. pp.56.
> *in progress?*

A[NDRÉ] STEYERT and F[ORTUNÉ] ROLLE, Inventaire-sommaire des archives hospitalières antérieures à 1790. . . . Ville de Lyon. La Charité ou Aumône-générale. Lyon 1874–1908. pp.[xv]. 12.31.399 + [iii].232.75.24.111 + [iii].439 + [iii]. 336.31.176.18+[v].135. [500,000.]

J. J. GRISARD, Notice sur les plans et vues de la ville de Lyon de la fin du xve au commencement du xviiie siècle. Lyon 1891. pp.[iii].216. [50.]

SÉBASTIEN CHARLÉTY, Bibliographie critique de l'histoire de Lyon. Université de Lyon: Annales (n.s. II. 9, 11): Lyon 1902–1903. pp.vii.357+vi. 259. [4827.]

[ALICE JOLY and HENRY JOLY], Le XVIIIᵉ siècle à Lyon. Rousseau, Voltaire et les sociétés de pensée. Exposition. Bibliothèque: Lyon 1962. pp.31. [150.]

Maashees.

P. M. F. RIETER, Inventaris van . . . het oud-archief van Maashees en Holthees. [*s.l.*] 1917. pp.42.

Maastricht.

[JEAN CHRISTIAN ANTOINE] ALEX[ANDRE] SCHAEP-KENS, Notice sur des anciens diplomes relatifs à Maestricht. Gand 1848. pp.15. [5.]

G. D. FRANQUINET, Beredeneerde inventaris der oorkonden en bescheiden van het kapitel van O. L. Vrouwekerk te Maastricht. Beredeneerde inventaris der oorkonden en bescheiden berustende op 't Provinciaal archief van Limburg (vols.ii–iii): Maastricht 1870–1877. pp.iv.415+ [iii].305. [1000.]

G. D. FRANQUINET, Beredeneerde inventaris der oorkonden en bescheiden van het klooster der Predikheeren te Maastricht. Beredeneerde inventaris der oorkonden en bescheiden berustende op het provinciaal archief van Limburg (vol.v): Maastricht 1880. pp.vi.191. [164.]

H[ERMAN] HARDENBERG, Inventaris der archieven van het arrondissement Maastricht en van het departement van de Nedermaas (1794–1814). Rijksarchief in Limburg [Maastricht]:'s- Gravenhage 1946. pp.[ii].cxxvi.291. [large number.]

Mâcon.

[L. MICHON], Inventaire sommaire des archives communales antérieures à 1790. . . . Ville de Mâcon. Mâcon 1878. pp.[iii].3.4.38.48.14.26.23. 105.9.5.7.31.6. [50,000.]

Made.

INVENTARIS van het archief der gemeente Made en Drimmelen. Oosterhout 1897. pp.17.

Madrid.

AGUSTÍN MILLARES CARLO, Índice y extractos del Libro de horadado del Consejo madrileño (siglos xv–xvi). Segunda edición. Revista de la biblioteca, archivo y museo: Publicaciones (vol. ii): Madrid 1927. pp.92. [260.]

AGUSTÍN MILLARES CARLO, Índice y extractos de los libros de cédulas y provisiones del Archivo municipal de Madrid (siglos xv–xvi). Madrid 1929. pp.89. [499.]

ANGELÁ GONZÁLEZ [PALENCIA SIMÓN], Colección de documentos sobre Madrid. Instituto de estudos madrileños: Biblioteca de estudos madrileños (vol.iii): Madrid 1953. pp.[v].743. [1546.]
the title is misleading; this is a catalogue.

Maidenhead.

J. W. WALKER, A calendar of the ancient charters and documents of the corporation of Maidenhead. Borough of Maidenhead: 1908. pp.[127]. [500.]

Maine-et-Loire.

INVENTAIRE-sommaire des archives départementales. . . . Maine-et-Loire. Paris [*afterwards:* Angers]. [very large number.]
Séries A, C–E. Par Célestin Port. 1863–1871. pp.xiii.31+472.
Série B. Par J. Levron. 1933. pp.23.

Séries E, E supplément. Par C. Port [et Marc
Saché et Jacques Levron]. 1885–1935. pp.
436+472+[ii].382.

Série G. 1880. pp.335.

Série H. Par C. Port [Marc Saché]. 1880–
1898. pp.276+xii.603.

Série H, supplément. 1870. pp.xxii.166.

Série I. Par M. Saché. 1931. pp.xxiv.64.

Série L. 1951. pp.148.

Série P. 1937. pp.25.

Série T. 1948. pp.49.

JACQUES LEVRON, Les inventaires, répertoires et
catalogues des archives de Maine-et-Loire (archives départementales, communales et hospitalières). Angers 1943. pp.39. [200.]

—— Supplément (1944–1953). 1954. pp.30.
[50.]

Mainz.

JOHANN FRIEDRICH BÖHMER, Regesta archi-
episcoporum maguntinensium. Regesten zur geschichte der mainzer erzbischöfe von Bonifatius
bis Uriel von Gemmingen, 742?–1514. . . . Bearbeitet und herausgegeben von Cornelius Will.
Innsbruck 1877–1886. pp.[vii].lxxx.400+[vii].
xci.467. [5000.]

Malaga.

FRANCISCO BEJARANO [ROBLES], Catálogo de los documentos del reinade de los reyes católicos existentes en el Archivo municipal de Málaga. Consejo superior de investigaciones científicas: Biblioteca "Reyes católicos": Inventarios y catálogos (no.viii): Madrid 1961. pp.iii–xiii.211. [943.]

Malines.

INVENTAIRE des archives de la ville de Malines. Administration communale: Malines.

    i–ii. [Chartes. Octrois]. Par P.-J. van Doren. 1859–1862. pp.xv.338+[ii].v.427. [1711.]

    iii–v. [Lettres missives]. 1865–1868. pp.[v]. 304+[v].367+[v].200. [1399.]

    vi. [Affaires civiles et ecclésiastiques]. Par V[ictor] Hermans. 1876. pp.vi.388. [large number.]

    [vii]. Nouvelle série, i. [Lettres missives]. 1885. pp.[vi].409. [900.]

    viii. [Registres et rouleaux]. 1894. pp.xvi.456. [large number.]

[GUILLAUME JOSEPH CHARLES PIOT], Inventaire des archives de la cour féodale du pays de Malines. Inventaires des archives de la Belgique: Inventaires divers: Bruxelles 1879. pp.[ii].xxii.77. [5000.]

A[RTHUR] GAILLARD, Inventaire des mémoriaux du Grand conseil de Malines. Inventaires des archives de la Belgique: Bruxelles 1900–1903. pp. viii.311+[iii].503. [3000.]

Manche.

INVENTAIRE-sommaire des archives départementales. . . . Manche. Saint-Lô. [very large number.]

> Série A. Par [François] Dubosc. 1865–1925. pp.iii.421+6.180.
> Série G. Par P. Le Cacheux. 1913. pp.37.
> Série H. Par P. Le Cacheux [F. Dubosc; F. Dolbet et P. Le Cacheux]. [*c.*1860]–1914. pp.294+388+xxxi.376+[iii].66.
> Série L. 1920. pp.xc.92.
> Série U. Par Gustave Eury. 1913. pp.4.
> Série V. 1912. pp.35.
> Série Y. 1913. pp.11.

in progress.

[Y. N.], Répertoire des bibliothèques et archives de la Manche. Société d'archéologie et d'histoire de la Manche: Saint-Lô [1963]. pp.87. [large number.]

Manchester, city and diocese of.

ERNEST AXON, Index to the Owen mss. in the

Free reference library. Public libraries: Occasional lists (no.6): Manchester 1900. pp.25. [4000.]

[A SURVEY of the ecclesiastical archives of the diocese of Manchester.] Pilgrim trust: Survey of ecclesiastical archives: [1952]. ff.12. [large number.]*

J[ACK] LEE, Maps and plans of Manchester and Salford, 1650 to 1843. A handlist. Altrincham 1957. pp.43. [65.]

Manosque.

D. ARBAUD, Rapport à m. le préfet des Basses-Alpes sur les archives municipales de Manosque. I. Les privilèges. Digne 1844. pp.32. [12.]

Mans, Le.

GUSTAVE RENÉ ESNAULT, Inventaire des minutes anciennes des notaires du Mans (xviie & xviiie siècles). . . . Publié . . . par Em.-Louis Chambois. Le Mans 1895–1898. pp.[v].324+[iii].319+[iii].320 + [iii].321 + [iii].324 + [iii].294 + [v].406. [5000.]

LÉONCE CELIER, Catalogue des actes des évêques du Mans jusqu'à la fin du xiiie siècle. 1910. pp.[iii].lxxvii.404. [762.]

Marche.

[AUGUSTE] ALFRED LEROUX, Chroniqueurs et historiens de la Marche et du Limousin avant la révolution. Limoges 1886. pp.59. [193.]

Marienthal, convent of.

G. D. FRANQUINET, Beredeneerde inventaris der oorkonden en bescheiden van de abdij Kloosterrade en van de adellijke vrouwenkloosters Marienthal en Sinnich. Beredeneerde inventaris der oorkonden en bescheiden berustende op't Provinciaal archief van Limburg (vol.i): Maastricht 1869. pp.viii.311. [Marienthal: 100.]

Marle.

AUGUSTE MATTON, Inventaire sommaire des archives hospitalières antérieures à 1790. . . . Ville de Marle. Laon 1889. pp.[ii].9.17. [10,000.]

Marne.

GEORGES HÉRELLE, Répertoire général et analytique des principaux fonds anciens conservés aux archives départementales de la Marne. Arcis-sur-Aube 1884. pp.242. [4600.]

INVENTAIRE-sommaire des archives départementales. . . . Marne. [very large number.]

Série C. Par [N.] Hatat, A. Vétault et Paul Pélicier. Châlons-sur-Marne 1884. pp.xv. 474.

Séries C–F. Par C. Pélicier. 1892. pp.viii.427.

Série G. Par L. Demaison [et Gaston Robert; Paul Pélicier]. Reims [1899–] 1900–1931. pp.xv.380+xii.366+   +viii.486.

Série H. Par P. Pélicier, Just Berland, René Gandilhon. 1949. pp.viii.382.

Série M. 1940–1961. pp.198+178.

Série O. 1946. pp.615.

Série V. 1911. pp.13.

Série X. 1947. pp.360.

Série Y. 1947. pp.38.

in progress.

Marne, Haute-.

INVENTAIRE-sommaire des archives départe-mentales. . . . Haute-Marne. Paris [*afterwards:* Chaumont]. [very large number.]

Série A. Par P. Chéron. 1864. single leaf.

Série C. Par A. Arcelin. 1865–1866. pp.40.

Série F. Par P. Gautier et J. Massiet Du Biest. 1923. pp.v.116.

Série G. Par [Alphonse] Roserot [*and others*]. 1909. pp.481.

Série L. Par René Tolmer, Roger Gény et Jean Gigot. 1948. pp.[39].

Série M. Par R. Gény et Léon Delessard.
1934. pp.84.
Série S. 1920. pp.40.
Série T. 1926. pp.23.
Série U. 1928. pp.23.
Série V. 1930. pp.28.
in progress.

ALPHONSE ROSEROT, Répertoire historique de la
Haute-Marne, contenant la nomenclature des
ouvrages, articles, dissertations et documents
imprimés concernant l'histoire de ce département.
1892–1901. pp.318. [5000.]

A[LPHONSE] ROSEROT, Catalogue des actes
royaux conservés dans les archives de la Haute-
Marne. Besançon [printed] 1905. pp.175. [566.]

Marseilles.

INVENTAIRE sommaire des archives hospitalières
antérieures à 1790. . . . Hospices de Marseille.
Marseille 1872. pp.[iii].164. [50,000.]

[ANTOINE CHARLES MARIUS] OCTAVE TEISSIER,
Inventaire des archives historiques de la Chambre
de commerce de Marseille. Marseille 1878. pp.
[vii].515. [10,000.]

[ANTOINE CHARLES MARIUS] OCTAVE TEISSIER, Inventaire des archives modernes de la Chambre de commerce. Marseille 1882. pp.[v].382. [100,000.]

[PHILIPPE MABILLY], Inventaire sommaire des archives communales. . . . Ville de Marseille. Marseille 1907–1909. pp.[iii].101+[iii].[239 large number.]
limited, incompletely, to series AA and BB; no more published.

ÉMILE ISNARD, Inventaire-sommaire des archives communales postérieures à 1790. . . . Ville de Marseille. Série 1D. Délibérations du conseil municipal, 1790–1830. Marseille 1925–1932. pp.[iii].334+312. [large number.]

ÉMILE ISNARD, Inventaire sommaire chronologique des chartes, lettres-patentes, lettres missives et titres divers antérieurs à 1500. Ville de Marseille: Marseille 1939. pp.[iii].188. [965.]

Massa-Carrara.

ERNESTO LASINIO, Regesto delle pergamene del Regio archivio di stato in Massa. Pistoia 1916. pp.xix.342. [998.]

SEZIONE di Archivio di stato di Massa. Inventario sommario dell'Archivio di stato. Ministero dell'interno: Pubblicazioni degli archivi di stato (vol.viii): Roma 1952. pp.xii.131. [very large number.]

Maurienne.

GABRIEL PÉROUSE, Inventaire sommaire des Archives départementales de la Savoie. . . . Archives ecclésiastiques: Série G. Diocèses de Tarentaise, de Grenoble et de Maurienne: Chambéry 1915. pp.[vi].55. [large number.]

Mayenne.

INVENTAIRE-sommaire des archives départementales. . . . Mayenne. Laval [very large number.]
> Séries A, C–E, G–H. Par J. Noël et L. Maître. [1864–1866].
> Série B. Par V[ictor] Duchemin et [Louis George] A[lfred] de Martonne [et Ernest Laurain]. 1882–1904. pp.xxxiii.439+iv.412.
> Série L. Par Marcel Wéber. 1940. pp.99.
> Série Q. Par M. Wéber et M. Chanteux. 1936. pp.83.
in progress.

[LOUIS GEORGES] A[LFRED] DE MARTONNE, Rapport sur les archives du département de la

Mayenne. Laval 1880–1889. pp.23. [large number.]

A. DE MARTONNE, Inventaire sommaire des archives communales antérieures à 1790. Ville de Mayenne. Laval 1888. pp.24.
incomplete; no more published.

Melcombe.

H[ENRY] J[OSEPH] MOULE, Descriptive catalogue of the charters, minute books and other documents of the borough of Weymouth and Melcombe Regis, A.D. 1252 to 1800. Weymouth 1883. pp.xv.224. [2000.]

Mellingen.

WALTHER MERZ, Inventar des stadtarchivs Mellingen. Aarau 1917. pp.24. [5000.]

Mende.

FERDINAND ANDRÉ, Inventaire sommaire des archives communales antérieures à 1790. . . . Ville de Mende. Mende 1885. pp.[iii].iv.5.35.71.5.7.10. 26.3.7.24.6.2. [40,000.]

Messines.

I. L. A. DIEGERICK, Inventaire analytique &

chronologique des chartes et documents appartenant aux archives de l'ancienne abbaye de Messines. [Société d'émulation:] Bruges 1876. pp. [iii].cviii.351.ccxii. [800.]

Metz.

[ÉTIENNE J. LECOUTEUX], Catalogue des manuscrits et documents originaux relatifs à l'histoire de la ville de Metz et du pays messin . . . provenant du cabinet de feu monsieur le comte [Jean Louis Claude] Emmery [de Grosyeulx]. Metz 1850. pp.vi.262. [1233.]

— CLERCX, Catalogue des manuscrits relatifs à l'histoire de Metz et de la Lorraine. Bibliothèque de la ville: Metz 1856. pp.[iii].238. [2000.]

[— NICOLAS, — JACQUIN, and — DISS], Inventaire-sommaire des archives communales antérieures à 1790. Ville de Metz. Metz 1880. pp.vii. 213.39. [100,000.]

ÉDOUARD SAUER, Inventaire des aveux et dénombrements déposés aux archives départementales à Metz. Metz 1894. pp.xviii.232. [1617.]

CATALOGUE des collections manuscrites et imprimées relatives à l'histoire de Metz et de la

Lorraine léguées par m. Auguste Prost. Bibliothèque nationale: 1897. pp.114. [2500.]

HENRI [AUGUSTE] OMONT, Collections Emmery et Clouët-Buvignier sur l'histoire de Metz et de la Lorraine conservées à la Bibliothèque nationale. Inventaire. Société nationale des antiquaires de France: Mettensia (vol.vii): 1919. pp.[vii].156. [20,000.]

RENÉ PAQUET, Bibliographie analytique de l'histoire de Metz pendant la Révolution (1789–1800). Imprimés et manuscrits. 1926. pp.1504.118. [25,000.]

Meurthe-et-Moselle.

HENRI LEPAGE, Coup d'œil sur les archives départementales de la Meurthe. Nancy 1853. pp.50. [200.]

HENRY LEPAGE, Inventaire des archives de la Meurthe. Nancy 1855. pp.68. [200.]

HENRI LEPAGE, Archives communales et hospitalières de la Meurthe. 1858. pp.279. [3000.]

INVENTAIRE-sommaire des archives départementales. . . . Meurthe-et-Moselle. Nancy. [very large number.]

i–ii. Série B. Par H[enri] Lepage. 1870–1875.
pp.xx 359+384.

iii. Séries B–E. 1877. pp.387.49.10.40.

— Série B. Lettres patentes . . . 1608–1929.
Index alphabétiques. Par Étienne Delcambre. 1962. pp.[iii].307.

iv–v. Séries G–H. 1880–1883. pp.xxxiv.186
+189.

vi. Tables. 1884–1891. pp.181+165+162.

vii–x. Série E, supplément. Par E[mile]
Duvernoy. 1896–1929. pp.324+415+615
+441.

in progress.

É[MILE] DUVERNOY, Catalogue des documents
des archives de Meurthe-et-Moselle antérieurs à
1101. Besançon 1907. pp.29. [99.]

Meuse.

INVENTAIRE-sommaire des archives départementales. . . . Meuse. Paris [*afterwards:* Bar-le-Duc]
1875. [very large number.]

i. Série B. Par Ad[olphe] Marchal. 1875.
pp.xii.451.

ii. Série C. Par A. Marchal, A. Lesort et
P. d'Arbois de Jubainville. 1918. pp.681.

Série G. Par Henri-François Buffet et Jean
Rigault. 1943. pp.40.

Série H. Par Noël Becquart et Jean Colnat. 1958. pp.[i].548.

Série K. 1916. pp.10.

Série L. 1942. pp.43.

Série M. Par Michel Trizac. 1944. pp.16.

Série N. Par Léon Thevenin. 1911. pp.6.

Série O. Par J. Colnat, Geneviève Grégoire-Soyer, André Norguin et Jacques Brisson. 1956. pp.133.

Série P. 1915. pp.8.

Série Q. 1917. pp.71.

Série R. 1911. pp.8.

Série S. 1910. pp.7.

Série T. 1910. pp.7.

Série V. 1910. pp.5.

Série X. 1911. pp.8.

Série Y. 1943. pp.5.

in progress.

Mézières.

ED[MOND] SÉNEMAUD, Inventaire-sommaire des archives communales antérieures à 1790. . . . Ville de Mézières. Mézières 1873. pp.vii.10.16.26.4.3.3. 16.2.3. [40,000.]

[JEAN] PAUL LAURENT, Inventaire sommaire des archives hospitalières de la ville de Mézières. Charleville 1891. pp.76. [10,000.]

Middelburg.

J. H. DE STOPPELAAR, Inventaris van het oud-archief der stad Middelburg, 1217–1581. Middelburg 1883. pp.964.

M. H. VAN VISVLIET, Inventaris der rechterlijke archieven van Middelburg. Middelburg 1906. pp.138.

C. DE WAARD, De archieven berustende onder het bestuur der godshuizen te Middelburg . . . 1313–1812. Middelburg 1907. pp.522.

W[ILLEM] S[YBRAND] UNGER, De archieven van kerken en kloosters in het archief der gemeente Middelburg. Middelburg 1926. pp.12.

W. S. UNGER, De archieven der gilden en beurzen in Middelburg. Middelburg 1930. pp.88.

W. S. UNGER, Het archief der Middelburgsche commercie compagnie. 's-Gravenhage 1951. pp. 122. [1777.]

Middelburg, abbey of.

R[OBERT] FRUIN, Het archief der o. l. v. abdij te Middelburg. Rijks archief-depôt in de provincie Zeeland: 's-Gravenhage 1901. pp.643. [2338.]

Middlesex.

W[ILLIAM] P[HILLIMORE] W[ATTS] PHILLIMORE, A calendar of inquisitiones post mortem for Middlesex and London returned into the court of Chancery 1 Henry VII. to 20 Charles I., 1485–1645. 1890. pp.54. [2250.]

W[ILLIAM] J[OHN] HARDY and W[ILLIAM] PAGE, A calendar to the feet of fines for London & Middlesex. . . . Richard I. to Richard III. [to 11 and 12 Elizabeth]. 1892–1893. pp.[iv].240.lxiii+ [iii].159.xxxv. [5000.]

W[ILLIAM] J[OHN] HARDY, Calendar of the sessions books, 1689 to 1709. Middlesex county records: 1905. pp.xxvi.404. [3500.]

MIDDLESEX in maps and surveys. Catalogue of exhibition of manuscript plans and estate surveys, 15th to 19th century, chiefly from the County record office. British record association: Middlesex standing joint committee: [1957]. pp.[67]. [66.]*

Milan.

DAMIANO MUONI, Le cinque giornate di Milano. Saggio bibliografico. Seconda edizione. Milano 1878. pp.68. [250.]

L[ÉON] G[ABRIEL JEAN BAPTISTE] PÉLISSIER, Les sources milanaises de l'histoire de Louis XII. Trois registres de lettres ducales de Louis XII aux archives de Milan. 1892. pp.80. [300.]

LUDOVICO [LODOVICO] FRATI, I codici [Carlo] Morbio della R. biblioteca di Brera. Forlì 1897. pp.3–219. [3000.]

ANTONIO VISMARA, Bibliografia storica delle cinque giornate e degli avvenimenti politico-militari in Lombardia nel 1848. Municipio di Milano: Milano 1898. pp.xi.275. [3750.]

[EMILIO MOTTA], Saggio bibliografico di cartografia milanese fino al 1796. Archivo storico Lombardo: Supplementi (no.2): Milano 1901. pp.vii.63. [750.]

E[LIA] LATTES, Repertorio diplomatico visconteo. Documenti dal 1263 al 1402 raccolti e pubblicati in forma di regesto. Milano 1911[1910]–1918. pp.[iv].152+[iv].153–400. [3373.]
to 1385 only; no more published.

ETTORE VERGA, Catalogo ragionato della raccolta cartografica. Archivio storico: Milano 1911. pp. iii–xii.191. [175.]

ALLEN B[ANKS] HINDS, Calendar of state papers and manuscripts in the archives and collections of

Milan. Vol.1. 1912. pp.lx.758. [1055.]*
covers the period 1385–1618.

INVENTARI e regesti del R. archivio di stato in Milano. Milano.

    i. I registri viscontei. [By Cesare Manaresi]. 1915. pp.lii.172. [1500.]

    ii. Gli atti cancellereschi viscontei. [By Giovanni Vittani]. 1920–1929. pp.xv.248+ viii.305. [2875.]

    iii. I registri dell'Ufficio degli statuti. [By Nicola Ferorelli]. 1920. pp.xv.410. [10,000.]

CATERINA SANTORO, I registri dell'Ufficio di provvisione e dell'Ufficio dei sindaci sotto la dominazione viscontea. Inventari e regesti dell'Archivio civico (vol.i): Milano 1929–1932. pp. iii–xxiii.815. [5000.]

Milan cathedral.

E[TTORE] VERGA, L'archivio della fabbrica del duomo di Milano. Milano 1908. pp.iii–viii.102. [25,000.]

Modena.

ARCHIVIO segreto estense. Sezione "Casa e stato". Pubblicazioni degli archivi di stato (vol.

xiii: Archivio di stato di Modena): Roma 1953. pp.li.318. [2500.]

Moissac.

CHARLES DUMAS DE RAULY and ALFRED GAN-DILHON, Inventaire-sommaire des archives communales et hospitalières de Moissac. Montauban 1906–1907. pp.viii.268. [25,000.]

Monkbretton, priory of.

J. W. WALKER, Abstracts of the chartularies of the priory of Monkbretton. Yorkshire archæological society: Record series (vol.lxvi): Leeds [printed] 1924. pp.x.252. [885.]

Monmouth.

[J. CONWAY DAVIES], Report on the records of quarter sessions of the county of Monmouth in the Muniments room, the Session house, Usk. [*s.l.*] 1939. ff.[ii].37.22. [50,000.]

W. H. BAKER, Guide to the Monmouthshire record office. Montmouthshire archives committee: Newport 1959. pp.126. [large number.]

Mons, city of.

LÉOPOLD DEVILLERS, Inventaire des archives de

la ville de Mons. Première partie. — Chartes. Mons 1882. pp.xlviii.287. [486.]

Mons, province of.

LÉOPOLD DEVILLERS, Notice sur le Dépôt des archives de l'état, à Mons. Cercle archéologique: Mons 1871. pp.459. [25,000.]

Montargis.

[FRÉDÉRIC ALEXANDRE] HENRI STEIN, Inventaire sommaire des archives de la ville de Montargis. Société historique et archéologique du Gâtinais: Documents (vol.iv): 1893. pp.xiv.233. [large number.]

Montbéliard.

L. SPACH, Inventaire sommaire des archives départementales. . . . Doubs. Série E. [Comté de Montbéliard]. Strasbourg 1867. pp.v.157.2. [1500.]

JULIEN MAUVEAUX, Inventaire sommaire des archives communales antérieures à 1793. . . . Suivi de l'inventaire sommaire des archives hospitalières. . . . Ville de Montbéliard. Montbéliard 1910. pp.xv.264. [100,000.]

LÉON NARDIN and JULIEN MAUVEAUX, Archives et archivistes de la principauté de Montbéliard. 1918. pp.[iii].73. [250,000.]

JULIEN MAUVEAUX, Le fonds Beurnier aux archives communales de Montbéliard. Inventaire sommaire. 1919. pp.79. [4317.]

Montbrison.

AUGUSTE CHAVERONDIER and J[OSEPH DE LA POIX] DE FRÉMINVILLE, Inventaire sommaire des archives départementales. . . . Loire. Série E, supplément. Tome I. Arrondissement de Montbrison. Saint-Étienne 1899. pp.57.547. [large number.]

Montélimar.

ANDRÉ LACROIX, Inventaire sommaire des archives communales . . . de Valence . . . et . . . de Die et Montélimar. Valence 1914. pp.xv.420. xl. [Montélimar: 10,000.]

Montelparo.

GIOVANNI CICCONI, Le pergamene dell'archivio municipale di Montelparo. Le pergamene dell'archivio domenicano di s. Lucia di Fabriano, a cura di Romualdi Sassi. R. deputazione di storie patria per le Marche: Fonti per la storia della Marche: Fermo 1939. pp.193. [500.]

Montesa, order of.

VICENTE VIGNAU [Y BALLESTER] and FRANCESCO RAFAEL DE UHAGÓN [Y GUARDAMINO], Índice de pruebos de los caballeros que han vestido el hábito de Calatrava, Alcántara y Montesa desde el siglo XVI hasta la fecha. Madrid 1903. pp.[ii].vii.361. [Montesa: 750.]

AUREA L. JAVIERRE MUR, Privilegios reales de la orden de Montesa en la edad media. Catálogo de la serie existente en el Archivo histórico nacional. Madrid [1961]. pp.3–361. [783.]

Montfoort.

R[OBERT] FRUIN and A[RTHUR] LE COSQUINO DE BUSSY, Catalogus van het archief der heeren van Montfoort. Rijks-archieven in de provincie Utrecht: Utrecht 1920. pp.[iv].335. [771.]

Montluçon.

INVENTAIRE sommaire des archives communales antérieures à 1790. Département de l'Allier. Ville

de Montluçon. Moulins. [very large number.]
  i. AA–CC. Rédigé par Paul Dupieux. pp.47.
in progress.

Montmajour, abbey of.

ÉDOUARD BARATIER, Inventaire-sommaire des archives départementales. . . . Abbaye de Montmajour. 1959. pp.[i].xiv.83. [large number.]

Montmartre.

EUGÈNE LE SENNE, Essai de bibliographie historique de Montmartre avant 1800. Société le vieux-Montmartre: 1907. pp.[iii].32. [269.]
  25 copies printed.

Montpellier.

[JOSEPH DUPONT], Inventaire des titres et pièces justificatives de l'état et existence de l'Ordre archihospitalier du saint-esprit de Montpellier et des biens d'iceluy. [1707]. pp.11. [40.]

EUGÈNE THOMAS, Sommaires historiques sur les anciennes archives ecclésiastiques du diocèse de Montpellier (clergé séculier). Montpellier 1852. pp.36. [large number.]

ARCHIVES de la ville de Montpellier. Inventaires et documents. Publiés par les soins de l'adminis-

tration municipale. Montpellier. [large number.]
  i[–ii]. Notice sur les anciens inventaires [by
    Ferdinand Castets and Joseph Berthelé].
  Inventaire du Grand chartrier [compiled
    in 1662–1663 by Pierre Louvet, edited by
    J. Berthelé]. 1895–1899. pp.[v].cxliii.403.
  iii. Inventaire des cartulaires de Montpellier
    (980–1789), cartulaire seigneurial et cartu-
    laires municipaux [by J. Berthelé]. 1901–
    1907. pp.iii–xix.679.
  vi–ix. Inventaire de [F.] Joffre [1662].
    Archives du greffe de la maison consulaire.
    Édité avec corrections et compléments par
    m. Oudot de Dainville. 1934–1949. pp.
    [iii].484+[iii].372+   +xix.257.
  vols.iv–v are not calendars.

EUGÈNE MARTIN-CHABOT, Les archives de la
Cour des comptes, aides et finances de Montpellier. Université de Paris: Bibliothèque de la
Faculté des lettres (vol.xxii): 1907. pp.[ii].xxxii.
227. [620.]

Moravia.

B[EDA] DUDÍK, J. P. Ceroni's handschriftensammlung. . . . Erste abtheilung: die landes-
geschichte im allgemeinen. Erste folge: der poli-
tische theil derselben. Mährens geschichtsquellen

(vol.i): Brünn 1850. pp.xxxi.511. [200.]
no more published.

P[ETER] VON CHLUMECKÝ, Die regesten oder die chronologischen verzeichnisse der urkunden in den archiven zu Iglau, Trebitsch, Triesch, Gross-Bitesch, Gross-Meseritsch und Pirnitz. . . . 1. bandes 1. abtheilung. Die regesten der archive im markgrafthume Mähren (vol.i): Brünn 1856. pp.[viii]. xli.223.335. [1500.]
no more published.

P[ETER] VON CHLUMECKÝ and J. CHYTIL, Bericht über das mähr. ständ. landes-archiv . . . für das jahr 1857. Brünn 1858. pp.111. [175.]

B[EDA] DUDÍK, Bibliothek und archiv im fürst-erzbischöflichen schlosse zu Kremsier. Wien 1870. pp.xxi.134. [large number.]

B[EDA] DUDÍK, Forschungen in Schweden für Mährens geschichte. Brünn 1852. pp.xvi.478. [1500.]

B[EDA] DUDÍK, Iter romanum. Wien 1855. pp. xx.368+232. [2500.]
on mss., papal archives &c. relating to Moravia.

Moray.

JOHN GRAHAM DALYELL, A brief analysis of the

ancient records of the bishopric of Moray. Edinburgh 1826. pp.viii.82. [100.]

Morbihan.

INVENTAIRE-sommaire des archives départementales. . . . Morbihan. Paris [*afterwards:* Vannes] 1877. [very large number.]

> Série B. Par [Louis] Rosenzweig [F. Pourchasse; Pierre Thomas-Lacroix]. 1877–1941. pp.418+123+56.
>
> Série C. 17 C. 1932. pp.68.
>
> Série E, supplément. Par [L.] Rosenzweig [F. Pourchasse; L. Rosenzweig et Ch. Estienne]. 1881–1911. pp.xcii.329+148+367.
>
> Série G. Par Ch. Estienne [Jules de la Martinière, G. Duhem, P. Thomas-Lacroix]. 1901–1940. pp.iv.527+viii.552.
>
> Série K. 1914. pp.36.
>
> Série T. 1914. pp.61.
>
> *in progress.*

Mortagne-du-Nord.

JULES FINOT and [J.] VERMAERE, Inventaire sommaire des archives communales antérieures à 1790. . . . Ville de Mortagne-du-Nord. Lille 1896. pp.[iii].xxxviii.40. [10,000.]

Moscow.

P[ETR VASILEVICH] KHAVSKY, Указатель источниковъ исторіи и географіи Москвы съ древнимъ ея уѣздомъ, расположеніямъ и царствованіямъ россійскихъ государей, со включеніемъ царствованія государя императора Николая Павловича. Москва 1839. pp.[viii].xii.367. [2038.]

A[LEKSYEI] I[VANOVICH] SOBOLEVSKY, Переводная литература Московской Руси XIV–XVII вѣковъ. Библіографическіе матеріалы. С.-Петербургъ 1903. pp.viii.460. [2000.]

[Z. P. GONCHAROVA and B. V. ZLATOUSTOVSKY], История города Москвы с XII в. до 1917 г . . . Под редакцией К. В. Сивкова. Государственная ордена Ленина библиотека [&c.]: Что читать к 800-летию Москвы: 1947. pp.96. [300.]

[Z. P. GONCHAROVA and B. V. ZLATOUSTOVSKY], Москва в истории революционного движения (1648–1917). . . . Под редакцией Г. Д. Костомарова. Государственная ордена Ленина [&c.]: Что читать к 800-летию Москвы: Москва 1947. pp.64. [150.]

V. N. SHUMILOV, Обзор документальных материалов Центрального государственного архива древних актов СССР по истории г. Москвы с древнейших времен до XIX в. Москва 1949. pp.[ii].187. [large number.]

S[OKRAT] A[LEKSANDROVICH] KLEDIKOV, Библиография печатных планов города Москвы XVI–XIX веков. Москва 1956. pp.123. [242.]

Moselle, department of the.

INVENTAIRE sommaire des archives départementales. . . . Moselle. Metz. [very large number.]

Séries A–E. Par É[douard] Sauer. 1890. pp. 7.49.127.12.124.

Série AL. Par Jean Rigault. 1954. pp.xlii.211.

Série G. 1879. pp.284.

Série H. [By É. Sauer and G. Wolfram]. 1895. pp.v.455.

Série J. 1948–1949. pp.23.16.9.

Série K. 1921. pp.8.

Série L. 1931. pp.30.

Série M. 1921. pp.16.

Série N. 1920. pp.7.

Séries P–Y. 1931. pp.40.

in progress.

P. D'ARBOIS DE JUBAINVILLE, Catalogue des inventaires et cartulaires conservés à Metz dans les dépôts d'archives. Metz [*c.*1925]. pp.29. [200.]

ERNST HAUVILLER, Les archives révolutionnaires du département de la Moselle à Metz. 1910. pp.33. [large number.]

RAYMOND LECOMTE, Répertoire des cartes et plans formant dans le dépôt une collection spéciale. Archives départementales de la Moselle: Metz 1931. pp.[v].29. [2181.]

Moulins.

[J. B.] CONNY and [MARTIAL ALPHONSE] CHAZAUD, Inventaire-sommaire des archives communales antérieures à 1790. . . . Ville de Moulins. Moulins 1882. pp.[iii].iv.121. [40,000.]

F. CLAUDON, Les archives de la Chambre des notaires de Moulins. Moulins 1902. pp.28. [large number.]

F. CLAUDON, Inventaire-sommaire des archives départementales. . . . Allier. Tome III. Série E, supplément, tome I. (Arrond^t de Moulins). Moulins 1906. pp.xviii.796. [very large number.]

Moutiers.

GABRIEL PÉROUSE, Inventaire des archives an-

ciennes antérieures à l'année 1793. Ville de
Moutiers. Chambéry 1912. pp.67. [5000.]

Mühldorf am Inn.

EDGAR KRAUSEN, Stadtarchiv Mühldorf am Inn.
Bayerische archivinventare (no.13): München
1958. pp.xi.136. [large number.]

Mulhouse.

BERNHARD PROST and ÉDOUARD BENNER, Verzeichnis u. inhaltsangabe der bestände des stadt-
archives von Mühlhausen i. E., 1236–1798. Mühlhausen 1910. pp.ix.562.

Munich.

J. K. STADLER, Das erzbistum München und
Freising. Bayerische archivverwaltung: Bayerische pfarrbücherverzeichnisse (vol.i): München
1938.

Münster.

HEINRICH BÖRSTING, Inventar des bischöflichen
diözesanarchivs in Münster. Archivberatungsstelle
der provinz Westfalen: Inventare der nichtstaatlichen archive der provinz Westfalen (beiband iii):

Münster i. W. 1937. pp.xii.524. [very large number.]

Namur, city and province of.

STANISLAS BORMANS, Cartulaire des petites communes. Analyse des pièces. Namur 1878. pp.11.136. [650.]

[GUILLAUME JOSEPH CHARLES PIOT], Inventaire des chartes des comtes de Namur anciennement déposées au château de cette ville. Inventaires des archives de la Belgique: Bruxelles 1890. pp.[ii]. xiii.520. [1417.]

L. LAHAYE, Inventaire sommaire des archives des anciens greffes scabinaux de la province de Namur. [Brussels c.1910]. pp.66. [large number.]

D. D. BROUWERS, Inventaire sommaire des archives des communes de la province de Namur conservées au dépôt des archives de l'état à Namur. [Brussels c.1910]. pp.25. [large number.]

D. D. BROUWERS, Inventaire sommaire des archives ecclésiastiques de la province de Namur. [Brussels c.1910]. pp.51. [large number.]

F. COURTOY, Inventaire sommaire des archives modernes conservées au dépôt des archives de l'état à Namur. [Brussels *c.*1910]. pp.45. [large number.]

L. LAHAYE, Inventaire sommaire des archives notariales conservées au dépôt des archives de l'état à Namur. [Brussels *c.*1910]. pp.37. [large number.]

D. D. BROUWERS, Inventaire sommaire des archives du souverain bailliage de Namur. [Brussels *c.*1910]. pp.6. [10,000.]

D. D. BROUWERS, Inventaire sommaire des archives des cours féodales conservées aux archives de l'état à Namur. [Brussels *c.*1910]. pp.6. [200.]

D. D. BROUWERS, Inventaire sommaire des archives des fiefs et des seigneuries de la province de Namur. [Brussels *c.*1910]. pp.7. [200.]

L. GENICOT, C[ECILE] DOUXCHAMPS-LEFÈVRE and J. BOVESSE, Inventaire des archives de la Commission d'assistance publique de Namur an v — 1870. Archives de l'état à Namur: Bruxelles 1959. pp. 105. [large number.]

JEAN BOVESSE, Inventaire général sommaire des archives ecclésiastiques de la province de Namur. Archives de l'état à Namur: Bruxelles 1962. pp. xxviii.339. [100,000.]

Nancy.

[HUBERT F.] SOYER-WILLEMET, Note sur les anciens plans de la ville de Nancy, conservés à la bibliothèque publique. Nancy 1866. pp.8. [16.]

INVENTAIRE sommaire des manuscrits de la bibliothèque publique. Nancy 1882. pp.17. [612.]

Nantes.

S[TÉPHANE PRAUD] DE LA NICOLLIÈRE-TEIJEIRO [vol.iii: RENÉ BLANCHARD], Inventaire sommaire des archives communales antérieures à 1790. . . . Ville de Nantes. Nantes 1888–1919. pp.[iii]. xxiii.400+[iii].xii.510+[ii].xi.392.ii. [250,000.]

Naples.

LORENZO GIUSTINIANI, La biblioteca storica e topografica del regno di Napoli. Napoli 1793. pp.xv.242. [1750.]

BARTOLOMMEO CAPASSO, Catalogo ragionato dei libri, registri e scritture esistenti nella sezione antica o prima serie dell'Archivio municipale di Napoli (1387–1806). 1876–1899. pp.lix.156+ix. 355. [25,000.]

PAUL DURRIEU, Les archives angevines de Naples. Étude sur les registres du roi Charles 1er (1265–

1285). Écoles françaises d'Athènes et de Rome:

Bibliothèque (vols.xlvi, li): 1886–1887. pp.[iii]. 324+[vi].420. [5000.]

BARTOLOMMEO CAPASSO, Le fonti della storia delle provincie napolitani dal 568 al 1500. . . . Con note . . . del d.r E. Oreste Mastrojanni. Napoli 1902. pp.[ii].vii.281. [1000.]

[LUIGI LUBRANO], Contributo alla bibliografia storica napoletana. Libri ed opuscoli su Napoli e l'antico reame delle due Sicile. Napoli 1919. pp. vii.190. [1361.]

A[LLEN] B[ANKS] HINDS, Descriptive list of state papers, foreign: Sicily and Naples (S.P.93). Public record office: 1933. ff.i.6. [125.]*
covers the period 1584–1679.

JOLE MAZZOLENI, Regesto delle pergamene di Castelcapuano, a. 1268–1789. R. deputazione napoletana di storia patria: Documenti per la storia dell'Italia meridionale (vol.iii): Napoli 1942. pp.xv.432.

RICCARDO FILANGIERI DI CANDIDA, I registri della cancelleria angioina ricostruiti. Napoli.
    i. 1265–1269. 1950. pp.xv.352. [1200.]
    ii. 1265–1281. 1951. pp.xi.339. [1000.]

iii. 1269–1270. 1951. pp.xi.323. [1500.]

iv. 1266–1270. 1952. pp.xv.259. [1300.]

v. 1266–1272. 1953. pp.xv.311. [1200.]

vi. 1270–1271. 1954. pp.xi.428. [1904.]

vii. 1269–1272. 1955. pp.xi.325. [1500.]

viii. 1271–1272. 1957. pp.xi.343. [1400.]

ix. 1272–1273. 1957. pp.xiii.335. [1400.]

x. 1272–1273. 1957. pp.xv.324. [1100.]

xi. 1273–1277. 1958. pp.xiii.419. [1500.]

xii. 1273–1276. 1959. pp.xi.329. [1200.]

xiii. 1275–1277. 1959. pp.xv.376. [1200.]

xiv. 1275–1277. 1961. pp.xi.320. [1000.]

xv. 1266–1277. 1961. pp.xiii.155. [400.]

the title refers to the war-time destruction of the archives; in progress.

JOLE MAZZOLENI, Regesto della cancelleria aragonese di Napoli. Archivi di stato: Pubblicazioni (vol.vii): Napoli 1951. pp.xxii.343. [1192.]

ARCHIVIO di stato di Napoli. Archivi privati. Inventario sommario. Pubblicazioni degli archivi di stato (vol.xi &c.): Roma 1953 &c.
in progress.

SALVATORE VITALI, Fogli volanti di Napoli e Sicilia del 1848–49, Biblioteca di storia moderna e contemporanea. Ministero della pubblica istruzione: Indici e cataloghi (n.s., vol.iii): [Rome] 1956. pp.[iii].175. [902.]

ARCHIVIO di stato di Napoli: Archivio borbone. Inventario sommario. Pubblicazioni degli archivi di stato (vol.xliii &c.): Roma 1961 &c.
in progress.

Narberth.

HENRY OWEN, A calendar of the public records relating to Pembrokeshire. Vol.II. The castles, towns, and lordships of Cilgerran and Narberth. Honourable society of Cymmrodorion: Cymmrodorion record series (no.7): 1914. pp.[viii]. 149. [Narberth: 100.]

Narbonne.

H. FAURE, Inventaire sommaire des archives hospitalières antérieures à 1790. . . . Narbonne 1855–1863. pp.[iii].166+vii.154. [large number.]

H. FAURE, Inventaire sommaire des archives hospitalières postérieures à 1790. . . . Narbonne. Narbonne 1856. pp.iv.206. [large number.]

GERMAIN MOUYNÈS, Inventaire des archives communales antérieures à 1790. . . . Ville de Narbonne. Narbonne 1871–1879. pp.xx.476+

479+906+1016+88. [large number.]
limited to series AA and BB; no more published.

MANUSCRITS de Narbonne. Bibliothèque municipale: [Narbonne] 1961. pp.[10]. [16.]
an exhibition catalogue.

Nassau.

[JOHANN HERMANN STEUBING], Versuch einer nassauischen geschichts-bibliothek. Hadamar &c. 1799. pp.257. [1000.]

A[NTONIUS] VON DER LINDE, Die nassauer brunnen-litteratur der Königlichen landesbibliothek. Wiesbaden 1883. pp.vi.102. [830.]

GEORG VOGEL, Nassauische bibliographie. Das schrifttum der jahre 1936–1940. Nassauische annalen (vol.lx, no.2): Wiesbaden 1948. pp.vii. 176. [5288.]

Navarre.

GUSTAVE BASCLE DE LAGRÈZE, Le trésor de Pau. Archives du château d'Henri IV. Pau 1851. pp.365. [7500.]

JOSÉ RAMÓN CASTRO, Catálogo de la sección de comptos. Documentos. Archivo general de Navarra: Diputación foral: Pamplona.

Europe

i. 842–1331. 1952. pp.487. [952.]

ii. 1332–1357. 1952. pp.497. [1090.]

iii. 1358–1361. 1953. pp.499. [1139.]

iv. 1362–1363. 1953. pp.751. [1736.]

v. 1364–1365. 1953. pp.619. [1410.]

vi. 1366–1367. Adiciones: 1303–1365. 1954. pp.507. [1105.]

vii. 1368–1369. 1954. pp.501. [1098.]

viii. 1370–1372. 1954. pp.471. [1016.]

ix. 1373–1375. 1954. pp.455. [989.]

x. 1376–1377. 1955. pp.471. [1059.]

xi. 1378. Adiciones: 1355–1377. 1955. pp.434. [971.]

xii. 1379. 1955. pp.567. [1318.]

xiii. 1380–1381. 1955. pp.525. [1166.]

xiv. 1382–1383. 1956. pp.417. [898.]

xv. 1384–1385. 1956. pp.599. [1272.]

xvi. 1386–1387. 1956. pp.791. [1754.]

xvii. 1388–1390. 1956. pp.475. [1005.]

xviii. 1391. 1957. Adiciones: 1341–1390. 1957. pp.503. [1082.]

xix. 1392. 1957. pp.505. [1022.]

xx. 1393–1394. 1957. pp.514. [1062.]

xxi. 1395–1396. 1958. pp.679. [1421.]

xxii. 1397–1398. 1958. pp.597. [1205.]

xxiii. 1399–1400. 1959. pp.493. [979.]

xxiv. 1401. Adiciones: 1385–1400. 1959. pp.485. [1012.]

xxv. 1402–1404. 1960. pp.625. [1215.]

xxvi. 1405–1406. 1960. pp.793. [1560.]

xxvii.

xxviii. 1409–1411. 1961. pp.821. [1485.]

in progress.

Neder-Hemert.

P. N. VAN DOORNINCK, Inventaris van het oud archief der heerlijkheid en gemeente Neder-Hemert. Haarlem 1892. pp.192.

— — Supplement. 1893. pp.30.

Neisse.

ERICH GRABER, Die inventare der nichtstaatlichen archive Schlesiens. Neisse. Verein für geschichte Schlesiens: Codex diplomaticus Silesiae (vol. xxxvi): Breslau 1933 &c.

in progress?

Netherlands.

Europe

1. *Cartography*

CATALOGUS van eene verzameling kaarten, berustende op de bibliotheek der Utrechtsche hoogeschool. Koninklijk instituut van ingenieurs: Verhandelingen: Bijlage: ['s-Gravenhage] 1850. pp.20. [575.]

RÉPERTOIRE des cartes du royaume des Pays-Bas et des colonies néerlandaises. Institut royal des ingénieurs néerlandais [Koninklijk instituut van ingenieurs]: La Haye 1865. pp.186. [293.]

P. L. PUTTERS, Catalogus van het kaarten-archief der afdeeling waterstaat van het Departement van binnenlandsche zaken. [s.l.] 1868. pp.276. [4000.]

[J. H. HINGMAN], Inventaris der verzameling van kaarten berustende in het Rijks-archief. Tweede gedeelte. 's Gravenhage 1871. pp.x.429. [3847.]
the Eerste gedeelte is entered under Cartography, above.

J. F. NIERMEYER, Zur geschichte der kartographie Hollands in den drei vorigen jahrhunderten. Erasmiaansch gymnasium: Programma: Rotterdam 1893. pp.32. [25.]

2. *Foreign relations*

i. *General*

CORNELIS JOHANNES ELIAS BOSMANS and M. VISSER, Répertoire des traités et engagements internationaux concernant les Pays-Bas, 1845–1900. La Haye 1928. pp.xv.204. [696.]

JOH[ANNES] THEUNISZ, Bibliographie van nederlandsche en belgische geschriften betreffende de vestiging van Nederlanders in midden- en oost-Europa. Volksche werkgemeenschap: Volksche wacht (special no.1): [The Hague 1941]. pp.20. [106.]

B. VAN 'T HOFF and M. W. JURRIAANSE, Het archief van Anthonie Heinsius. Allgemeen rijksarchief: 's-Gravenhage 1950. pp.246. [2500.]

Europe

A[LEXANDER] M[ARIE] STUYT, Repertorium van
door Nederland tussen 1813 en 1950 gesloten ver-
dragen. 's-Gravenhage 1953. pp.403. [2847.]

ii. *Countries*

Brazil

JOSÉ HONÓRIO RODRIGUES, Historiografia e
bibliografia do domóno holandês no Brasil.
Instituto nacional do livro: Coleção B1: Bibliografia (vol.vi): Rio de Janeiro 1949. pp.3–490.
[1098.]

France

[FRANÇOIS JOSEPH FERDINAND] MARCHAL, Notice
sur plusieurs manuscrits inédits de l'ancienne
bibliothèque de Bourgogne concernant les négo-
ciations des États-généraux des Pays-Bas avec les
rois de France Henri III et Henri IV jusqu'à la trève
de 1609. [*s.l.* 1846]. pp.19. [6.]

BARON [FRÉDÉRIC AUGUSTE FERDINAND THOMAS]
DE REIFFENBERG, Notices et extraits des manuscrits
de la bibliothèque dite de Bourgogne relatifs aux
Pays-Bas. . . . Première partie. Académie royale
des sciences et belles-lettres: Bruxelles 1829. pp.
[iii].iii.135. [100.]
no more published.

Europe

P[IETER] J[OHANNES] BLOK, Verslag aangaande
een voorloopig onderzoek te Parijs naar archivalia
belangrijk voor de geschiedenis van Nederland.
's-Gravenhage 1897. pp.54. [1000.]

G[ÉDÉON] BUSKEN HUET and J. S. VAN VEEN,
Verslag van onderzoekingen naar archivalia te
Parijs, belangrijk voor de Geschiedenis van Neder-
land. 's Gravenhage 1899. pp.vi.145. [1000.]
— — Tweede verslag . . . door G. B. Huet.
1900. pp.[vi].150. [1000.]
— — Derde verslag. 1901. pp.[vi].124. [700.]

Germany and Austria

P[IETER] J[OHANNES] BLOK, Verslag aangaande
een onderzoek in Duitschland naar archivalia
belangrijk voor de geschiedenis van Nederland.
's-Gravenhage 1888. pp.[ii].ii.296. [2000.]

P[IETER] J[OHANNES] BLOK, Verslag aangaande
een onderzoek in Duitschland en Oostenrijk naar
archivalia belangrijk voor de geschiedenis van
Nederland. 's-Gravenhage 1889. pp.xx.91. [1500.]

DUITSCH-NEDERLANDSCHE betrekkingen in den
loop der eeuwen. Catalogus: Tentoonstelling van
handschriften, boek- en plaatwerken. Rijksuniver-
siteit: Bibliotheek: Utrecht 1941. pp.54.

Europe

JOSEPH RUWET, Les archives et bibliothèque de Vienne et l'histoire de Belgique. Académie royale des sciences, des lettres et des beaux-arts de Belgique: Commission royale d'histoire: Bruxelles 1956. pp.iii–xi.963. [large number.]

BERNHARD VOLLMER, Inventare von quellen zur deutschen geschichte in niederländischen archiven. Allgemeines reichsarchiv in 's Gravenhage, reichsarchiv der provinz Gelderland in Arnheim. Archivalische zeitschrift: Archiv und wissenschaft (vol.i): München 1957. pp.xv.180. [large number.]

Great Britain

P[IETER] J[OHANNES] BLOK, Verslag aangaande een voorloopig onderzoek in Engeland naar archivalia, belangrijk voor de geschiedenis van Nederland. 's-Gravenhage 1891. pp.[iii].31. [large number.]

H[AJO] BRUGMANS, Verslag van een onderzoek in Engeland naar archivalia, belangrijk voor de geschiedenis van Nederland. 's-Gravenhage 1895. pp.[v].iv.516.viii.63. [25,000.]

G[EORGE] N[ORMAN] CLARK, List of authorities on british relations with the Dutch, 1603–1713. [s.l.] 1920. pp.18.

Europe

A[LLEN] B[ANKS] HINDS, Descriptive list of state papers, foreign: Holland. Public record office: 1939–1947. ff.i.163+i.253+[i].171. [12,500.]*
covers the period c.1560–1659.

Italy and the Vatican

P[IETER] J[OHANNES] BLOK, Verslag van onder-zoekingen naar archivalia in Italië belangrijk voor de geschiedenis van Nederland. 's Gravenhage 1901. pp.[iii].87. [1000.]

GISBERT BROM, Archivalia in Italië belangrijk voor de geschiedenis van Nederland. Rijks geschiedkundige publicatiën (Kleine serie, vol.ii, &c.): 's-Gravenhage.

 i. Rome. Vaticaansch archief . . . (vols.ii, vi): 1908–1909. pp.xxxi.464 + [v].465–1116. [2650.]

 ii. Rome. Vaticaansche bibliotheek . . . (vol. ix): 1911. pp.xiv.550. [399.]

 iii. Rome. Overige bibliotheken en archieven . . . (vol.xiv): 1914. pp.lxxxviii.732. [533.]

ALFRED CAUCHIE and LÉON VAN DER ESSEN, Inventaire des Archives farnésiennes de Naples au point de vue de l'histoire des Pays-Bas catho-liques. Académie r. de Belgique: Commission r. d'histoire: Publications in octavo (vol.xxx): Bruxelles 1911. pp.ccxxvii.557. [2068.]

Europe

LOUIS JADIN, Les Actes de la Congrégation consistoriale concernant les Pays-Bas, la principauté de Liége et la Franche-Comté, 1593–1787. Institut historique belge de Rome: Bulletin (fasc. xvi): Rome 1935. pp.622. [2500.]

Russia

FREDERIK MULLER, Essai d'une bibliographie néerlando-russe. Amsterdam 1859. pp.viii.176. [1243.]

a facsimile was published, Amsterdam 1960.

C. C. UHLENBECK, Verslag aangaande een onderzoek in de archieven van Rusland ten bate der nederlandsche geschiedenis. 's-Gravenhage 1891. pp.vi.280. [2000.]

includes B. Cordt, 'Beiträge zu einer russisch-niederländischen bibliographie'.

Scandinavia and the Baltic

G. W. KERNKAMP, Verslag van een onderzoek in Zweden, Noorwegen en Denemarken naar archivalia belangrijk voor de geschiedenis van Nederland. 's-Gravenhage 1903. pp.xii.376. [3000.]

G. W. KERNKAMP, Baltische archivalia. Onderzoek naar archivalia, belangrijk voor de geschiedenis van Nederland, in Stockholm, Kopenhagen en de duitsche oostzeesteden. Rijks geschiedkundige publicatiën (Kleine serie, vol.iv): 's-Gravenhage 1909. pp.xxii.364. [10,000.]

A. HULSHOF, Verslag van een onderzoek te Rostock naar handschriften, drukwerken en bescheiden belangrijk voor de geschiedenis van Nederland. 's-Gravenhage 1909. pp.x.90. [500.]

B. A. MEULEMAN, Norge i Nederland. Katalog over bøker og tidsskriftartikler om norske forhold. Norsk bibliografisk bibliothek (vol.iii, no.2): Leiden 1937. pp.69. [1000.]

Spain

TH. BUSSEMAKER, Verslag van een voorloopig onderzoek te Lissabon, Sevilla, Madrid, Escorial, Simancas en Brussel naar archivalia belangrijk voor de geschiedenis van Nederland. 's Gravenhage 1905. pp.viii.208. [4000.]

JULIÁN PAZ, Archivo general de Simancas. Secretario de estado. Catálogo de los documentos de las negociaciones de Flandes, Holanda y Bruselas, 1506–1795. Paris 1915. pp.185. [5000.]

United States

MATERIALS in the national archives relating to Belgium, France and the Netherlands. National archives: Reference information circular (no.3):

[Washington] 1942. pp.12. [very large number.]*

[ROBERT BENAWAY BROWN], The Netherlands and America. [William L.] Clements library: Bulletin (no.1): Ann Arbor 1947. pp.64. [70.]

DUTCH in the United States: a brief selection of references. Library of Congress: Washington 1947. ff.6. [51.]*

3. *History*

i. *Bibliographies*

OVERZICHT van de inventarissen der oude rijksarchieven in Nederland. 's-Gravenhage 1884. pp.iii.50. [400.]

OVERZICHT van de door bronnenpublicatie aan te vullen leemten der nederlandsche geschiedkennis. Commissie van advies voor 's rijks geschiedkundige publicatiën: 's-Gravenhage 1904. pp.ix.108. [62.]

[A. LE COSQUINO DE BUSSY, W. J. FORMSMA and B. VAN 'T HOFF], Gids voor de archieven van gemeenten en waterschappen in Nederland. Groningen 1942-1945. pp.51+vi.88. [500.]

J[URRIAAN] VAN TOLL, Gedrukte archivaliën. Proeve van een overzicht der tot dusver in druk verschenen nederlandsche kerkregisters, graf-

schriften: poorter- en burgerboeken, belasting-
cohieren e.a. Amsterdam 1943. pp.92. [1450.]

W[IEBE] J[ANNES] FORMSMA and B[ERT] VAN
'T HOFF, Repertorium van inventarissen van nederlandsche archieven. Groningen 1947. pp.100.
[1162.]

ii. *Manuscripts*

AUBERTUS MIRAEUS [AUBERT LE MIRE], Elenchus
historicorum Belgii nondum typis editorum.
Antverpiae 1606. pp.15. [50.]

LISTE et extraits de divers actes d'apel au future
concile général interjettez par les églises, princes,
estats, communautez ecclésiastiques & séculières
des Pays-Bas autrichiens & françois. [*s.l.*] 1718.
pp.[xvii].9. [35.]

CHRONOLOGISCH register op het vervolg van het
groot-charterboek van van Mieris, aanwezig op
het Rijks-archief te 's Hage. Provinciaal utrechtsche genootschap van kunsten en wetenschappen:
Utrecht 1859. pp.ix.187. [1500.]

L. PH. C. VAN DEN BERGH, Register van hol-
landsche en zeeuwsche oorkonden, die in den
charterboeken van van Mieris en Kluit ontbreken.
Eerste afdeeling, tot het uitsterven van het Hol-

landsche huis. Amsterdam 1861. pp.viii.143.
[1000.]

[LOUIS PROSPER] GACHARD, Actes des états généraux des Pays-Bas, 1576–1585. Notice chronologique et analytique. Commission royale d'histoire:
Bruxelles 1861–1866. pp.[v].xlvi.490+[v].540.
[2384.]
the British museum copy contains numerous ms.
corrections and notes.

P[IETER] L[ODEWIJK] MULLER, Regesta hanno-
nensia. Lijst van oorkonden betreffende Holland
en Zeeland uit het tijdvak der regeering van het
Henegouwsche huis, 1299–1345, die in het charter-
boek van van Mieris ontbreken. Koninklijke aca-
demie van wetenschappen: 's Gravenhage 1881
[on cover: 1882]. pp.[iii].viii.342. [3000.]

[E. DE BREYNE, ARTHUR GAILLARD and EDGAR
DE MARNEFFE], Inventaires sommaires des archives
des anciens gouvernements des Pays-Bas conservés aux Archives générales du Royaume. Tome I.
Archives de l'état en Belgique: Bruxelles 1906.
pp.7.38.91.21.22.30.29.7.27.14.6. [5000.]
no more published.

PLAC[IDE] and JOS[EPH] LEFÈVRE, Inventaire des
archives du Conseil du gouvernement général.

Inventaire des archives de la Belgique: Bruges 1925. pp.146. [30,000.]

R. BIJLSMA, De Regeeringsarchieven der geüniëerde en der nader geüniëerde nederlandsche provinciën, 1576 September–1588 Mei. Algemeen rijksarchief: 's-Gravenhage 1926. pp.v.192. [5000.]

P[ETRUS] A[NNE] MEILINK, Archieven van de staten van Holland en de hen opgevolgde gewestelijke besturen. Eerste deel. Archieven van de staten van Holland vóór 1572. 's-Gravenhage 1929. pp.xii.641. [10,000.]

a supplement by the author appears in the Inventarissen van rijks- en andere archieven (*1931*), *iv.159–161.*

S. W. A. DROSSAERS, He archief van den nassauschen [nassause] domeinraad. Algemeen rijksarchief: 's-Gravenhage.

    i. [i]. Het archief van den raad en rekenkamer te Breda tot 1581. Inventaris. 1948. pp. xxxix.272. [1549.]

    i. ii–iv. — Regestenlijst . . . (1170–1427 [–1581]). 1948. pp.[iv].331+[iv].308+[iv]. 315. [3533.]

i. v. — Repertorium op de leenregisters van de lek en polanen 1309–1576 en index. 1949. pp.viii.432. [556.]

ii. i. Stukken betreffende de rechten en goederen van Anna van Buren. Inventaris. 1955. pp.x.252. [1301.]

ii. ii–iii. Regestenlijst van oorkonden . . . (*c.*1166–1459[–1580]). 1955. pp.[iii].255+ [iii].276. [1966.]

iii. iv–v. Regestenlijst van brieven . . . (1467–1542[–1548]). 1955. pp.[iv].266+[iii].272. [1459.]

DENISE VAN DERVEEGHDE and CÉCILE LEFÈVRE, Inventaire des archives du conseil d'état de régence, 1706–1716. Archives générales du royaume: Bruxelles 1950. pp.31. [506.]

H. BONDER, De archieven van inspecteurs en commissies van de waterstaat in Nederland vóór 1850. Algemeen rijksarchief: 's-Gravenhage 1952. pp.144. [25,000.]

J. L. VAN DER GOUW, Stukken afkomstig van ambtenaren van het centraal bestuur tijdens de regering van Karel V gedeponeerd ter charterkamer van Holland. Algemeen rijksarchief: 's-Gravenhage 1952. pp.167. [1233.]

Europe

DE RIJKSARCHIEVEN in Nederland. Overzicht van de inhoud van de rijksarchief bewaarplaatsen. Ministerie van onderwijs, kunsten en wetenschappen: 's Gravenhage 1953. pp.vii.404. [many million.]

G. FRADCOURT, Inventaires. I. Inventaire des archives de la conférence ministérielle, 20 mai 1793–12 juin 1794. II. Inventaire des archives de la Commission pour la liquidation des dettes de 1789–1790. III. Inventaire des archives de la loterie aux Pays-Bas autrichiens. Archives générales du royaume: Bruxelles 1957. pp.23. [5000.]

iii. General

JOHANNES VAN ABKOUDE, Lyst of register van alle tractaten, gedichten, predicatien . . . enz. enz. uytgekomen ter gelegentheid van het huwelyk . . . den . . . heere Willem Carel Hendrik Friso . . . prince van Oranje en Nassaw. . . . Als ook over de geboorte en doop van . . . Willem de v. graaf van Buren. . . . Als mede over het jubeljaar van de hondertjaarige vreede . . . als ook op de gelooten vreede te Aaken, den 18 October 1748. Leiden 1750. pp.72. [500.]

also issued as a supplement to the second supplement of the author's Naamregister.

Europe

A[DRIAAN] KLUIT, Index chronologicvs, . . . sive prodromvs, ad primas lineas historiae federvm Belgii federati. Lvgduni Batavorvm 1789. pp. xvi.312. [1270.]

[J. ERMENS], Description bibliographique de la bibliothèque de Joseph Ermens. [Bruxelles c.1800]. [8116.]

S[AMUEL] DE WIND, Bibliotheek der neder-landsche geschiedschrijvers. . . . Eerste deel. Be-vattende de inlandsche geschiedschrijvers der Nederlanden, van de vroegste tijden tot op den Munsterschen vrede (970–1648). Middelburg [1831–]1835. pp.[iii].xxix.608. [400.]
— — Aanhangsel. Naamlijst der nederlandsche geschiedschrijvers, sedert den jare 1648 tot 1815. [?1840]. pp.31. [200.]

H[ENDRIK] C[ORNELIUS] ROGGE, Beschrijvende catalogus der pamfletten-verzameling van de boekerij der Remonstrantsche kerk te Amsterdam, stuk III. [Stukken betreffende de geschiedenis van Nederland]. Amsterdam 1862. pp.[vi].70. [1250.]

R[OBERT] FRUIN [and others], Repertorium der verhandelingen en bijdragen, betreffende de ge-schiedenis des vaderlands, in mengelwerken en tijdschriften tot op 1860 verschenen. Maatschap-pij der nederlandsche letterkunde: Commissie

voor geschied- en oudheidkunde [v: Rijks-
commissie van advies in zake het bibliotheek-
wezen]: Leiden 1863. pp.[iii].xi.400. [8566.]

—— [second edition]. Repertorium . . . tot op
1900. . . . Door Louis D[avid] Petit. 1907. pp.10.
[vi].xxix.coll.1638. [30,000.]

—— Tweede deel . . . 1901–1910. 1913. pp.9.
[vi].xvii.coll.884. [17,500.]

—— Derde deel . . . 1911–1920. Door
H[illetje] J[acoba] A[dolphin] Ruys. 1928. pp.
xxix.coll.904. [17,500.]

—— Vierde deel . . . 1921–1929. 1933. pp.
xxx.coll.1132. [22,500.]

—— Vijfde deel . . . 1930–1939. 1953. pp.
xxxiii.coll.764. [15,000.]

[*continued as:*]

Repertorium van boeken en tijdschriftartikelen
op het gebied van de geschiedenis van Nederland.
Nederlandsch comité voor geschiedkundige wetenschappen: Groningen [Leiden].

1940. Door Aleida Gast en N[icolaas] B[er-
nardus] Tenhaeff. 1943. pp.viii.210. [1833.]

1941. Door A. Gast. 1945. pp.viii.180. [1078.]

1942–1944. 1947. pp.viii.254. [2477.]

1945–1947. Door A. Gast en J. Brok-Ten
Broek. 1953. pp.viii.263. [2628.]

1948–1950. Door J. Brok-Ten Broek. 1954.
pp.viii.436. [3433.]

1951–1953. 1959. pp.iii–xx.442. [4318.]
1954–1956. 1963. pp.xi.484. [4392.]
in progress.

CATALOGUS van het geschiedkundig gedeelte der Gemeente-bibliotheek van Delft. 1865. pp.39. [300.]

[WILLEM NIKOLAAS DU RIEU], Register van academische dissertatien en oratien betreffende de geschiedenis des vaderlands. Maatschappij der nederlandsche letterkunde: Commissie voor geschied- en oudheidkunde: Leiden 1866. pp.[iii]. iv.104. [1601.]
—— Supplement. 1882. pp.[viii].47. [800.]

J. K. VAN DER WULP, Catalogus van de tractaten, pamfletten, enz. over de geschiedenis van Nederland, aanwezig in de bibliotheek van Isaac Meulman. Amsterdam [printed] 1866–1868. pp.[viii]. 431+[iii].383+[vi].311. [9407.]
privately printed.

1572 — 1 April — 1872. Lijst van boeken, brochuren, platen, muziek, enz. uitgegeven ter gelegenheid van het feest van Nêerlands onafhankelijkheid. Nederlandsche bibliographie (1872: bijvoegsel): Utrecht 1872. pp.xxvii. [500.]
— 1e vervolg. . . . (1873): 1873. pp.[ii].xxix-xlix. [400.]

ᴋᴀᴛᴀʟᴏɢᴜs der boekerij van het Historisch genootschap gevertigd te Utrecht. Derde uitgave. Utrecht 1872. pp.iv.155. [2500.]

— Supplement-katalogus. 1882. pp.[iv].68.14. [1500.]

— Tweede supplement-catalogus. [By P. J. D. van Dokkum]. 's Gravenhage 1895. pp.[iv].148. [2500.]

s[ᴀᴍᴜᴇʟ] ᴍᴜʟʟᴇʀ, Lijst van noord-nederlandsche kronijken, met opgave van bestaande handschriften en litteratuur. Historisch genootschap: Werken (new ser., no.31): Utrecht 1880. pp.x.97. [2000.]

ɢ. ᴠᴀɴ ʀɪᴊɴ [vol.viii &c.: and ᴄ. ᴠᴀɴ ᴏᴍᴍᴇʀᴇɴ], Atlas van Stolk. Katalogus der historie-, spot- en zinneprenten betrekkelijk de geschiedenis van Nederland verzameld door A. van Stolk. Amsterdam ['s-Gravenhage] 1895–1933. pp.viii. 365 + vi.352 + [vi].356 + vi.385–501 + [iii].354 + vi.381.480*–480** + vi.358 + [iii].319.ff.321–333 + pp.vii.390.ff.391–420 + pp.vii.348 + [vii].84. [10,000.]

ᴄᴀᴛᴀʟᴏɢᴜs der geschiedenis. De Nederlanden (noord en zuid). Koninklijke bibliotheek: [The Hague] 1901. pp.[v].194. [7000.]

Europe

BEKNOPTE catalogus van de geschiedenis der
Nederlanden (noord en zuid) in der Koninklijke
bibliotheek. Eerste deel. 's-Gravenhage 1922. pp.
[vii].459. [6330.]
covers the period to 1813; no more published.

JURRIAAN VAN TOLL, Gedrukte archivaliën.
Proeve van een overzicht der tot dusver in druk
verschenen nederlandsche kerkregisters, graf-
schriften, poorter- en burgerboeken, belasting-
cohieren e.a. Amsterdam 1943. pp.92. [1400.]

[FRANZ UNTERKIRCHER], Manuscrits et livres
imprimés concernant l'histoire des Pays-Bas,
1475–1600. Biblos-schriften (vol.33): Bruxelles
1962. pp.xv.112. [159.]
*the catalogue of an exhibition in the Bibliothèque
royale de Belgique of books from the Nationalbibliothek, Vienna.*

iv. *Miscellaneous*

JAN [MARIUS] ROMEIN, Geschiedenis van de
noord-nederlandsche geschiedschrijving in de
middeleeuwen. Haarlem 1932. pp.xxxi.248. [250.]

4. *Topography*

J[OHANNES] T[IBERIUS] BODEL NIJENHUIS, Topo-
graphische lijst der plaatsbeschrijvingen van het

koningrijk der Nederlanden. Amsterdam 1862. pp.[iv].354. [3700.]

—— Toevoegsel. Bibliographie der plaats-beschrijvingen [&c.]. 1868. pp.[vi].111. [1000.]

P[IETER] A[NTON] TIELE, Nederlandsche biblio-graphie van land- en volkenkunde. Frederik Muller-fonds: Bijdragen tot eene nederlandsche bibliographie (vol.i): Amsterdam 1884. pp.vii. 288. [1254.]

R. VAN DER MEULEN, Algemeene aardrijks-kundige bibliographie van Nederland. . . . Eerste deel. Algemeene en plaatselijke beschrijving. Nederlandsch aardrijkskundig genootschap: Lei-den 1888. pp.xiv.271. [4000.]

WOUTER NIJHOFF, Bibliographie van noord-nederlandsche plaatsbeschrijvingen tot het ende der 18e eeuw. Frederik Muller-fonds: Bijdragen tot eene nederlandsche bibliographie (vol.iv): Amsterdam 1894. pp.vii.112. [342.]

—— Tweede druk. Bewerkt . . . door F. W. D. C. A. van Hattum. 's-Gravenhage 1953. pp. viii.125. [356.]

J. N. JACOBSEN JENSEN, Reizigers te Amsterdam. Beschrijvende lijst van reizen in Nederland door vreemdelingen voor 1850. Genootschap Amstelo-

damum: Amsterdam 1919. pp.xvi.259. [349.]
—— Supplement. 1936. pp.91. [100.]

CATALOGUS van gidsen, brochures en kaarten
ten dienste van het toerisme in Nederland. Algemeene nederlandsche vereeniging voor vreem-
delingenverkeer:'s-Gravenhage 1922. pp.78.

NEDERLAND in woord en beeld. Catalogus van
boekwerken, prenten en kaarten betreffende de
provincies en gemeenten van Nederland. Leiden
1924. pp.662.

BINNEN de landgrens. Een keuze van boeken
voor den reiziger in eigenland. Bibliotheek en
leeszalen der gemeente: Rotterdam [1940]. pp.35.

E. HÉLIN, J. GRAUWELS and M[ARIE] R[OSE]
THIELEMANS, Inventaire des archives de la Jointe
des terres contestées. Archives générales du
royaume: Bruxelles 1952. pp.xiv.66. [675.]

Neuburg a. d. Donau.

HERIBERT STURM, Staatsarchiv Neuburg a. d.
Donau. Bayerische archivinventare (no.1): München 1952. pp.[iv].123. [large number.]

JOSEF HEIDER, Seminararchiv Neuburg a. d.
Donau. Bayerische archivinventare (no.7): München 1957. pp.[v].74. [2177.]

Neustadt.

ERICH GRABER, Die inventare der nichtstaatlichen archive Schlesiens. Kreis Neustadt. Verein für geschichte Schlesiens: Codex diplomaticus Silesiae (vol.xxxiii): Breslau 1928. pp.[viii].247. [10,000.]

Neuvy.

BERNARD JARRY and PAUL CRAVAYAT, Inventaire sommaire des archives départementales antérieures à 1790. Cher. Série E, supplément. Tome v. . . . Neuvy-Deux-Clochers, Neuvy-le-Barrois Neuvy-sur-Barangeon. Bourges 1943. pp.[viii]. coll.430. [7500.]

Nevele.

ROBERT SCHOORMAN, Inventaire sommaire des archives de la baronnie de Nevele [Brussels *c.*1910]. pp.12. [2000.]

Nevers.

[CHARLES ANTOINE] PARMENTIER, Archives de Nevers ou inventaire historique des titres de la ville. 1842. pp.[iii].lxiii.328[*sic,* 428] + [iii].338. [large number.]

G. EYSENBACH, Inventaire des titres de la

Chambre des comptes de Nevers. Nevers [*c.*1870]. pp.50.

[MICHEL] DE MAROLLES, Inventaire des titres de Nevers . . . suivi d'extraits des titres de Bourgogne et du Nivernois, d'extraits des inventaires des archives de l'église de Nevers et de l'inventaire des archives des Bordes. Publié et annoté par le c^te [George] de Soultrait. Société nivernaise: Nevers 1873. pp.xxiii.coll.1058. [20,000.]

[FRANÇOIS] BOUTILLIER, Inventaire-sommaire des archives communales antérieures à 1790. . . . Ville de Nevers. Nevers 1876. pp.[iii].7.2.16.137. 5.5.10.48.6.6.2.4.7.15.19. [50,000.]

F. BOUTILLIER, Inventaire-sommaire des archives hospitalières antérieures à 1790. . . . Ville de Nevers. Nevers 1877. pp.xvi.3–25.2.5.3.3.7.12. [2500.]

RENÉ [LEBLANC] DE LESPINASSE, Chartes nivernaises du comte de Chastellux. Nevers 1896. pp. 238. [2500.]

RENÉ DE LESPINASSE, Chartes nivernaises originales provenant de m. Grangier de la Marinière aujourd'hui à la Bibliothèque nationale. Nevers 1898. pp.19. [3.]

Newcastle upon Tyne, city and diocese of.

[A SURVEY of the ecclesiastical archives of the diocese of Newcastle]. Pilgrim trust: Survey of ecclesiastical archives: [1952]. ff.7. [large number.]*

New college, Oxford.

T. F. HOBSON, A catalogue of 'manorial documents' preserved in the Muniment room of New college, Oxford. Manorial society's publications (no.16): 1929. pp.vii.71. [5000.]

New Forest.

[CHARLES JANE GALE, JAMES BARSTOW and JOHN DUKE COLERIDGE], New Forest. Register of decisions on claims to forest rights by the commissioners. 1858. pp.[iv].500. [1311.]

HEYWOOD SUMNER, A New Forest bibliography & list of maps. Southampton [1925]. pp.15. [175.]
— — Second edition. Edited by W. Frank Perkins. Lymington &c. 1935. pp.30. [350.]

Nice. [*see also* Piedmont.]

ROBERT LATOUCHE, Répertoire numérique du fonds sarde, 1814–1860. [1re partie. Intendance

générale de Nice]. Archives des Alpes-maritimes: Nice 1928. pp.xviii.31. [large number.]
  the cover is dated 1930.

R[OBERT] LATOUCHE and L[ÉO] IMBERT, Inventaire sommaire du fonds "Città e contado di Nizza" des Archives d'état de Turin. Département des Alpes-maritimes: Cannes 1937. pp.xvi.206. [very large number.]

ERNEST HILDESHEIMER, Inventaire sommaire du fonds du chapitre, cathédrale de Nice. Département des Alpes-maritimes: Cannes 1955. pp. xxxxiv.74. [large number.]

Nieuwpoort.

L. M. VAN WERVEKE, Stad Nieuwpoort. Inventaris ven het archief van het oude regime. Nieuwpoort. 1937. pp.xvii.190. [large number.]

Nièvre.

INVENTAIRE sommaire des archives départementales. . . . Département de la Nièvre. Nevers. [very large number.]
  Série B. Par [Henri] de Flamare. 1891–1898. pp.467+357.
  Sous-série 2 C. Par P. Destray. 1920. pp.31.
  Série D. pp.27.

Série E, supplément. 1919. pp.viii.401.
Série 1F. Par P. Destray. 1927. pp.vii.197.
Série 2F. Par P. Destr^y et A. Biver. 1932.
pp.vii.207.
in progress.

Nijmegen.

P. NIJHOFF, Inventaris van het oud archief der gemeente Nijmegen. Arnhem 1864. pp.140. [very large number.]

J. M. VAN PABST VAN BINGERDEN, Inventaris van het oud-archief van het Oud-burger-gasthuis te Nijmegen. Nijmegen 1871. pp.63.

W. VAN DE POLL, Inventaris van het oudrechter-lijk archief der gemeente Nijmegen. Nijmegen 1890. pp.118.

J. G. C. JOOSTING, Inventaris van het oud archief der nijmeegsche broederschappen. Nijmegen 1891. pp.615.

H[ERMAN] D[IEDERIK] J[OHAN] VAN SCHEVI-CHAVEN, Repertorium noviomagense. Proeve van een register van boekwerken en geschriften betrekking hebbende op de stad en het rijk van Nijmegen. Nijmegen 1906.

L. SORMANI, Inventaris van de archieven van het borger-kinderenweeshuis, het arme-kinderhuis en de beide weeshuizen te Nijmegen. Nijmegen 1915. pp.384.

J. A. B. M. DE JONG, Voorloopige inventaris van het oud-archief der gemeente Nijmegen. Gestene 1942. pp.97. [very large number.]

Ninove.

ROBERT SCHOORMAN, Inventaire sommaire des archives de l'abbaye de Ninove. [Brussels *c.*1910]. pp.5. [750.]

Niort.

APOLLIN BRIQUET, Fragments d'un nouvel inventaire des archives de la ville de Niort. Niort 1844. pp.52. [165.]

Nivernais.

LÉON MIROT, Bibliographie des articles de géographie publiés dans les revues savantes du Nivernais. Nevers [printed] 1936. pp.35. [283.]

Nogent-le-Rotrou.

STANISLAS PROUST, Inventaire-sommaire des

archives des hospices de Nogent-le-Rotrou depuis leur fondation jusqu'à 1890. Nogent-le-Rotrou 1869. pp.226. [10,000.]

Nontron.

F[ERDINAND] VILLEPELET, ADUMAS and G[ÉRAUD] LAVERGNE, Inventaire sommaire des archives départementales. . . . Dordogne. Série E, supplément. Tome II. Arrondissement de Nontron. Périgueux 1915 [1923]. pp.ix.362. [large number.]

Noordholland.

P[IETER] SCHELTEMA, Inventaris van het provinciale archief van Noord-Holland. Haarlem 1873. pp.[iii].xiv.266.ii. [20,000.]

G. VAN ES and H. L. DRIESSEN, Inventaris der doop-, trouw-, begraaf- en successie-registers, berustende in het rijksarchief-depôt in Noord-Holland. 's-Gravenhage 1922. pp.64. [791.]

Nord.

A[NDRÉ JOSEPH GHISLAIN] LE GLAY [*and others*], Inventaire-sommaire des archives départementales. . . . Nord. Lille.

Série B. 1863 &c.
Série G. Par Anne-Marie Pietresson de Saint-Aubin. 1960. pp.xii.607+277.
Série H. Par Max Bruchet et Pierre et A. M. Pietresson de Saint-Aubin. 1928–1943. pp. ix.521+x.761.
Série L. 1911. pp.xxxv.269.
in progress.

LÉO VERRIEST, Les archives départementales du Nord à Lille. . . . Première partie. Bruxelles 1913. pp.181. [very large number.]

Norfolk.

SAMUEL WOODWARD, The Norfolk topographer's manual: being a catalogue of the books and engravings hitherto published in relation to the county. . . . Revised and augmented by W. C. Ewing esq. To which are appended, a catalogue of the drawings, prints, and deeds, collected for the illustration of the county history and antiquities, by Dawson Turner, esq. And also lists of the Norfolk chartularies known to be in existence; and of the manuscripts and drawings, relating to Norfolk, in the British museum. 1842. pp.viii.276. [1000.]

WALTER RYE, An index to Norfolk topography.

Index society: Publications (vol.x): 1881. pp.xxx. 416. [12,500.]

— — Appendix . . . forming an index to . . . books published or written since. Rye's Norfolk handlists (2nd ser., no.1): Norwich 1916. pp.35. [700.]

WALTER RYE, A short calendar of the feet of fines for Norfolk, in the reigns of Richard I., John, Henry III., . & Edward I. [Edward II.– Richard III.]. 1885–1886. pp.[ii].218+[iii].iii.219– 502. [7254.]

[W. RYE], A catalogue of fifty of the Norfolk manuscripts in the library of mr. Walter Rye. Norwich [printed] 1889. pp.[iii].ff.35. [1000.]

A SHORT catalogue of the records of the county of Norfolk, preserved in the Shirehall. Norwich 1904. pp.[ii].5. [5000.]

WALTER RYE, A catalogue of the topographical and antiquarian portions of the Free library. Norwich 1908. pp.[ii].81. [1500.]

T[HOMAS] CHUBB, A descriptive list of the printed maps of Norfolk, 1574–1916 . . . and a descriptive list of Norwich plans, 1541–1914, by Geo. A. Stephen. Norwich 1928. pp.xvi.289. [Norfolk: 600.]

Normandy.

[THOMAS CARTE], Catalogue des rolles gascons, normans et françois, conservés dans les Archives de la Tour de Londres. Londres 1743. pp.[iii]. viii.463+[iii].407. [norman: 7000.]

Carte's preface was removed by order of the french government and replaced by another written by J. P. de Bougainville; a copy in the Bibliothèque nationale contains both prefaces.

ÉDOUARD FRÈRE, Catalogue des manuscrits de la Bibliothèque municipale de Rouen relatifs à la Normandie. Rouen 1874. pp.[iii].xvi.208. [1000.]
100 copies printed.

PAUL CHEVREUX and JULES VERNIER, Les archives de Normandie et de la Seine-Inférieure. État général des fonds. Rouen 1911. pp.xvi.50. [very large number.]

ÉM[ILE] SEVESTRE, Essai sur les archives municipales et les archives judiciaires des chefs-lieux de département et de district en Normandie pendant l'époque révolutionnaire (1787–1801). 1912. pp. 201. [large number.]

ÉM[ILE] SEVESTRE, Étude critique des sources de l'histoire religieuse de la révolution en Normandie (1787–1801). 1916. pp.vii.276. [large number.]

MICHEL NORTIER, Les sources de l'histoire de Normandie au département des manuscrits de la Bibliothèque nationale. Nogent-sur-Marne. [large number.]★

    [i]. Le Fonds des nouvelles acquisitions latines. 1959. pp.x.228.

    ii. Quittances et pièces diverses de comptabilité, du règne de Philippe le Bel à celui de Louis XVI. [1962–1963]. pp.84.

    [iii]. Le fonds des nouvelles acquisitions françaises. [1960–1963]. pp.116.

in progress.

Northamptonshire.

HAROLD WHITAKER, A descriptive list of the printed maps of Northamptonshire, A.D. 1576–1900. Northamptonshire record society: Publications (vol.xiv): 1948. pp.xvi.216. [691.]

Northumberland.

LIST of documents of public interest filed in the office of the Clerk of the peace for the county [of Northumberland]. [Newcastle-on-Tyne] 1922. pp.[ii].90. [10,000.]

JOSEPH WALTON, The Greenwell deeds preserved in the Public library, Newcastle upon

Tyne. Society of antiquaries of Newcastle upon Tyne: Archaeologia aeliana (4th ser., vol.iii): Newcastle 1928. pp.iii–xxiv.237. [467.]

[A. M. OLIVER], Northumberland and Durham deeds from the Dodsworth mss. in Bodley's library, Oxford. Newcastle upon Tyne records committee: Publications (vol.vii): Newcastle 1929. pp.iii–xi.333. [1250.]

HAROLD WHITAKER, A descriptive list of the maps of Northumberland, 1576–1900. Society of antiquaries and Public libraries committee: Newcastle upon Tyne 1949. pp.iii–xvi.219. [707.]

Norway. [*see also* Scandinavia.]

1. *Cartography*

RÉPERTOIRE des cartes de la Suède, de la Norvège et du Danemark. Institut royal des ingénieurs néerlandais [Koninklijk instituut van ingenieurs]: La Haye 1859. pp.[iii].74. [177.]

Europe

KATALOG over landkarter. [Norges geografiske opmaaling:] Kristiania 1909. pp.26. [100.]
— [another edition]. 1919. pp.18. [250.]

CATALOG of nautical charts and publications. Region 4. Norway, Baltic and U. S. S. R. Washington 1962. pp.[21]. [250.]

2. Foreign relations

A[UGUSTE] GEFFROY, Notices et extraits des manuscrits concernant l'histoire ou la littérature de la France qui sont conservés dans les bibliothèques ou archives de Suède, Danemark et Norvège. 1855. pp.[iii].216. [250.]

ARNE GALLIS and SLOBODAN KOMADINIĆ, Jugoslavia–Norge. En bibliografi. Oslo 1953. pp.70. [692.]

NORDISK utenrikspolitikk etter 1945. Et utvalg böker og tidsskriftartikler. Nobelinstitutt: Bibliotek: Oslo 1958. ff.[ii].12. [300.]*

3. History

NICOLAUS PETRUS SIBBERN, Bibliotheca historica dano-norvegia, sive de scriptoribus rerum dano-norvegicarum commentarius historico literarius. Hamburgi &c. 1716. pp.[viii].454.[xiii]. [1000.]

Europe

GUSTAV LUDVIG BADEN, Dansk-norsk historisk bibliothek, indeholdende efterretning om de skrifter, som bidrage til dansk-norsk historie-kundskab. Odense 1815. pp.[xiv].358. [3500.]

BIBLIOGRAFI til Norges historie. Norske historiske forening: Oslo.

    1916–1925. Ved Wilhelm Munthe, Leiv Amundsen, Jonas Hauer. 1927. pp.[iii].596. [7452.]

    1926–1935. Ved Jonas Hauer, Reider Omang, Harald L. Tveterås. 1938. pp.v.583. [6950.]

    1936–1945. Ved Harald L. Tveterås, Finn Erichsen og Gunnar Christie Wasberg. 1939–1952. pp.[iii].745. [8601.]

    1946–1955.

    1956–1957. Av H. Falck Myckland. 1959. pp.115. [1930.]

    1958–1959. 1960. pp.117–215. [1616.]

in progress.

KAARE HAUKAAS, Litteraturen om 1905. Ein bibliografi. Historiske bibliografiar (no.1): Oslo 1956. pp.67. [500.]

CECILIE BONAFEDE, Den norske politiske brosjyrelitteraturen 1880–1890. Ein bibliografi. Historiske bibliografiar (no.3): Oslo 1961. pp.62. [400.]

Europe

4. Topography

HJALMAR PETTERSEN, Udlændingers reiser i Norge. Kgl. norske Frederiks universitet: Bibliothek: Aarbog (1895 [supplement]): Christiania 1897. pp.[iii].69. [1000.]

KATALOG over de af Norges geografiske opmaling udgivne karter og bøger. Kristiania 1902. pp.31.

[IVAR SÆTER and ARNE ARNESEN], Register til en del norske tidsskrifter. 1. Topografi. Deichmanske bibliothek: Kristiania 1908. pp.vi.192. [5000.]

JOHAN SCHWEIGAARD, Norges topografi. Bibliografisk fortegnelse over topografisk og lokalhistorisk literatur. Kristiania 1918. pp.viii.291. [10,000.]

— — Tillæg 1917-1927. Ved W[ilhelm] P[reus] Sommerfeldt. Oslo 1930. pp.[iv].250. [7000.]

KATALOG over sjøkarten og fariannsbeskrivelser vedkommende den norske kyst m.v. Norges sjøkartverk: Oslo 1947. pp.12. [300.]

MORTEN HANSEN, Utenlandske privattryck om reiser i Norge. Småskrifter for bokvenner (no. 83): Oslo 1956. pp.93. [100.]
400 copies printed.

ERLAND SCHEEN, Utenlandske bøker op reiser i Norge. Oslo 1961. pp.107. [25.]
33 copies printed.

Norwich, city and diocese of. [*see also* **Norfolk.**]

WILLIAM HUDSON and JOHN COTTINGHAM TINGEY, Revised catalogue of the records of ᵗhe city of Norwich. Norwich [1898]. pp.132. [100,000.]

WALTER RYE, A short calendar of the deeds relating to Norwich enrolled in the court rolls of that city, 1285–1306. Norfolk and Norwich archæological society: Norwich 1903. pp.[iii].xix. 136. [1750.]

WALTER RYE, Depositions taken before the mayor & aldermen of Norwich, 1549–1567. Extracts from the court books of the city of Norwich, 1666–1688. Norfolk and Norwich archæological society: Norwich 1905. pp.[iii].205. [1000.]

WALTER RYE, Calendar of Norwich deeds enrolled, etc., etc. [*s.l.*] 1910. pp.[ii].v.coll.112. pp. 113–172. [2750.]

WALTER RYE, A calendar of Norwich deeds enrolled in the court rolls of that city, 1307–1341. Norfolk and Norwich archæological society: Norwich 1951. pp.[ii].xvii.248. [3000.]

[A SURVEY of the ecclesiastical archives of the diocese of Norwich]. Pilgrim trust: Survey of ecclesiastical archives: [1952]. ff.19. [large number.]*

WINIFRED M. RISING and PERCY MILLICAN, An index of indentures of Norwich apprentices enrolled with the Norwich assembly, Henry VII–George V. Norfolk record society: Publications (vol.xxix): [Norwich] 1959. pp.xiv.210. [4500.]

Nottinghamshire.

NOTTINGHAMSHIRE. County library local history collection. [Nottingham] 1953. pp.[ii].29. [300.]

P. A. KENNEDY, Guide to the Nottinghamshire county record office. Nottinghamshire county council: [Nottingham] 1960. pp.xii.180. [very large number.]

Noyelles-lez-Seclin.

THÉODORE [HENRI JOSEPH] LEURIDAN, Inventaire-sommaire des archives communales de

Noyelles–lez–Seclin antérieures à 1790. Lille [printed] 1890. pp.18. [500.]

Noyon.

ARMAND RENDU, Inventaire analytique du cartulaire du chapitre cathédral de Noyon. Beauvais 1875. pp.72. [800.]

ARMAND RENDU, Exposé du premier volume de l'inventaire-sommaire des archives de l'Oise. Les trois évêchés et chapitres cathédraux de Beauvais, Noyon et Senlis. Beauvais 1880. pp.45. [1000.]

MARIE JOSÈPHE GUT, Répertoire numérique des archives hospitalières antérieures à 1790. Hôpital de Noyon. Département de l'Oise: Beauvais 1960. pp.16. [large number.]

Nuremberg.

GEORG ANDREAS WILL, Bibliotheca norica williana, oder kritisches verzeichniss aller schriften, welche die stad Nürnberg angehen. Altdorf.

    i. Scriptorvm ad historiam politicam pertinentivm sectio I[–II]. 1772. pp.[iii].xxiv. 328+xviii.326. [1498.]

    ii. Scriptorvm ad historiam ecclesiasticam pertinentivm. 1773. pp.[iii].vi.362. [1567.]

iii. Scriptorvm ad hist. literariam. Pars iiii. Ad hist. natvralem et mixtam pertinentivm. 1774. pp.xxxvi.271. [1168.]

v. Scriptorvm ad hist. altorfinam pertinentivm. 1775. pp.[x].xvi.260. [1475.]

vi. Indices completos nominalem et realem continens. 1778. pp.viii.312.

vii. Continens svpplementa ad historiam, politicam et ecclesiasticam nor. 1792. pp. viii.360. [1506.]

viii. Continens svpplementa ad hist. liter. nat. et mixtam nor. atqve altorfinam. 1793. pp. xvi.349. [3500.]

JOHANNES MÜLLER, Katalog der historisch-geographischen ausstellung des 16. Deutschen geographentages. Nürnberg 1907. pp.80. [323.]

the exhibition consisted in the main of maps of Germany, with special reference to Nürnberg.

KARL FISCHER, Verzeichnis der von 1941 bis 1950 erschienenen schriften zur geschichte der stadt Nürnberg und ihres ehemaligen gebietes. Nürnberg 1951. pp.91. [920.]

[PETER STRIEDER], Kaiser Maximilian I, 1459–1519, und die Reichsstadt Nürnberg. Ausstellung. Germanisches nationalmuseum: Nürnberg 1959. pp.32. [137.]

[KARLHEINZ GOLDMANN], Melanchton und Nürnberg. Ausstellung aus anlass der 400. wiederkehr seines todestages. Stadtbibliothek: Ausstellungskatalog (no.15): Nürnberg 1960. pp.[16]. [171.]

[KARLHEINZ GOLDMANN], Die literarischen und wissenschaftlichen beziehungen zwischen Nürnberg und Grossbritannien im 17. und 18. jahrhundert. Stadtsbibliothek: Ausstellungs-katalog (no.18): Nürnberg [1960]. pp.[12]. [95.]

Oberhessen.

HEINRICH EDUARD SCRIBA, Regesten der bis jetzt gedruckten urkunden zur landes- und ortsgeschichte des grossherzogthums Hessen. . . . Zweite [vierte, no.2] abtheilung: die regesten der provinz Oberhessen enthaltend. Darmstadt 1849–1853. pp.[iv].276+[ii].112. [5115.]

Obernai.

[JOSEPH MEINRAD] GYSS, Inventaire-sommaire des archives communales antérieures à 1790. . . . Ville d'Obernai: Strasbourg 1868. pp.[iii].ii.9.8. 14.19.5.8.10. [15,000.]

Oedelem.

BARON A. VAN ZUYLEN VAN NYEVELT, Inventaire

sommaire des archives de la baronne de Praet et de la paroisse d'Oedelem conservées au dépôt des archives de l'état, à Bruges. [Brussels *c.*1910]. pp.8. [446.]

Oise.

ARMAND RENDU, Catalogue de la bibliothèque administrative de la préfecture et des archives de l'Oise. Beauvais 1878. pp.68. [897.]

— — Premier supplément. Par É[mile Louis] Coüard-Luys. 1883. pp.36. [450.]

— — Deuxième supplément. Par Ernest [Victor Henri] Roussel. 1889. pp.55.

INVENTAIRE-sommaire des archives départe-mentales. . . . Oise. Beauvais. [very large number.]

Série G. Par Gustave Desjardins et Armand Rendu. 1878. pp.viii.478.

Série H. Par A. Rendu et É[mile Louis] Coüard-Luys [Ernest (Victor Henri) Roussel]. 1888–1897. pp.xvi.495+xiv.478.

in progress.

ERNEST [VICTOR HENRI] ROUSSEL, Répertoire des plans conservés aux archives départementales de l'Oise. Avec l'état sommaire des plans, intéressant des localités de l'Oise, déposés aux Archives

nationales et aux archives des départements limi-
trophes. Beauvais 1899. pp.127. [2500.]

Oisterwijk.

R. A. VAN ZUYLEN, Inventaris van het oud-
archief der gemeente Oisterwijk [*s.l.*] 1917. pp.29.

Olargues.

J. SAHUC, Inventaire sommaire des archives
communales. Communes du canton d'Olargues.
[Montpellier *c.*1870]. pp.71. [large number.]

Oldenzaal.

J. I. VAN DOORNINCK, Tijdrekenkundige lijst
van stukken, welke thans nog het oud-archief
der gemeente Oldenzaal uitmaken. Vereeniging
tot beoefening van overijsselsch regt en geschiedenis: Werken: Zwolle 1874. pp.72.

—— IIᵉ lijst van stukken behoorende tot het
oud-archief der stad Oldenzaal. [By] J. W. F. van
Harten. Oldenzaal 1938. pp.114.

B. H. HOMMEN, Het archief der gemeente Oldenzaal van 1811–1917. Oldenzaal 1937. pp.79.

W. J. FORMSMA, De archivalia van de olden-
zaalsche oudheidskammer. Oldenzaal 1940. pp.89.

— — 1e annvulling. Door B. H. Hommen.
1943. pp.55.

Ollières.

— PAIX, Inventaire sommaire des archives communales antérieures à 1790. . . . Commune
d'Ollières. Draguignan 1889. pp.[iii].51. [7500.]

Oosterhout.

C[ORNELIUS] C[ATHARINUS] N[ICOLAAS] KROM,
Inventaris van het oud-archief der gemeente
Oosterhout. Oosterhout 1885. pp.31.

Ootmarsum.

R. E. HATTINK, Register op het oud-archief van
Ootmarsum. Vereeniging tot beoefening van
overijsselsch regt en geschiedenis: Werken:
Zwolle 1878. pp.80.

W. J. FORMSMA, Het oud-archief der gemeente
Ootmarsum. Assen 1943. pp.144.

Orange, France.

L[ÉOPOLD] DUHAMEL, Inventaire-sommaire des
archives municipales antérieures à 1790 de la ville

d'Orange. Orange 1917. pp.iv.464. [large number.]
in progress?

Orchies.

JULES FINOT and J. VERMAERE, Inventaire sommaire des archives hospitalières antérieures à 1790. . . . Ville d'Orchies. Lille 1901. pp.[iii].xxii.40. [2500.]

Orléans, France.

PAUL VEYRIER DU MURAUD [*and others*], Inventaire sommaire des archives communales antérieures à 1790. . . . Ville d'Orléans. Orléans 1907–1920. pp.ii.338+399. [large number.]

J. DOINEL, Inventaire sommaire des archives hospitalières antérieures à 1790. Hospice d'Orléans. Revu et publié par Jacques Soyer. Orléans 1920. pp.v.115. [983.]

CAMILLE BLOCH and JACQUES SOYER, Inventaire sommaire des archives départementales antérieures à 1790. . . . Intendance de la généralité d'Orléans et assemblée provinciale de l'Orléanais. Orléans 1927. pp.xi.280. [large number.]

CAMILLE BLOCH and JACQUES SOYER, Inventaire sommaire des archives communales antérieures à 1790. Tome II, série GG. Cultes: registres des baptêmes, mariages et sépultures des paroisses d'Orléans...jusqu'en 1658. Orléans 1935. pp.399. [large number.]

Orne.

INVENTAIRE-sommaire des archives départementales. . . . Orne. Paris [*afterwards:* Alençon]. [very large number.]

    Série A. Par P. J. Gravelle-Desulis. [*c.1875*]. pp.88.

    Séries C–D. 1877. pp.10.426.24.5.

    Série H. Par Louis Duval. 1891–1910. pp. xxvi.378+xcii.265+lxviii.331+xxxv.343 +309.

    Série K. Par René Jouanne. 1924. pp.22.

    Série O. Par Max Fazy [*and others*]. 1911. pp.59.

    Série U. 1919. pp.7.

    Série V. 1912. pp.23.

  in progress.

R[ENÉ] JOUANNE, Répertoire critique des anciens inventaires des archives départementales de l'Orne. Alençon 1930. pp.103. [500.]

Oss.

C. C. D. EBELL and J[OSEPH] P[ETER] W[ILLEM] A[NTOON] SMIT, Inventaris van het oud-archief der gemeente Oss. [*s.l.*] 1916. pp.18.

Ossana.

GIOVANNI CICCOLINI, Inventari e regesti degli archivi parrochiali della Val di Sole. . . . Vol. primo. La Pieve di Ossana. Rerum tridentinarum fontes: Trento 1936. pp.xv.515. [5000.]

Oudegem.

C. WYFFELS, Inventarissen van het archief van de baronie van Eksaarde en van Oudegem. Rijksarchief te Gent: Brussel 1960. pp.48. [5000.]

Oudenarde.

P. DE MUYNCK, Inventaris der stad Oudenarde. Oud-archif. Oudenarde 1942 &c.*
in progress.

Oudenbourg.

J. YERNAUX, Inventaire sommaire des archives de l'abbaye d'Oudenbourg conservées au dépôt des archives de l'état, à Bruges. [Brussels *c.*1910]. pp.8. [500.]

Ouveilhan.

[GERMAIN] MOUYNÈS, Inventaire-sommaire des archives communales antérieures à 1790. . . . Ouveilhan. 1863. pp.[iii].7.6.2.2.2.9. [5000.]

Overijssel.

[JAN IZAAK VAN DOORNINCK], Tijdrekenkundig register op het oud provinciaal archief van Overijssel. Zwolle [printed].

    i. 1225–1393. 1857. pp.105. [250.]
    ii. 1393–1423. 1859. pp.268. [1000.]
    iii. 1424–1456. 1860. pp.144. [300.]
    iv. 1456–1496. 1865. pp.643. [2000.]
    — Aanhangsel, aº 1225–1496. 1874. pp.[ii].
    487. [1500.]
    v. 1496–1527. 1872. pp.[iv].559. [2500.]
    — Bladwijzer. 1875. pp.[iv].190.

A. BARON VAN DEDEM, Register van charters en bescheiden berustende bij de Vereeniging tot beoefening van overijsselsch regt en geschiedenis te Zwolle. Kampen 1913. pp.xix.432. [1049.]

Overloon.

P. M. F. RIETER, Inventaris van . . . het oud-archief van Maashees en Holthees . . . het oud-archief van Overloon. [*s.l.*] 1917. pp.42.

Oviedo.

SANTOS GARCÍA LARRAGUETA, Catálogo de los pergaminos de la catedral de Oviedo. Instituto de estudios asturianos: Oviedo 1957. pp.[xv].xx.504. [1318.]

Oxford, city, county, diocese and university of.

F[ALCONER] MADAN, Rough list of manuscript materials relating to the History of Oxford contained in the printed catalogues of the Bodleian and college libraries. Oxford 1887. pp.vii.170. [2000.]

H[ERBERT] E[DWARD] SALTER, The feet of fines for Oxfordshire, 1195–1291. Oxfordshire record society: Oxfordshire record series (vol.xii): Oxford 1930. pp.xi.286. [1250.]

[A SURVEY of the ecclesiastical archives of the diocese of Oxford]. Pilgrim trust: Survey of ecclesiastical archives: [1952]. ff.19. [large number.]*

Paderborn.

JOHANNES LINNEBORN, Inventar des archives des Bischöflichen generalvikariats zu Paderborn.

Historische kommission der provinz Westfalen: Inventare der nichtstaatlichen archive (beiband ii. 1): Münster 1920. pp.[xi].386. [7500.]

JOHANNES LINNEBORN, Inventare der nichtstaatlichen archive des kreises Paderborn. Historische kommission der provinz Westfalen (vol.iii, no.2): Münster 1923. pp.[iv].213. [4000.]

Palatinate. [*see also* **Bavaria.**]

STEPHAN EHSES, Quellen und literatur zur geschichte des bayrisch-pfälzischen oder landshuter erbfolgekrieges, 1504–1509. Würzburg 1880. pp.[iii].53. [150.]

MANFRED KREBS, Die kurpfälzischen dienerbücher, 1476–1685. Oberrheinische historische kommission: Zeitschrift für die geschichte des Oberrheins (vol.94, supplement): Karlsruhe 1942. pp.168. [3191.]

Paris.

J. B. MAROT, Inventaire-sommaire des archives hospitalières antérieures à 1790. . . . [Hospice des] Quinze-vingts. 1867. pp.[iii].12.3–7.396. [6580.]

[TOURNIER and LÉON BRIÈLE], Inventairesommaire des archives hospitalières antérieures à

1790. . . . Hôtel-Dieu [vol.iii: Hôpital saint-Jacques-aux-pèlerins. — Hôpital du saint-esprit-en-Grève. — Hôpital de la trinité. — Hôpital des enfants-rouges. — Hôpital des enfants-trouvés. — Hôpital sainte-Anastase]. Administration générale de l'assistance publique à Paris: [1881–]1882–1886. pp.[iii].xxxviii.411+[iii].343+[iii].372. [250,000.]

first printed in 1866–1870; the larger part of the impression was destroyed by fire in 1871.

— — Supplément. [1888–]1889. pp.[iii].lv.360. [20,000.]

contains inventories of the Hopital sainte-Catherine, the Hopital général, the Hospice des incurables, and a supplement to the Hotel-Dieu.

A[UGUSTE MARIE LOUIS ÉMILE] MOLINIER, Inventaire sommaire de la collection Joly de Fleury. 1881. pp.xlvi.114. [2555.]

VALENTIN DUFOUR, Bibliographie artistique, historique et littéraire de Paris, avant 1789. 1882. pp.[iii].viii.539. [4000.]

PAUL LACOMBE, Essai d'une bibliographie des ouvrages relatifs à l'histoire religieuse de Paris pendant la révolution (1789–1802). 1884. pp.[iii]. iii. [994.]

100 copies printed; in a copy in the Bibliothèque nationale the pressmarks of that library have been inserted in ms.

CATALOGUE des livres relatifs à l'histoire de la ville de Paris et de ses environs composant la bibliothèque de m. l'abbé L. A. N. Bossuet. 1888. pp.[ii].384. [2500.]

H[ENRI] OMONT, Manuscrits relatifs à l'histoire de Paris et de l'Ile-de-France conservés à Cheltenham dans la bibliothèque de sir Thomas Phillipps. 1889. pp.15. [100.]

MAURICE TOURNEUX, Bibliographie de l'histoire de Paris pendant la révolution française. Ville de Paris: Publications relatives à la révolution française: 1890–1913. pp.[iii].lxxviii.520+[iii].xliv. 822 + [iii].lviii.991 + [iii].xl.738 + [iii].vii.1024. [27,500.]

ALEXANDRE TUETEY, Répertoire général des sources manuscrites de l'histoire de Paris pendant la révolution française. Ville de Paris: Publications relatives à la révolution française.

 i–iii. États-généraux et Assemblée constituante. 1890–1894. pp.[iii].xlvi.482+[iii]. xxxix.588+[iii].xliv.725. [14,000.]

 iv–vii. Assemblée législative. 1890–1905. pp.[iii].xxxv.652 + [iii].lxv.718 + [iii]. lxxxvii.730+[iii].xxvii.528. [15,000.]

viii–xi. Convention nationale. 1908–1914. pp.[iii].847 + [iii].cxii.631 + [iii].849 + [iii].c.916. [11,000.]

MARIUS BARROUX, Inventaire sommaire des archives de la Seine. Partie municipale. . . . Ville de Paris. Période révolutionnaire (1789–an VIII). Fonds de l'Administration générale de la commune et de ses subdivisions territoriales (série D). 1892–1901. pp.[iii].iii.238. [2500.]
no more published.

M. THORLET, Inventaire sommaire des archives de la Seine. . . . Fonds des anciens arrondissements de Paris. Lois, décrets . . . relatifs à l'organisation et au mode de fonctionnement des services municipaux . . . depuis l'an VIII jusqu'au 31 décembre 1859. 1896. pp.xiv.184. [5983.]

PAUL LE VAYER, Les entrées solennelles à Paris des rois et reines de France, des souverains et princes étrangers, ambassadeurs, etc. Bibliographie sommaire. 1896. pp.47. [363.]

MARIUS BARROUX, Les sources de l'ancien état-civil parisien. Répertoire critique. 1898. pp.vii.136. [large number.]
a calendar of the documents prior to 1860 which survived the fires of 1871.

ÉMILE CAMPARDON and ALEXANDRE TUETEY, Inventaire des registres des insinuations du Châtelet de Paris: règnes de François Iᵉʳ et de Henri II. Histoire générale de Paris: 1906. pp. xlvii.1098. [5382.]

LÉON VALLÉE, Catalogue des plans de Paris et des cartes de l'Île de France, de la généralité, de l'élection, de l'archevêché, de la vicomté, de l'université, du Grenier de sel et de la Cour des aydes de Paris, conservés à la Section des cartes et plans. Bibliothèque nationale: 1908. pp.[ii].ii.579. [3592.]

ÉTIENNE CLOUZOT, Impressions du XVIᵉ siècle relatives à l'histoire de Paris et de la France. Ville de Paris: Catalogue méthodique de la bibliothèque (vol.i): 1908. pp.vi.coll.694.pp.697–698. [1750.]

MARIUS BARROUX, Essai de bibliographie critique des généralités de l'histoire de Paris. 1908. pp.vi.155. [815.]
320 copies printed.

[MARCEL POËTE *and others*], Paris sous la république de 1848. Exposition de la Bibliothèque et des travaux historiques de la ville de Paris. [1909]. pp.44. [24.]

[MARCEL POËTE *and others*], La transformation de Paris sous le second empire. Exposition de la

Bibliothèque et des travaux historiques de la ville de Paris. 1910. pp.69. [29.]

[MARCEL POËTE *and others*], Paris durant la grande époque classique (xviie siècle). Exposition de la Bibliothèque et des travaux historiques de la ville de Paris. [1911]. pp.80. [30.]

HISTOIRE de Paris. Université de Paris: Bibliothèque: 1912. pp.24. [350.]
reproduced from handwriting.

[MARCEL POËTE *and others*], Sur les boulevards. Madeleine-Bastille (depuis le xviie siècle jusqu'à la fin du second empire). Exposition de la Bibliothèque et des travaux historiques de la ville de Paris. 1912. pp.43. [12.]

GABRIEL HENRIOT, Quelques sources manuscrites privées de l'histoire contemporaine de Paris. Société des amis de la Bibliothèque de la ville de Paris. 1912. pp.11. [30.]

[MARCEL POËTE *and others*], Promenades et jardins de Paris (depuis le xve siècle jusqu'en 1830). Exposition de la Bibliothèque et des travaux historiques de la ville de Paris. [1913]. pp.61. [21.]

GABRIEL HENRIOT and JEAN DE LA MONNERAYE, Répertoire des travaux publiés par les sociétés d'histoire de Paris depuis leur fondation jusqu'au

31 décembre 1911. Dressé sous la direction de Marcel Poëte. Bulletin de la Bibliothèque et des Travaux historiques de la ville (vol.viii–ix): 1914. pp.vii.358. [3553.]

ÉTIENNE CLOUZOT, Dépouillement d'inventaires et de catalogues. Bibliothèque d'histoire de Paris: Répertoire des sources manuscrites de l'histoire de Paris (no.i): 1915–1916. pp.[iii].xxxv.519+ [iii].584+[iii].539. [25,000.]

ERNEST COYECQUE and HENRI PROST, Répertoire des fonds des insinuations de Paris et des bureaux des domaines de banlieue (C^6). . . . Révisé par Henri Lemoine. Archives du département de la Seine et de la ville de Paris: 1926. pp.xxvi.63. [595.]

HENRI LEMOINE, Table des registres du bureau de la ville de Paris de 1615 à 1643 conservés aux Archives nationales. Archives du département de la Seine et de la ville de Paris: Documents (3rd ser., vol.i): 1926. pp.24. [2000.]

LÉON MIROT, Inventaire analytique des hommages rendus à la Chambre de France. I. Prévôté et vicomté de Paris. Melun 1932. pp.[ii].247. [4412.]

ALBERT SOBOUL, Les papiers des sections de Paris, 1790–an IV. Répertoire sommaire. Commission de recherche et de publication des documents relatifs à la vie économique de la révolution française: 1950. pp.125. [1000.]

LÁSZLÓ GERÉB, A Párisi kommün az egykorú magyar irodalomban, 1870–1871–1872. Bibliográfia és repertórium jegyzetekkel. Fővárosi Szabó Ervin könyvtár: Tanulmányok: Új sorozat (no.1): Budapest 1951. pp.70. [500.]

ROBERT BARROUX, Inventaire sommaire de la série V.M$^{31-37}$ (édifices du culte de la Ville de Paris). Archives du département de la Seine et de la ville de Paris: 1952. pp.[ii].130. [10,000.]

GIUSEPPE DEL BO, La Comune di Parigi. Saggio bibliografico. Istituto Giangiacomo Feltrinelli: Bibliografie (vol.ii): Milano [1957]. pp.vi.143. [1000.]

Parma.

RAIMONDO [MELILUPI, MARCHESE] DI SORAGNA, Bibliografia storica e statutaria delle provincie parmensi. Reale deputazione di storia patria per le provincie parmensi: Parma 1886. pp.[ii].253. [1473.]
incomplete; no more published.

STEFANO LOTTICI and GIUSEPPE SITTI, Bibliografia

generale per la storia parmense. Parma 1904. pp.
x.3–427. [6168.]

GIOVANNI DREI, L'Archivio di stato di Parma.
Indice generale, storico, descrittivo ed analitico.
Bibliothèque des 'Annales institutorum' (vol.vi):
Roma 1941. pp.xi.283. [large number.]
250 copies printed.

Pas-de-Calais.

INVENTAIRE-sommaire des archives départementales. . . . Pas-de-Calais. Arras. [very large
number.]

Série A. Par Jules Marie Richard. 1878–1887.
pp.xv.378+xx.236.

Série B. Par A. Godin et J. A. Cottel. 1875.
pp.215.

Série C. Par J. A. Cottel. 1882. pp.iv.394.

Série G. Par Daniel Haigneré. 1891. pp.331.ii.

Série H. Par H. Loriquet et J. Chavanon [G.
Tison]. 1902–1911. pp.[iii].421 + 374 +
[iii].455.8.

Série K. Par R. Louis et Eugène Déprez. 1912.
pp.78.

Série L. Par H. Loriquet. 1895. pp.lxxvi.202.

Série Q. Par J.-B. Brunel et E. Déprez. 1914.
pp.60.

Série V. Par A. Lavoine et E. Déprez. [*c*.1910].
pp.65.
in progress.

Pembrokeshire.

HENRY OWEN, A calendar of the public records
relating to Pembrokeshire. Honourable society
of Cymmrodorion: Cymmrodorion record series
(no.7): 1911–1918. pp.xii.172+[viii].149+xvi.
268. [1500.]

Perche.

VISCOUNT O[LIVIER] DE ROMANET and H[ENRI]
TOURNOÜER, Sources de l'histoire du Perche.
Indication des documents et monuments de toute
nature relatifs à cette province. Documents sur la
province du Perche: Mortagne 1890. pp.8.72.
[500.]

Périgord.

[COUNT ERNEST DE MALEVILLE], Bibliographie du
Périgord, XVIᵉ siècle. 1861. pp.[v].59. [100.]
100 copies printed.

LÉONARD A[LBERT] DUJARRIC-DESCOMBES, Recherches sur les historiens du Périgord au XVIIᵉ
siècle. Périgueux 1882. pp.152. [50.]

Périgueux.

L. DESSALLES and F[ERDINAND] VILLEPELET, Inventaire sommaire des archives départementales. . . . Dordogne. Tome I. Sénéchaussée, présidial et maréchaussée de Périgueux. Périgueux 1882. pp. x.365. [large number.]

MICHEL HARDY, Inventaire sommaire des archives communales antérieures à 1790. . . . Ville de Périgueux. Périgueux 1894. pp.xxxv.543. [50,000.]

F[ERDINAND] VILLEPELET, Inventaire sommaire des archives départementales. . . . Dordogne. Série E, supplément. Tome I. Arrondissement de Périgueux. Périgueux 1906. pp.[ii].403.

Pernis.

H. C. HAZEWINKEL, De archieven der gemeenten Kralingen, Charlois en Katendrecht. Rotterdam 1909. pp.76.

Perugia.

GIOVANNI BATTISTA VERMIGLIOLI, Bibliografia storico-perugina, o sia catalogo degli scrittori che hanno illustrato la storia della città, del contado, delle persone, de' monumenti, della letteratura. Perugia 1823. pp.xiv.197. [1000.]

L. FUMI, Inventario e spoglio dei registri della Tesoreria apostolica di Perugia e Umbria dal R. archivio di stato in Roma. Perugia 1901. pp. lxviii.403. [25,000.]

ARCHIVIO storico del comune di Perugia. Inventario. Pubblicazioni degli archivi di stato (vol.xxi): Roma 1956. pp.xlii.474. [large number.]

Peterborough.

[A SURVEY of the ecclesiastical archives of the province of Peterborough]. Pilgrim trust: Survey of ecclesiastical archives: [1952]. ff.20. [large number.]*

Pézenas.

F[RANÇOIS] RESSEGUIER, Inventaire. . . . Archives de la ville de Pézenas. . . . Publié par Jos[eph] Berthelé. Montpellier 1907. pp.[iii].264. [1853.]
compiled in 1774.

Pfävers, abbey of.

KARL WEGELIN, Die regesten der Benedictinerabtei Pfävers and der landschaft Sargans. Regesten der archive in der Schweizerischen eidgenossenschaft (vol.i): Chur 1850. pp.[iv].112.xxiii. [916.]

Picardy.

HIP[POLYTE] COCHERIS, Notices et extraits des documents manuscrits conservés dans les dépôts publics de Paris, et relatifs à l'histoire de la Picardie. 1854–1858. pp.[iv].693+vi.626. [50,000.]

E[UGÈNE] DRAMARD, Bibliographie géographique et historique de la Picardie. Tome premier. 1869. pp.xxiii.494. [2000.]
no more published.

COUNT [ARTHUR] DE MARSY, Documents historiques et autographes concernant la Picardie. I. 1886. pp.16. [40.]
no more published.

Piedmont.

NICODEME BIANCHI, Le carte degli archivi piemontesi, politici, amministrativi, guidiziari, finanziari, comunali, ecclesiastici e di enti morali. Torino &c. 1881. pp.xxxix.568. [100,000.]

Pilsen.

MILOSLAV BĚLOHLÁVEK, Městský archiv v. Plzni. Průvodce po archivu. Prameny a příspěsky k dějinám Plzně a Plzeňska (vol.9): Plzeň 1954. pp.231. [large number.]

Plombières.

[LOUIS JOUVE], Bibliographie de Plombières. Remiremont 1866. pp.[ii].43. [152.]

[MARIE] ANDRÉ PHILIPPE, Inventaire-sommaire des archives de l'Hôpital notre-dame. . . . Ville de Plombières. Épinal 1925. pp.[ii].viii.18. [500.]

Plymouth.

R. N. WORTH, Calendar of the Plymouth municipal records. Plymouth 1893. pp.xi.308. [100,000.]

Poblet, monastery of.

SIEGFRIED BOSCH and MANUEL CRUELLS, Catalog de l'exposició de documents jurídics de l'arxiu de Poblet. Congrès jurídics català: Barcelona 1936. pp.3–80. [233.]

Podolia.

MIKOLA BILINSKII, NINA SPIVOCHENSKA and VAN KREVETSKII Часописи Поділля. Історично-бібліографічний збірник. Вінницька Філія всенародньої Бібліотеки України при Українській академії наук: Матеріяли до історії друку та до бібліографії Поділля (vol.i): Винниці 1927–1928. pp.146.21.4.v. [529.]

Poitiers.

LOUIS [FRANÇOIS XAVIER] RÉDET and [GUY] ALFRED RICHARD, Inventaire sommaire des archives départementales. . . . Vienne. Série G. Poitiers 1883. pp.xv.266. [large number.]
deals with the archives of the bishopric, chapter, ecclesiastic chamber, seminaries and collégiales *of Poitiers.*

E. BRICAULD DE VERNEUIL, Inventaire sommaire des archives départementales. . . . Vienne. Série E, supplément. Arrondissement de Poitiers. Poitiers 1921. pp.viii.347. [large number.]

Poitou.

[VICTOR BUJEAUD], Catalogue des pièces les plus importantes contenues dans les registres du parlement de Paris concernant l'Angoumois, la Saintonge et le Poitou. (Archives de l'Empire). 1770–1785. Niort 1865. pp.28. [200.]

[GUY] ALFRED RICHARD, Archives seigneuriales du Poitou. Inventaire analytique des archives du château de La Barre. Saint-Maixent 1868. pp.[iii]. xlvi.292+[iii].506+[iii].xlvii–ccv. [7500.]

[GUY] ALFRED RICHARD, Notes pour servir à la bibliographie des états généraux de 1789 en Poitou. Melle 1888. pp.31. [110.]

Europe

MADELEINE DILLAY, Les chartes de franchises du Poitou. Société d'histoire du droit: Catalogue des chartes de franchises de la France (vol.i): 1927. pp.[vii].xxvii.106. [100.]

Poland.

1. *Cartography*

BARON EDWARD RASTAWIECKI, Mappografia dawnej Polski. Warszawa 1846. pp.[iv].xiv.159. [424.]

LUDOMIR SAWICKI, Spis map Archiwum wojennego w Wiedniu odnoszących się do ziem polskich. [Wjskowy instytut naukowo-wydawiczy:] Przyczynki do bibljografji kartograficznej ziem polskich: Warszawa 1920. pp.xxii. 242.iii. [2488.]

BOLESŁAW OLSZEWICZ, Polska kartografja wojskowa. Wojskowy instytut naukowo-wydawniczy: Warszawa 1921. pp.199.lxxx. [2500.]

BOLESŁAW OLSZEWICZ, Polskie zbiory karto-
graficzne. Towarzystwo bibljofilów polskich:
Warszawa 1926. pp.120.

KATALOG map i innych wydawnictw W.I.G.
ze skorowidzami i wzórami. Wojskowy instytut geograficzny: Warszawa 1927. pp.17. [50.]

BOLESŁAW OLSZEWICZ, Kartografja polska xv i
xvi wieku (przegląd chronologiczno–bibliograficzny). Lwów &c. 1930. pp.28. [41.]

KATALOG wystawy zbiorów kartograficznych.
Bibljoteka narodowa: Katalogi wystaw (vol.iv):
Warszawa 1934. pp.114. [232.]

2. *Foreign relations &c.*

SEBASTIANO CIAMPI, Bibliografia critica delle
antiche reciproche corrispondenze politiche,
ecclesiastiche, scientifiche, letterarie, artistiche
dell'Italia colla Russia, colla Polonia ecc. Firenze
1834–1842. pp.[vi].v.366 + xii.326 + [vi].137.
[2500.]

A REVIEW of the british war literature on the
polish problem. Translated from Uwagi. Polish
information committee: 1916. pp.22. [25.]

Europe

STANISLAS WĘDKIEWICZ, La Suède et la Pologne. Essai d'une bibliographie des publications suédoises concernant la Pologne. Stockholm 1918. pp.[iii].112. [1000.]

WOJCIECH MEISELS, Italja a powstanie styczniowe. Bibliografja. Kraków 1926. pp.31. [230.]
205 copies printed.

KATALOG wystawy rękopisów i druków polsko-węgierskich xv i xvi wieku. Bibljoteka jagiellońska: Kraków 1928. pp.59. [101.]

CASIMIR [KAZIMIERZ] SMOGORZEWSKI, Abrégé d'une bibliographie relative aux relations germano-polonaises. Problèmes politiques de la Pologne contemporaine (vol.iii, supplément): 1933. pp.115. [800.]

WALTER SCHINNER, Polen. Nach den beständen der Weltkriegsbücherei unter besonderer berücksichtigung der deutsch-polnischen beziehungen in vergangenheit und gegenwart bearbeitet. Weltkriegsbücherei: Bibliographische vierteljahrshefte (no.1): Stuttgart 1934. pp.80. [2000.]
—— Nachtrag. 1934. pp.81–90. [250.]

FELIKS LIBERT, Materjały do bibljografji wojny polsko-sowieckiej. Wojskowe biuro historyczne: Warszawa 1935. pp.[ii].xiv.162. [2720.]

A[LLEN] B[ANKS] HINDS, Descriptive list of state papers, foreign: Poland (S.P. 88), 1586–1661. Public record office: 1937. ff.i.47. [1000.]*

[MAX GUNZENHÄUSER], Bibliographie zur aussen-politik der republik Polen, 1919–1939, und zum feldzug in Polen 1939. Institut für weltpolitik: Bibliographie der weltkriegsbücherei (no.33): Stuttgart 1942. pp.97. [2500.]

[MAX GUNZENHÄUSER], Bibliographie zur ge-schichte der deutsch-polnischen beziehungen und grenzlandfragen, 1919–1939. Weltkriegsbücherei: Bibliographien (no.34/36): Stuttgart 1942. pp.205. [4000.]

V. MEYSZTOWICZ, Repertorium bibliographicum pro rebus polonicis archivi secreti Vaticani. Uni-versitas regia bathorea: Studia teologiczne (vol.xi): Città del Vaticano 1943. pp.20. [135.]

PIETRO SAVIO, De actis nuntiaturae Poloniae quae partem archivi secretariatus status consti-tuunt. Città del Vaticano 1947. pp.156. [3375.]

MARIA and MARINA BERSANO BEGEY, La Polonia in Italia. Saggio bibliografico, 1799–1948. Univer-sità di Torino: Istituto di cultura polonica: Pubbli-cazione (vol.ii): Torino 1949. pp.295.

Europe

ALPHONSE S. WOLANIN, Polonica americana. Annotated catalogue of the archives of the Polish roman catholic union. Chicago 1950. pp.295. [2500.]

JOSEF BLEHA and JAROSLAV KUNC, Polsko. Bibliografický ukazatel literatury. Bibliografický katalog ČSR: Praha 1954. pp.24. [300.]

MARIA WALENTYNOWICZ and ANDRZEJ WĘDZKI, Bibliografia zawartości przeglądu zachodniego 1945–1955. Biblioteka przeglądu zachodniego (vol.7): Poznań 1957. pp.125. [1440.]

VICTOR TUREK, Polonica canadiana. A bibliographical list of the canadian polish imprints, 1848–1957. Canadian polish congress: Polish research institute in Canada: Studies (no.2): Toronto 1958. pp.138. [789.]

JAN KOWALIK, Polska w bibliografi niemieckiej 1954–1956. Oraz uzupełnienia do okresu 1945–1953. "Kultura": Biblioteka: Paryż 1958. pp.3–115. [500.]
   the bibliography for 1945–1953 was published in Kultura (*nos.86–90*).

WŁADISŁAW CHOJNACKI and JAN KOWALIK, Bibliografia niemieckich bibliografii dotyczących

Polski 1900–1958. Instytut zachodni: Poznań 1960. pp.252. [1281.]

WIKTOR TUREK, Z przeszłosci Polskiej w Kanadzie. Przyczynki do dziejów polaków w Kanadzie i do historii stosunków polsko-kanadyjskich. Kongres polonii kanadyjskiej: Instytut polski w Kanadzie: Prace (no.3): Toronto 1960. pp.138. [844.]

новая литература по европейским странам…. Польша. Академия наук СССР: Фундаментальная библиотека общественных наук: Москва.

   1960. pp.[ix].59.54.56.57.44.52.55.45.43.34. 48.54. [7570.]
   1961. pp.[vii].47.46.55.42.48.41.39.57.44.41. 41. [6003.]
             [*continued as:*]
новая литература по Польше.
   1962. pp.[vii].41.59.51.46.43.75.42.28.46.48. 41. [6194.]
in progress.

WOJCIECH ZAMECZNIK, Polskie zabytki cechowe archiwalia. Museum historyczne m. st. Warszawy: Warszawa 1961. pp.328. [2026.]

BIBLIOGRAPHIE sur la Pologne, pays — histoire — civilisation. [Stowarzyszenie bibliotekarzy

Europe

polskich:] Varsovie 1963. pp.231. [1228.]

3. *History*

i. *Manuscripts*

INVENTARIUM omnium et singulorum privilegiorum, litterarum, diplomatum, scripturorum et monumentorum quæcunque in archivo regni in arce Cracoviensi continentur. Lutetiæ Parisiorum &c. 1862. pp.xv.483. [1000.]

COUNT ALEXANDER PRZEZDZIECKI, Énumération et description sommaire de 64 manuscrits, 6 fragments et.10 abrégés de l'histoire de Pologne de Jean Dlugosch (dit Longin). Cracovie 1870. pp. [ii].9. [80.]

JÓZEF KORZENIOWSKI [vol.ii: STANISLAUS (STANISŁAW) KUTRZEBA], Catalogus codicum manu scriptorum Musei principium Czartoryski cracoviensis. Cracoviæ 1887–1913. pp.[iii].385+ [v].385. [20,000.]

WŁADISLAW ABRAHAM, Sprawozdanie z poszukiwan w archiwach i bibliotekach rzymskich a szyǵólniej w archiwum waty kanskiem. Archiwum Komisyi historycznej (vol.v: Kraków 1888. pp.53. [225.]

JÓZEF KORZENIOWSKI, Catalogus actorum et documentorum res gestas Poloniae illustrantium, quae ex codicibus manu scriptis in tabulariis et bibliothecis italicis servatis expeditionis Romanae cura MDCCCLXXXVI–MDCCCLXXXVIII deprompta sunt. Cracoviae 1889. pp.[ii].lxiv. [1000.]

JAN CZUBEK, Katalog rękopisów Akademii umiejętności. Krakowie 1906. pp.[ii].v.313. [1588.]
— — Zbigniew Jabłonski [and] Alojzy Preissner, Katalog rękopisów. Sygnatury 1811–2148. Polska akademia nauk w Krakowie: Biblioteka: Wrocław 1962. pp.xii.318. [5000.]

A. WARSCHAUER, Mitteilungen aus der handschriftensammlung des Britischen museums zu London, vornehmlich zur polnischen geschichte. Mitteilungen der K. preussischen archivverwaltung (no.13): Leipzig 1909. pp.[iii].80. [2000.]

JAN SMOŁKA, Katalog starożytnego Archiwum miejskiego i Towarzystwa przyjaciół nauk w Przemyślu. Przmyśl 1921 &c.
in progress.

JOSEPH SIEMIEŃSKI, Guide des archives de Pologne. 1. Archives de la Pologne ancienne.

Archives de l'état. Varsovie 1933. pp.120. [very large number.]
also published with a polish title.

HELENA WIĘCKOWSKA, Zbiory batignolskie i Towarzystwa przyjaciół Polski w Londynie. Katalog rękopisów bibljoteki narodowej (vol.iii): Warszawa 1933. pp.232. [2500.]

FELIKS POHORECKI, Catalogus diplomatum bibliothecae Instituto ossoliniani nec non Bibliothecae pawlikowianae inde ab anno 1327 usque ad annum 1505. Leopoli 1937. pp.151. [288.]
—— Adam Fasnacht, Catalogus diplomatum bibliothecae Instituti ossoliniani. Supplementum I. Wratislaviae 1951. pp.vi.57. [101.]

JADWIGA JANKOWSKA, Akta Komisji policji obojga narodów i Komisji policji koronnej, 1791–1794. Archiwum główne akt dawnych (vol.i): Warszawa 1949. pp.39.

ADAM FASTNACHT, Katalog dokumentów biblioteki Zakładu narodowego im. ossolińskich. Wrocław.
    i. 1507–1700. 1953. pp.viii.328. [821.]
in progress.

JADWIGA ŁUCZAKOWA, Katalog "Papierów po Leonardzie Niedźwieckim" i archiwum dwizji

kozaków sułtańskich w bibliotece kórnickiej.
Kórnik 1959. pp.[ii].241–367. [10,000.]

ii. *General*

SAMUEL JOACHIM HOPPIUS [HOPPE], De scriptoribus historiae polonicae schediasma. Dantisci
[1707]. pp.[iv].136. [1000.]
—— [another edition]. Lipsiae 1711. pp.[ii].
176. [1000.]

[SEBASTIANO CIAMPI], Catalogo di documenti
manoscritti e stampati relativi alla storia politica,
militare, ecclesiastica e letteraria del regno di
Pollonia raccolti negli anni 1823, 1824, 1825 dal
professore Sebastiano Ciampi. [Florence 1825].
pp.[ii].27. [250.]
—— Supplimento. [*c.*1825]. pp.5. [30.]

КАТАЛОГ ИСТОРИЧЕСКИМЪ ПАМЯТНИКАМЪ, собраннымъ и изданнымъ Павломъ Муханo-
вымъ. Москва 1836. pp.[iv].ii.34. [221.]

A[LEKSANDER] HIRSCHBERG, Bibliografia powstania narodu polskiego z r. 1830–1831. Lwowie
1882. pp.ix[*sic*, xi].124. [750.]

M. E. SOSNOWSKI and L[UDWIG] KURTZMANN,
Katalog der Raczyńskischen bibliothek in Posen.
Dritter band. Polnische geschichte und literatur.

Posen 1885. pp.xi.667. [7000.]
the library was that of count Eduard Raczyński.

ANATOLI LEWICKI, Index actorum saeculi xv ad
res publicas Poloniæ spectantium. [Akademija
umiejętności]: Monumenta medii aevi historica
res gestas Poloniae illustrantia (vol.xi): Cracoviae
1888. pp.[ii].xvi.583. [5118.]

LUDWIG FINKEL, Bibliografia historyi polskiej.
Akademija umiejętności: Krakowie [1891–]1906.
pp.xlviii.2150. [34,305.]
*a facsimile was issued Warszawa 1955; corrections
and additions by M[ax] Perlbach appear in the* Central-
blatt für bibliothekswesen (*1892*), *ix.361–370.*

— — Dodatek II.-zeszyt I. (lata 1901–1910
obejmujący). 1914. pp.175. [3675.]
*dodatek 1 forms part of the main work; no more
published.*

— — Wydanie drugie . . . przejrzał i uzupełnił
Karol Maleczyński. Polskie towarzystwo historyczne: Lwów.
  i. [1931–] 1937. pp.564. [13,137.]

KATALOG wystawy zabytków epoki jagiel-
lońskiej w 500 rocznicę odnowienia Uniwersy-
tetu jagiellońskiego zorganizowanej. Kraków
1910. pp.viii.71. [1500.]

Europe

[LEON WASILEWSKI and ZENON WIERZCHOWSKI], Wydawnictwa Naczelnego komitetu narodowego, 1914–1917. Spis bibliograficzny. Naczelny komitet narodowy: Kraków 1917. pp.[iv].170. [300.]

W. RECKE and A. M. WAGNER, Bücherkunde zur geschichte und literatur des königreichs Polen. Warschau 1918. pp.xi.242. [history: 1000.]

JANUSZ GĄSIOROWSKI, Bibljografja druków dotyczących powstania styczniowego 1863–1865. Wydawnictwa Centralnej bibljoteki wojskowej (vol.vii): Warszawa 1923. pp.394.iv. [4168.]

KAZIMIERZ TYSZKOWSKI, Informacyjna bibliografja historji polskiej za rok 1925. Zakład Narodowy imienia Ossolińskich: Lwów &c. 1926. pp.51. [1250.]

BIBLJOGRAFJA historji polskiej. Polskie towarzystwo historyczne: Kwartalnik historyczny: Dodatek: Lwów [1948–   : Wrocław].
    1926. Opracowali Marja Mazankówna i Kazimierz Tyszkowski. pp.58. [1500.]
    1927. pp.55. [1500.]
    1928. pp.72. [1825.]
    1929. Opracowała Marja Mazankówna-Friedbergowa. pp.86. [2174.]

Europe

1930–1931. Opracowali Marja i Marjan Friedbergowie. pp.[iii].171. [3638.]

1932. pp.[iii].68. [1574.]

1933–1934. Opracowała Marja Friedbergowa. pp.[iii].176. [3872.]

1948. Opracował Jan Baumgart. 1952. pp. vi.90. [2055.]

1949. 1954. pp.vii.147. [1813.]

1950–1951. 1955. pp.vi.232. [3020.]

1952–1953. 1956. pp.x.330. [4280.]

1954. 1957. pp.xxi.249. [3190.]

1955. 1958. pp.xxvii.307. [3738.]

1956–1957. 1960. pp.x.386. [4396.]

1958. Opracowali J. Baumgart i Anna Malcówna. 1960. pp.x.202. [2259.]

1959. 1961. pp.x.242. [2518.]

1960. 1962. pp.x.274. [2861.]

in progress; earlier issues formed part of the Kwartalnik.

ANDRZEJ WOJTKOWSKI, Bibljografja historji Wielkopolski. Towarzystwo miłosników historji: Poznań.

i. A–Pożegowo. 1934–1936. pp.484. [14,715.] *in progress?*

HALINA BACHULSKA, MARCELI HANDELSMAN and RYSZARD PRZELASKOWSKI, Bibliografia historii

polskiej XIX w. Warszawa 1939.
only a small fragment was published.
—— [another edition]. Bibliografia historii Polski, 1815–1914.

> [i]. Tom wstępny. [By H. Bachulska *and others*]. 1954. pp.x.237. [5315.]

BIBLIOGRAFIA rewolucji 1905–7 w królestwie Polskim. T.I. Pisma ulotne. Biblioteka narodowa: Zakład informacji naukowej: Warszawa 1955. pp.47. [256.]
in progress?

JÓZEF TRYPUĆKO, Polonica vetera upsaliensia. Catalogue des imprimés polonais ou concernant la Pologne des XVe, XVIe, XVIIe et XVIIIe siècles conservés à la bibliothèque de l'université royale d'Upsala. Acta bibliothecae R. universitatis upsaliensis (vol.xiii): Uppsala 1958. pp.xvi.186. [2885.]

BIBLIOGRAFIA historii Polski XIX wieku. Polska akademia nauk: Instytut historii: Wrocław &c.

> i. 1815–1831. Pod readkcją Stanisława Płoskiego. 1958. pp.xlii.662. [8943.]

in progress.

4. Topography

KAROL HOFFMAN, Krajoznawcy Polscy. . .

Zeszyt 1-szy, od A do D. Warszawa 1909. pp.24.
[200.]
no more published.

BIBLIOGRAFIA geografii polskiej. Polska akademia nauk: Instytut geografii: Warszawa.

    1936–1944. Opracowali Stanisław Leszczycki, Janina Piasecka, Bogodar Winid. 1959. pp.316. [3925.]

    1945–1951. [By] S. Leszczycki i B. Winid. 1956. pp.220. [3353.]

    1952–1953. Polska akademia nauk: Instytut geografii: 1957. pp.100. [1329.]

    1954. 1957. pp.68. [742.]

        [*continued as:*]

Polska bibliografia analityczna. Geografia.

    i. 1956. pp.88. [168.]

    ii. 1957. pp.105. [299.]

    iii. 1958. pp.127. [408.]*

    iv. 1959. pp.94. [333.]*

    v. 1960. pp.159. [525.]*

Pomerania.

JOHANN CARL CONRAD OELRICHS, Zuverlässige historisch-geographische nachricht vom herzogthum Pommern und fürstenthum Rügen, welche ein historisch-kritisches verzeichniss aller diese länder angehenden geographischen schriften, auch land- und fürnehmsten see-charten . . . in sich enthält. Berlin 1771. pp.[iv].xxxiv.112. [100.]

JOHANN CARL CONRAD OELRICHS, Verzeichnis der [Friedrich] von Dregerschen übrigen sammlung pommerscher urkunden. Alten-Stettin 1795. pp.xii.124. [1500.]

Pontarlier.

JULES MATHEZ, Inventaire sommaire des archives communales antérieures à 1790. Ville de Pontarlier. Besançon 1889. pp.x.146. [50,000.]

Pontoise.

LÉON [ADRIEN] THOMAS, Bibliographie de la ville et du canton de Pontoise. Société historique et archéologique de l'arrondissement de Pontoise et du Vexin: Mémoires (vol.v): Pontoise 1883. pp. [iii].viii.207. [1266.]

F. ROCQUAIN, Inventaire sommaire des archives hospitalières. . . . Hôtel-dieu de Pontoise. Pontoise 1924. pp.231. [large number.]
this inventory was compiled in 1858.

Porto.

JOSÉ GASPAR DE ALMEIDA, Inventário do cartório

do cabido da sé do Pôrto e dos cartórios anexos. Arquivo distrital do Pôrto: Publicações: Pôrto 1935. pp.[iii].A–L.xiv.258. [very large number.]

Portsmouth, diocese of.

[A SURVEY of the ecclesiastical archives of the diocese of Portsmouth]. Pilgrim trust: Survey of ecclesiastical archives: [1952]. ff.8. [large number.]*

Portugal.

[*bibliographies dealing with both Spain and Portugal are entered only under Spain.*]

1. Cartography, 1057.
2. History, 1058.
3. Topography, 1062.

1. *Cartography*

RANESTO DE VASCONCELLOS, Exposição de cartographia nacional. . . . Catálogo. Sociedade de geographia: Lisboa 1904. pp.xxxix.279. [1194.]

CATÁLOGO das cartas publicadas pela Comissão de cartografia 1883–1925. Ministerio das colónias: Lisboa 1926. pp.3–18. [150.]

CATÁLOGO das cartas. Instituto geográfico e cadastral: Lisboa [*c.*1935]. pp.[12]. [200.]
— [another edition]. 1946. pp.[12]. [300.]

CATÁLOGO das cartas e planos hidrograficos da costa de Portugal e ilhas adjacentes em depósito na Direcção dos serviços de hidrografia, navegação e meteorologia nautica. [Lisbon 1948]. pp.[11]. [100.]
— 2.ª edição. Catálogo . . . Portugal continental, ilhas adjacentes e províncias ultramarinas. 1956. *consists of key maps.*

CARTAS e planos hidrográficos de provincías ultramarinas portuguesas publicados pelos Junta das missões geográficas e de investigações do ultramar o pela antiga Comissão de cartografia. Lisboa 1959. pp.[33].
consists largely of key maps.

2. *History*

[JOSÉ CARLOS PINTO DE SOUSA], Bibliotheca histórica de Portugal e seus dominios ultramarinos. Lisboa 1801. pp.[xxvi].xiii.408.100. [500.]

VISCOUNT [MANUEL FRANCISCO DE BARROS] DE SANTAREM, Notícia dos manuscriptos pertencentes ao direito público externo diplomático de Portugal . . . que existem na Bibliotheca r. de Paris, e outras, da mesma capital, e nos archivos de França. Lisboa 1827. pp.[iii].105. [1000.]

—— Secunda edição. 1863. pp.128. [1000.]

[VISCOUNT] JORGE CESAR DE FIGANIERE, Bibliographia historica portugueza, ou catalogo methodico dos auctores portuguezes, e de alguns estrangeiros domiciliarios em Portugal, que tractaram da historia . . . d'estes reinos e seus dominios. Lisboa 1850 [*on cover:* 1851]. pp.ix.349.[ix]. [1658.]

[F. A. V.], Succinta indicação de alguns manuscriptos importantes respectivos ao Brazil e a Portugal, existentes no Museo britannico em Londres, e não comprehendidos no catalogo-Figanière. Habana 1863. pp.15. [500.]

INVENTARIO. Secção XIII — manuscriptos. Collecção pombalina. Biblioteca nacional: Lisboa 1889 [*on cover:* 1891]. pp.[352]. [10,000.]

ERNESTO CANTO, Ensaio bibliographico. Catalogo das obras nacionaes e estrangeiras relativas aos successos de Portugal, nos annos de 1828-34. Segunda edição. Ponta Delgada 1892. pp.viii.314. [1686.]

—— [supplement]. Antonio de Portugal de Faria, a lucta de 1828-34. Tentativa de auxiliar bibliographico. Leorne 1897. pp.16. [32.]

[MANOEL JOSÉ DE LACERDA and EDUARDO MARQUES PEIXOTO], Índice da correspondencia da corte de Portugal com os vice-reis do Brasil no Rio de Janeiro de 1763 a 1807. Publicações do Archivo público nacional (vol.iii): Rio de Janeiro 1901. pp.c.204. [2000.]

PEDRO A. D'AZEVEDO and ANTONIO BAIÃO, O Archivo da Tôrre do tombo. Annaes da academia de estudos livres [vol.xi]: Lisboa 1905. pp.[iv].223. [several million.]

A[NTONIO] MESQUITA DE FIGUEIREDO, Arquivo nacional da Tôrre do tombo. Roteiro prático. Lisboa 1922. pp.100. [several million.]
300 copies printed.

MARTINHO [AUGUSTO FERREIRA] DA FONSECA, Elementos bibliográficos para a história das guerras chamadas da restauração (1640–1668). Coimbra 1927. pp.vii.129. [791.]

FRANCISCO MANUEL ALVES, Catálogo dos manuscritos de Simancas respeitantes à história portuguesa. Coimbra 1933. pp.168. [large number.]

ANTÓNIO AUGUSTO FERREIRA DA CRUZ, Catálogo dos manuscritos da restauração da biblioteca da universidade de Coimbra. Coimbra 1936. pp.viii.79. [300.]

A[LLEN] B[ANKS] HINDS, A descriptive list of state papers, foreign: Portugal (S.P. 89), [1577-] 1660. Public record office: 1936. ff.i.16. [300.]*

EDGAR PRESTAGE, Portugal & the war of the spanish succession. A bibliography. Cambridge 1938. pp.viii.44. [100.]

EXPOSIÇÃO bibliográfica da restauração. Catálogo. Biblioteca nacional: Lisboa 1940–1941. pp. [viii].452+592. [9000.]

ANTONIO IBOT, Un tesoro bibliográfico, Fuentes históricas españolas en la biblioteca del Palacio nacional de Mafra (Portugal). Colección bibliográfica (vol.ii): Madrid 1942. pp.157. [574.]

BULLETIN of british historical publications on Spain and Portugal. No.1. Hispanic and Luso-Brazilian councils: Canning house library: 1951. pp.4. [12.]*
merged into the Bulletin of british historical publications on latin America and West Indies.

[JESÚS ERNESTO MARTÍNEZ FERRANDO, *ed.*], Catálogo de la documentación de la cancillería regia de Pedro de Portugal (1464–1466). Archivo de la corona de Aragón: Madrid 1953–1954. pp.3–254 +3–263. [3323.]

JEAN MEYRIAT, Le Portugal depuis la seconde guerre mondiale. Fondation nationale des sciences politiques: Centre d'étude des relations internationales: États des travaux (ser. B, no.10): 1957. pp.646–658. [85.]

GUIA da bibliografia histórica portuguesa. Academia portuguesa da história: Lisboa 1959 &c. *in progress.*

ERNST GERHARD JACOB, Deutschland und Portugal. Ihre kulturellen beziehungen, rückschau und ausblick. Eine bibliographie. Leiden 1961. pp. xv.88. [1500.]

3. *Topography*

[PEDRO WENCESLAU DE] BRITO ARANHA, Bibliographie des ouvrages portugais pour servir à l'étude des villes, des villages, des monuments, des institutions, des mœurs et coutumes, etc. du Portugal, Açores, Madère et possessions d'outremer. Exposition universelle [Paris]: Section portugaise: Lisbonne 1900. pp.90. [625.]

EDUARDO ROCHAD IAS, Monographias e outras obras referentes a varias localidades e monumentos do continente de Portugal. Real associação dos architectos civis e archeologos portuguezes:

Boletim (vol.xi, appenso): Lisboa 1908. pp.[v]. 82. [1206.]

[ANTÓNIO MESQUITA DE FIGUEIREDO], Subsidios para a bibliografía da história local portuguêsa. Bibliotheca nacional: Lisboa 1933. pp.[ii].xii.425. [4000.]

HERMANN LAUTENSACH and MARIANO FEIO, Bibliografia geográfica de Portugal. Instituto para a alta cultura: Lisboa 1948. pp.viii.256. [2347.]

Poschiavo.

REGESTI degli archivi della valle di Poschiavo. Pro Grigioni italiano: Regesti degli archivi del Grigioni italiano (vol.iii): Poschiavo [printed] 1955. pp.119. [564.]

Poznań.

ADOLF WARSCHAUER, Die städtischen archive in der provinz Posen. Mittheilungen der K. preussischen archivverwaltung (no.5): Leipzig 1901. pp.xli.324. [50,000.]

ANDRZEJ WOJTKOWSKI, Bibliografia historii miasta Poznania. Towarzystwo miłośników historii: Poznań 1938. pp.[viii].144. [3481.]

Europe

MARIA SZYMÁNSKA, Bibliografia historii Poznania. Polski twarzystwie historyczny: Oddział w Poznania: Poznań [1960]. pp.272. [3841.]

INWENTARZE mieszczańskie z wieku XVIII z kziąg miejskich i grodzkich Poznania. Polskie towarzystwo historyczne: Oddział w Posnaniu: Materiały sekcji historii Poznania: Poznań.

    i. 1700–1758. Przygotowali do druku Józef Burszta i Czesłav Łuczak. 1962. pp.xvi.435. [141.]

in progress.

Prague.

VÁCLAV HLAVSA, Pražeské matriky farní 1584–1870. Archiv hlavního města Prahy: Katalogy (vol.1): Praha 1954. pp.116. [very large number.]

VÁCLAV HLAVSA, *ed.* Archiv hlavního města Prahy. Průvodce po fondech a sbírkách. Archivní správa ministeriva vnitra: Praha 1955. pp.175. [large number.]

JIŘÍ ČAREK [*and others*], Městeské a jiné úřední knihy archivu hlavního města Prahy. Přehled. Archivni správa Ministerstva vnitra: Praha 1956. pp.223.

Prato.

R. PIATTOLI, Guida storica e bibliografica degli archivi e delle biblioteche d'Italia. . . . Volume I. Provincia di Firenze. Parte I. Prato. Real istituto storico italiano: Roma 1932. pp.xv.180. [large number.]

RUGGERO NUTI, Inventario dell'archivo antico. Comune di Prato: Prato 1939. pp.255. [very large number.]

GUIDO PAMPALONI, Inventario sommario dell'archivio di stato di Prato. Deputazione di storia patria per la Toscana: Firenze 1958. pp.iii–xxix. 141. [large number.]

Preston.

H[ENRY] W[ORDSWORTH] CLEMESHA, A bibliography of the history of Preston in Amounderness. Preston 1923. pp.24. [500.]

Provence.

C. U. ISNARD, Inventaire sommaire des archives départementales. . . . Basses-Alpes. Série C. Démembrement du fonds de l'intendance de Provence. 1863. pp.10. [large number.]

[LOUIS] BLANCHARD, Inventaire sommaire des archives départementales. . . . Bouches–du–Rhône. Série B. Cour des comptes de Provence. Paris [*vol.ii:* Marseilles] 1875–1879. pp.13.459+556. [large number.]

[LOUIS] BLANCHARD, Inventaire sommaire des archives départementales. . . . Bouches–du–Rhône. Série C. États de Provence. Marseille 1884–1892. pp.504+524. [large number.]

F. REYNAUD, Inventaire sommaire des archives départementales. . . . Bouches–du–Rhône. Série C. Tome III. Intendance de Provence. Marseille 1904. pp.540. [large number.]

M[ARIE] Z[ÉPHIRINE] ISNARD, État documentaire & féodal de la Haute-Provence. . . . État sommaire des documents d'archives communales antérieures à 1790. Bibliographies. Digne 1913. pp.[iii].xxiii.496. [20,000.]

R[AOUL] BUSQUET, Inventaire sommaire des archives départementales. . . . Bouches–du–Rhône. Série B. Tome III. Parlement de Provence. Lettres royaux, 1366–1660. Marseille 1919. pp.xxxii.381.
— — Supplément . . . 1660–1680. Par Maurice Raimbault et Paul Moulin. 1950. pp.[iii].coll.100. [1500.]

Europe

RAOUL BUSQUET, Inventaire sommaire des archives départementales. . . . Bouches-du-Rhône. Intendance de Provence. Marseille 1934. pp.[i]. v.299. [large number.]

LES FONDS des archives départementales des Bouches-du-Rhône, archives centrales de Provence. Marseille. [large number.]
  i. Dépôt principal de Marseille, séries anciennes A à F. Par Raoul Busquet. 1937. pp.xv.299.
  ii. Dépôt annexe d'Aix-en-Provence. Série B. Par R. Busquet [Augustin Roux]. 1939–1954. pp.viii.196+186.

Prussia.
Cartography and topography

R[UDOLF] REICKE, E[MIL] REICKE and — VON SCHACK, Die landeskundliche litteratur der provinzen Ost- und Westpreussen. . . . Heft 1. Allgemeine darstellungen und allgemeine karten. Geographische gesellschaft: Königsberg 1892. pp.[v]. 71. [681.]
  no more published.

History

M[AX POLLUX] TÖPPEN, Geschichte der preussischen historiographie von P. v. Dusburg bis auf

K. Schütz. Oder nachweisung und kritik der gedruckten und ungedruckten chroniken zur geschichte Preussens unter der herrschaft des deutschen ordens. Berlin 1853. pp.x.290. [100.]

KARL KLETKE, Quellenkunde der geschichte des
Preussischen staats. Berlin.

> [i]. Die quellenschriftsteller zur geschichte
> des Preussischen staats nach ihrem inhalt
> und werth dargestellt. 1858. pp.ix.614.
> [2000.]

> [ii]. Urkunden-repertorium für die ge-
> schichte des Preussischen staats. 1861. pp.
> xii.704. [25,000.]

ALLGEMEINE bücherkunde des Brandenburgisch-
Preussischen staates. Berlin 1871. pp.[iii].108.
[10,000.]

HANDSCHRIFTEN geschichtlichen inhalts, welche
aus der universitätsbibliothek zu Frankfurt in die
zu Breslau gelangt sind. Verein für geschichte
Berlins: Berlin 1887. pp.45. [175.]

REINHARD LÜDICKE, Die königs- und kaiser-
urkunden der Königlichen preussischen staats-
archive und des Königlichen hausarchivs bis 1439.
Chronologisches gesamtverzeichnis der original-
ausfertigungen. Mitteilungen der K. preussischen

archivverwaltung (no.16): Leipzig 1910. pp.x.184. [3253.]

— — Nachträge und berichtigungen . . . (no. 20): 1912. pp.16. [150.]

DIE HANDSCHRIFTEN des finanzarchivs zu Warschau zur geschichte der ostprovinzen des Preussischen staates. Archivverwaltung bei dem Kaiserlich deutschen generalgouvernement Warschau: Veröffentlichungen (vol.i:) Warschau 1917. pp. xlix.290. [50,000.]

VERZEICHNIS der handschriftlichen chroniken bis zum ausgang des 17. jahrhunderts. Kleine führer der stadtbibliothek: Danzig 1926. pp.16. [197.]

ERNST WERMKE, Bibliographie der geschichte von Ost- und Westpreussen. Historische kommission für ost- und westpreussische landesforschung: Königsberg i. Pr. [1931–]1933. pp.iii–xviii.1098. [15,839.]

— — Neudruck . . . mit ergänzendem nachtrag. Königsberg 1962. pp.xv.1098.21. [supplement: 215.]

— — 1952–1956. Historische kommission für ost- und west-preussische landesforschung: Wissenschaftliche beiträge zur geschichte und landes-

kunde Ost-Mitteleuropas (no.37): 1958. pp.x.256.
[4053.]*

ERNST MÜLLER and ERNST POSNER [part 2: HEIN-
RICH OTTO MEISNER and GEORG WINTER; part 3:
REINHARD LÜDICKE], Übersicht über die bestände
des Geheimen staatsarchivs zu Berlin-Dahlem.
I–[XI]. Hauptabteilung. Mitteilung der Preussischen archivverwaltung (vols.xxiv–xxvi): Leipzig
1934–1939. pp.xii.217+xii.272+xi.195. [very
large number.]

LUDWIG DEHIO, ERWIN HOLK and KURT JAGOW,
Übersicht über die bestände des Brandenburg-
preussischen hausarchivs zu Berlin-Charlotten-
burg. Mitteilungen der Preussischen archivverwaltung (vol.xxvii): Leipzig 1936. pp.x.87. [large
number.]

EDUARD GRIGOLEIT, Verzeichnis der ostpreussi-
schen und danziger kirchenbücher, sowie der dissi-
denten- und judenregister. Görlitz 1939. pp.xv.
120. [large number.]

ERNST WERMKE, Bibliographie der geschichte
von Ost- und Westpreussen für die jahre 1939–
1942 nebst nachträgen zu den früheren jahren.
Königsberg 1944. pp.158.

—— 1939–1951. Johann Gottfried Herder-institut: Wissenschaftliche beiträge zur geschichte und landeskunde Ost-Mitteleuropas (no.11): Marburg a. d. Lahn 1953. pp.iii.294. [4538.]*

KURT DÜLFER, Gesamtübersicht über die bestände des staatsarchivs Marburg. Marburg 1949 &c.

in progress.

KAROL GÓRSKI, Inwentarz aktów sejmikowych Prus królewskich, 1600–1764. Fontes (no.34): Toruń 1950. pp.xxxiii.502. [4360.]

KURT FORSTREUTER, Das Preussische staatsarchiv in Königsberg. Ein geschichtlicher rückblick mit einer übersicht über seine bestände. Niedersächsische archivverwaltung: Veröffentlichungen (no. 3): Göttingen 1955. pp.114. [very large number.]

KATALOG des schrifttums über den deutschen osten. Band 1. Ostpreussen und Westpreussen. Niedersächsische landesbibliothek: Hannover 1958. pp.[iii].vi.242. [7500.]*

Putten.

B. H. SLICHER VAN BATH, Het archief van de kelnarij van Putten. Rijksarchief in Gelderland: 's-Gravenhage 1952. pp.103. [425.]

Puy-de-Dôme.

MICHEL COHENDY, Inventaire de toutes les chartes antérieures au XIIIe siècle, qui se trouvent dans les différents fonds d'archives du dépôt de la Préfecture du Puy-de-Dôme. Clermont-Ferrand 1855. pp.[iii].107. [100.]

INVENTAIRE sommaire des archives départementales. . . . Puy-de-Dôme. Clermont-Ferrand. [very large number.]

> Série A. Par Michel Cohendy. 1863. pp.45.
> Série C. Par M. Cohendy [G. Rouchon]. 1893–1916. pp.[iii].465+528+492+508+504+459.
> Série L, 1e partie. Par Gilbert Rouchon et Albert Combaud. 1925. pp.[ii].147.
> *in progress.*

P. F. FOURNIER, Répertoire de la collection Marcellin Boudet, sous-série 3F. Archives départementales du Puy-de-Dôme: Clermont-Ferrand 1938. pp.16. [large number.]

Pyrénées, Basses-.

INVENTAIRE-sommaire des archives départementales antérieures à 1790. . . . Basses-Pyrénées. [200,000.]

i. Séries A–B. Par P[aul] Raymond. 1863.
pp.[ii].5.401.

ii. Série B. 1876. pp.[v].460.

iii. Séries C–D. 1865. pp.[vi].146.298.[iii].7.

iv–v. Série E. 1867–1873. pp.[x].iii.419+[iii].
153.166.8.

vi. Séries G–H. 1879. pp.[iii].3.68.27.182.

Série L. Par Pierre Bayand. 1957. pp.30.

Série Q. 1950. pp.34.

in progress?

L[OUIS] SOULICE, Essai d'une bibliographie du
département des Basses Pyrénées . . . 1789–1800.
Pau 1874. pp.115. [467.]

Pyrénées, Hautes-.

INVENTAIRE-sommaire des archives départementales. . . . Hautes-Pyrénées. Tarbes. [very
large number.]

i. Séries A–B. Par Charles Durier, P. La-
brouche et M. Lanore. 1904. pp.xxxii.8.
321.

ii. Séries G–H. 1892. pp.vii.265.

iii. Séries C–D. [*c.*1880]. pp.41.2.

iv. Série L. Par Gaston Balencie. 1934. pp.
20.563.

Série I. Par Jean Pambrun et G. Balencie.
1914. pp.11.

Pyrénées-Orientales.

INVENTAIRE-sommaire des archives départementales. . . . Pyrénées-Orientales. Paris [*afterwards:* Perpignan]. [very large number.]

    Série B. Par [Bernard] Alart et A. Brutails.
       1868–1886. pp.ii.396.
    Série C. Par B. Alart. 1877. pp.iv.480.4.
    Série G. Par A. Brutails, E. Desplanque et
       B. Palustre. 1904. pp.xix.518.

in progress.

Quorndon.

GEORGE F. FARNHAM, Quorndon records. 1912.
pp.[iii].499. [1500.]
privately printed.

Rachamps.

É[TIENNE] HÉLIN, Inventaire des archives de la
seigneurie de Rachamps. Archives de l'état à
Arlon: Bruxelles 1957. pp.29. [5000.]

Raismes-Vicoigne.

M[AURICE] HÉNAULT, Inventaire sommaire des
archives communales antérieures à 1790. . . . Ville
de Raismes-Vicoigne. Lille 1902. pp.xii.48. [large
number.]

Rambervillers.

A[LEXIS] HENRIOT, Inventaire-sommaire des archives communales antérieures à 1790. . . . Ville de Rambervillers. Épinal 1869. pp.[iii].13.3.12.70. 4.2.7.3.3.4.8. [20,000.]

Ransdorp.

W. F. H. OLDEWELT, Inventaris van de archieven der voormalige gemeenten Ransdorp en Buiksloot. Amsterdam 1928. pp.100.

Rapperswil.

XAVER RIKENMANN, Die regesten des archivs der stadt Raperswyl im canton St. Gallen. Die regesten der archive in der Schweizerischen eidgenossenschaft (vol.i): Chur 1850. pp.35–44. [107.]

the index to this calendar is published with that devoted to Schanfigg, q.v.

Ravenna.

G. BOVINI, Principale bibliografia su Ravenna romana, paleocristiana e paleobizantina. Università degli studi di Bologna: Corsi di cultura soll'arte ravennate e bizantina: Ravenna 1959. pp.29. [350.]

Regensburg.

JOSEPH SCHMID, Die urkunden-regesten des Kollegiatstiftes u. l. frau zur alten kapelle. Regensburg 1911–1912. pp.xii.517+vii.436. [3357.]

Reichenau.

KARL BRANDI, Kritisches verzeichnis der reichenauer urkunden des VIII–XII jahrhunderts. Heidelberg 1890. pp.42. [90.]

Rennes.

GILLES DE LANGUEDOC, Inventaire des archives de la paroisse Saint-Sauveur de Rennes . . . 1720. [Edited by] Paul Parfouru. Rennes 1899. pp.82. [400.]

Rethel.

[CHARLES] HENRI JADART, Les anciens registres paroissiaux dans les arrondissements de Reims (Marne) et de Rethel (Ardennes). 1901. pp.20. [large number.]

Reuss.

HEINRICH ALFRED AUERBACH, Bibliotheca ruthenea. Die literatur zur landeskunde und geschichte

des fürstenthums Reuss. Gera 1892. pp.101. [1103.]
a supplement by the author appears in the Jahres-
bericht *of the Gesellschaft von freunden der natur-
wissenschaften (Gera 1896–1899), xxxix–xlii, 145–
232.*

Revel.

PIERRE and THÉRÈSE GÉRARD, Inventaire sommaire des archives antérieures à 1790. Archives de
la Haute-Garonne: Commune de Revel: Toulouse
1955. pp.25. [1000.]*

Revesby abbey.

[FRANK BESANT], Abstracts of the deeds and
charters relating to Reversby abbey, 1142–1539.
Horncastle 1889. pp.[viii].40. [150.]

Rheims.

PIERRE VARIN, Archives législatives et adminis-
tratives de la ville de Reims. Prolégomènes historiques et bibliographiques. 1839. pp.[iii].280.
[large number.]

LOUIS DE GRANDMAISON, Inventaire-sommaire
du fonds de Ch. M. Le Tellier, archevêque-duc de
Reims (mss. français 20707–20770). Bibliothèque
nationale: 1894. pp.29. [large number.]

L. DEMAISON [*and others*], Inventaire sommaire des archives départementales. . . . Marne. Série G. Tome I[–II]. Reims 1900–1931. pp.xv.380+xii. 366. [large number.]

these volumes deal with the archives of the archbishopric and chapter of Rheims.

[CHARLES] HENRI JADART, Les anciens registres paroissiaux dans les arrondissements de Reims (Marne) et de Rethel (Ardennes). 1901. pp.20. [large number.]

Rheinhessen.

HEINRICH EDUARD SCRIBA, Regesten der bis jetzt gedruckten urkunden zur landes- und ortsgeschichte des grossherzogthums Hessen. . . . Dritte [Vierte, no.3] abtheilung: die regesten der provinz Rheinhessen enthaltend. Darmstadt 1851– 1854. pp.[iv].360+[ii].73. [6205.]

Rhenen.

K. HEERINGA, Inventaris van het archief der gemeente Rhenen, 1337–1851. 1926. pp.134.

Rhin, Bas-.

F[RÉDÉRIC] C[HARLES] HEITZ, Catalogue des principaux ouvrages et des cartes imprimés sur le département du Bas-Rhin. Strasbourg 1858. pp. [ii].102. [2000.]

INVENTAIRE-sommaire des archives départementales. . . . Bas-Rhin. Strasbourg. [very large number.]

    i. Séries A–E. Par L[ouis Adolphe] Spach. 1863. pp.xi.2.51.67.18.397.

    ii. Séries E–F. 1867. pp.159.

    iii. Série G. 1868. pp.xiii.435.

    iv. Séries G–H. 1872. pp.134.263.

    Série J, première partie. Par François-J. Himly. 1958. pp.lv.531.

    Série M. Par Louis Martin. 1950. pp.335.

    Table générale des inventaires . . . 613 à 1789–1793. 1954. pp.517.

  in progress?

AUGUSTE ECKEL and LUCIEN METZGER, Répertoire critique des anciens inventaires des archives du Bas-Rhin. Strasbourg 1938. pp.52. [241.]

FRANÇOIS J. HIMLY, Catalogue des cartes et plans manuscrits antérieurs à 1790. Archives départementales du Bas-Rhin: Strasbourg 1959. pp.xv. 169. [2000.]★

Rhin, Haut-.

INVENTAIRE-sommaire des archives départementales. . . . Haut-Rhin. Colmar. [very large number.]

Série A, C, E. Par [Léon] Brièle [et F. Blanc]. 1863–1865. pp.404.

Série 1 E. Par Emile Herzog. 1952. pp.3–195. *in progress?*

ÉMILE HERZOG, État général par fonds des archives départementales. Département du Haut-Rhin. Colmar 1928. pp.[iv].cxxxii.75.7. [large number.]

ÉMILE HERZOG, Répertoire méthodique de la série V.E.: état civil. Archives départementales du Haut-Rhin: Colmar 1937. pp.xx.459. [45,000.]

ÉMILE HERZOG, Inventaire sommaire de la série E, supplément. Fascicule 3[–6]. Archives communales d'Appenwihr . . . Mittelwihr . . . Ostheim . . . Wihr-au-Val. Archives départementales du Haut-Rhin: Colmar 1949. pp.5–31. [2500.]

DOCUMENTS exposés lors de l'inauguration du nouvel hôtel des archives départementales du Haut-Rhin. Colmar 1959. ff.20. [68.]*

Rhine provinces. [*see also* **Rijn.**]

FRANZ RITTER [vol.ii: (JOSEPH GOTZEN)], Katalog der Stadtbibliothek in Koeln, abtheilung Rh.,

geschichte und landeskunde der Rheinprovinz.
Stadtbibliothek: Veroeffentlichungen (no.5–8):
Koeln 1894–1907. pp.xxviii.237 + xxviii.284.
[4500.]

ARMIN TILLE [vols.ii: A. TILLE and JOHANNES
KRUDEWIG; iii–iv: J. KRUDEWIG], Übersicht über
den inhalt der kleineren archive der Rheinprovinz.
Gesellschaft für rheinische geschichtskunde: Publikationen (no.xix): Bonn 1899–1915. pp.xii.3–340
+ix.385+ix.315+xii.515. [very large number.]
 also issued as Beiheft i, v, viii, ix of the Annalen
of the Historischer verein für den Niederrhein.

RICHARD KNIPPING, Niederrheinische archiva-
lien in der Nationalbibliothek und dem National-
archiv zu Paris. Mitteilungen der K. preussischen
archivverwaltung (no.8): Leipzig 1904. pp.viii.
126. [5000.]

MAX BÄR, Bücherkunde zur geschichte der
Rheinlande. Band i. Aufsätze in zeitschriften und
sammelwerken bis 1915. Gesellschaft für rheinische geschichtskunde: Publikationen (vol.
xxxvii): Bonn 1920. pp.lx.716. [16,051.]
 no more published.

CHARLES SCHMIDT, Les sources de l'histoire des
territoires rhénans de 1792 à 1814 dans les archives

rhénans & à Paris. Haut-commissariat de la république Française dans les provinces du Rhin: 1921. pp.[iii].ii.323. [1,000,000.]

DIE AMTLICHEN karten des landes Nordrhein-Westfalen. Landesvermessungsamt: Bad Godesberg [1956]. pp.20. [500.]
—Änderungen und nachträge. 1957. pp.3. [25.]

Rhône.

INVENTAIRE-sommaire des archives départementales. . . . Rhône. Paris [*afterwards:* Lyon]. [very large number.]

> Séries A–E. Par [J. P.] Gauthier. 1864. pp. xvii.1.32.119.104.213.10.
> Série E, supplément. Par G. Guigue. 1902–1906. pp.432+408.
> Série G. **Par** H. Hours [*and others*]. 1959. pp. lxxii.328.
> Série H. Par G. Guigue [et C. Faure]. 1895–1932. pp.391+xv.335.
> Série Q. Par René Lacour. 1951. pp.xii.134.
> *in progress.*

Europe

RÉPERTOIRE général des protocoles du notariat du département du Rhône. Lyon 1933. pp.184. [large number.]

Ribeauvillé.

[BERNARD] BERNHARD, Compte-rendu du classement et de l'inventaire des anciennes archives de Ribeauvillé [Haut-Rhin]. Colmar 1863. pp.[ii].33. [large number.]

Rijn, Neder-.

A[NTHONY] H[ENRIK] MARTENS VAN SEVENHOVEN, Het archief van het College tot de beneficieering von Neder-Rijn en Ijsel. 's-Gravenhage 1917. pp.49. [320.]

Rijnland.

W. C. D. OLIVIER, Alphabetisch register op de stukken van het oude archief van het hoogheemraadschap Rijnland. Leiden 1871. pp.315.

—— Supplement-catalogus ... door E. F. van Dissel. 1893. pp.123.

C. H. DEE, Inventaris van de atlassen, kaartboeken, kaarten en teekeningen in het archief van het hoogheemraadschap Rijnland. Leiden 1882. pp.126.

s. j. fockema andreae, De oude archieven van
het hoogheemraadschap van Rijnland, 1255–1857.
Leiden 1933. pp.295.

Riom.

françois boyer, Inventaire sommaire des
archives communales antérieures à 1790. . . . Ville
de Riom. Riom 1892. pp.[iii].xvi.194. [50,000.]

Ripon, diocese of.

[a survey of the ecclesiastical archives of the
diocese of Ripon]. Pilgrim trust: Survey of ecclesiastical archives: [1952]. ff.10. [large number.]*

Robertbridge, abbey of.

calendar of charters and documents relating
to the abbey of Robertbridge, co: Sussex, preserved at Penshurst among the muniments of lord
de Lisle and Dudley. 1873. pp.[iii].179. [411.]

Rochefort.

louis [marie de meschinet] de richemond,
Inventaire-sommaire des archives communales
antérieures à 1790. . . . Ville de Rochefort. 1877.
pp.[iii].6.96. [20,000.]

DICK LEMOINE, Répertoire numérique des archives de l'arrondissement maritime de Rochefort. Archives de la Marine: 1925. pp.60+22+40 +18+10. [1100.]

Rochester, diocese of.

[A SURVEY of the ecclesiastical archives of the diocese of Rochester. Pilgrim trust: Survey of ecclesiastical archives: 1952]. ff.14. [large number.]★

Rodez.

H[ENRI] AFFRE, Inventaire-sommaire des archives communales antérieures à 1790.... Ville de Rodez. Rodez 1877–1885. pp.6.2.16.80.4.2.6.9.2.5.13.49. 2.2.5.17.11.24. [50,000.]

Roermond.

[J. B. SIVRÉ], Inventaris van het oud archief der gemeente Roermond. 1869–1882.

the first part only of a new edition appeared in 1912.

Romania.

C. GÖLLNER, Anul revoluţionar 1858 în principatele română. O contribuţie bibliografică.

Bibliotheca bibliologică (vol.ii): Cluj 1934. pp.18. [209.]

INVENTARUL arhivelor statului: Bucureşti, Cernăuti, Chişinău, Cluj, Craiova, Iaşi, Năsăud, Timişoara, Braşov. Biblioteca arhivelor statului (vol.i): Bucureşti 1939. pp.420. [very large number.]

ION RADU MIRCEA, Catalogul documentelor tării românesti, 1369–1600 . . . dela Arhivele statului din Bucureşti. Biblioteca arhivelor statului (vol.ii): Bucureşti 1939. pp.xvi.323.

P[ETRE] CONSTANTINESCU-IAŞI, Realizările istoriografiei romîne între anii 1945–1955. Societatea de ştiinţe istorice şi filologice: Bucureşti 1955. pp.52. [304.]

F[REDDY] THIRIET, Régestes des délibérations du sénat de Venise concernant la Romanie. École pratique des hautes études: Documents et recherches sur l'économie des pays byzantins, islamiques et slaves (vol.i &c.).

    i. 1329–1399. . . . 1958. pp.247. [972.]
    ii. 1400–1430. . . . (vol.ii). 1959. pp.300. [1249.]
    iii. 1431–1463. . . . (vol.iv). 1961. pp.278. [976.]
  in progress.

G[EORGE] BAICULESCU, AL. DUTU and DOROTHEA SASSU-TIMERMAN, Echos ibériques et hispano-américains en Roumanie. Bibliographie littéraire sélective. Commission nationale de la République Populaire Roumaine pour l'Unesco: Bucarest 1959. pp.124. [1000.]*

Romans.

ANDRÉ LACROIX, Inventaire sommaire des archives hospitalières de la ville de Romans. Valence 1894. pp.[iii].vii.137. [25,000.]

[JEAN MARIE] CYPRIEN PERROSSIER, Essai de bibliographie romanaise. Évêques originaires de la Drôme. Valence 1910. pp.xviii.312.228. [349.] *incomplete, as left by the author at his death.*

Rome.

MARTIN HANKE, De romanarum rerum scriptoribus liber [liber secundus]. Lipsiae 1669–1675. pp.[xii].306.[lxxxii]+[xviii].424.[c]. [1500.]

PROSPERO MANDOSIO, Bibliotheca romana, sev romanorvm scriptorvm centvriae. Romae 1682–1692. pp.[viii].368+[viii].360. [4000.]

RUGGIERO BONGHI, Bibliografia storica di Roma antica. Roma 1879. pp.[ii].177. [3000.]

VINCENZO FORCELLA, Catalogo dei manoscritti riguardanti la storia di Roma che si conservano nelle biblioteche romane [vol.v: di Padova] publiche e private. Volume I[-IV]. Catalogo dei manoscritti . . . nella Biblioteca vaticana. Roma 1879–1885.   pp.xi.451+[iv].447+[iv].481+[iii].297+[v].vii.139. [10,000.]

ARNOLD [DIETRICH] SCHAEFER, Abriss der quellenkunde der griechischen und römischen geschichte. . . . Zweite abteilung. Die periode des römischen reiches. Leipzig 1881. pp.[iii].199. [1000.]

—— Zweite auflage, besorgt von Heinrich Nissen. 1885. pp.x.208. [1000.]

FRANCESCO CERROTI, Bibliografia di Roma medievale e moderna. . . . Accresciuta a cura di Enrico Celani. Volume I. Storia ecclesiastico-civile. Roma 1893. pp.xi.coll.606. [9292.]
300 copies printed; no more published.

MOSTRA di topografia romana. Biblioteca nazionale Vittorio Emanuele: Roma 1903. pp.22. [50.]

EMILIO CALVI, Bibliografia generale di Roma. Roma.
   i. Bibliografia di Roma nel medio evo. 1906. pp.xxiii.175. [3000.]

— Supplemento I. Con appendice sulle cata-
combe e sulle chiese di Roma. 1908. pp.
xxxiv.162. [3000.]

ii. Bibliografia di Roma nel cinquecento.
Tomo I. 1910. pp.[v].231. [3758.]

v. I. Bibliografia di Roma nel risorgimento.
Tomo I (1789–1846). 1912. pp.xii.159.
[2281.]

no more published.

OTTO SEECK, Regesten der kaiser und päpste für
die jahre 311 bis 476 n. Chr. Vorarbeit zu einer
prosopographie der christlichen kaiserzeit. Stuttgart 1919. pp.xi.488. [5000.]

OSKAR POLLAK and LUDWIG SCHUDT, Le guide di
Roma. Materialien zu einer geschichte der römischen topographie. Quellenschriften zur geschichte der barockkunst in Rom: Wien &c. 1930.
pp.xx.544. [1286.]

CHRISTIAN [CARL FRIEDRICH] HUELSEN, Saggio di
bibliografia ragionata delle piante sconografiche e
prospettiche di Roma dal 1551 al 1748. Edizione
riveduta e accresciuta dall'autore. Firenze 1933.
pp.3–122. [156.]

G[IOVANNI] SANNA, Bibliografia generale del-
l'età romana imperiale. Ente nazionale di cultura:
Firenze.

i. Parte generale. Raccolte di scritti vari. Collezione di fonti. Sussidi generali di studio. [1938]. pp.xvi.123. [1573.]
no more published.

LUIGI GUASCO, L'Archivio storico capitolino. Istituto di studi romani: Quaderni di studi romani: Gli istituti di cultura artistica romani (vol.ii): Roma 1946. pp.61. [large number.]

IOSEPHUS [GIUSEPPE] LUGLI, Fontes ad topographiam veteris vrbis Romae pertinentes. Università di Roma: Istituto di topografia antica: Roma 1952–1953. pp.iii–xvi.234+3–231. [4000.]

[ELIO LODOLINI], L'archivio della s. congregazione del buon governo (1592–1847). Inventario. Pubblicazioni degli archivi di stato (vol.xx: Archivio di stato di Roma): Roma 1956. pp.clxxxvi.471. [large number.]

VITTORIO E. GIUNTELLA, Bibliografia della Repubblica romana del 1798–1799. Istituto di studi romani: Roma 1957. pp.xliv.195. [900.]

ARMANDO LODOLINI, L'Archivio di stato di Roma. Epitome di una guida degli archivi dell'amministrazione centrale dello stato pontificio. Istituto di studi romani: Gli istituti culturali e

artistici di Roma (vol.iv): Roma 1960. pp.230.
[large number.]

GEROLD WALSER and THOMAS PEKÁRY, Die krise
des römischen reiches. Bericht über die forschungen zur geschichte des 3. jahrhunderts... von 1939
bis 1959. Berlin 1962. pp.xi.146. [1500.]

Romorantin.

FERNAND BOURNON, Inventaire sommaire des
archives communales antérieures à 1790. . . .
Ville de Romorantin. Blois 1884. pp.vi.138.
[25,000.]

L[UDOVIC] GUIGNARD DE BUTTEVILLE, Inventaires des titres de la châtellenie de Romorantin.
Vannes [printed] 1900. pp.56. [500.]

Rostock.

HEINRICH NETTELBLADT, Verzeichniss allerhand
mehrenteils ungedruckter zur geschichte und
verfassung der stadt Rostock gehöriger schriften,
münzen, verordnungen und urkunden. Rostock
1760. pp.[viii].28.108. [1500.]

Rotherham.

T. WALTER HALL, Sheffield and Rotherham from

the 12th to the 18th century. A descriptive catalogue of miscellaneous charters and other documents. Sheffield 1916. pp.viii.291. [400.]

Rotterdam.

H. C. H. MOQUETTE, Het archief van de weeskamer te Rotterdam. Rotterdam 1907. pp.120.

E. WIERSUM, De archieven der rotterdamsche gilden. Rotterdam 1926. pp.51.

Roubaix.

TH[ÉODORE DÉSIRÉ JOSEPH] LEURIDAN, Inventaire-sommaire des archives communales antérieures à 1790. . . . Ville de Roubaix. 1866. pp.5–12. 7.18.56.6.6.5.56.24.6.55. [50,000.]

Rouen.

[A. LE TAILLANDIER], Inventaire sommaire des archives hospitalières. Hospices civils de Rouen. Rouen 1866. pp.292.
incomplete; no more published.

CH[ARLES] DE ROBILLARD DE BEAUREPAIRE, Inventaire sommaire des archives départementales. . . . Seine-Inférieure. Série G. Paris [*afterwards:* Rouen]. [large number.]

i–ii. Archevêché de Rouen. 1868–1874. pp. 42.442+xii.468.

iii–v. Chapitre de Rouen. 1881–1892. pp.482 +490+479.

vi–vii. Paroisses [séminaire, secrétariat] de Rouen. 1896–1912. pp.479+180+198+ viii.102.

CH[ARLES] DE ROBILLARD DE BEAUREPAIRE [*and others*], Inventaire-sommaire des archives communales antérieures à 1790. . . . Ville de Rouen. Rouen 1887 &c.

in progress.

Rouergue.

CAMILLE COUDERC, Bibliographie historique du Rouergue. Rodez 1931–1934. pp.xii.641+[iii]. 658. [15,000.]

—— Supplément . . . par B[ernard] Combes de Patris. 1956. pp.xvi.352. [4500.]

Rousselare.

K. VANDEN HAUTE, Het oud archief der stad Rousselare. Brugge 1912. pp.97. [10,000.]

Rowington.

JNO. WM. RYLAND, Records of Rowington . . .

in the possession of the feoffees of the Rowington charities. Birmingham [printed] [1896]. pp.[x]. xxix.239. [300.]

Ruinen.

J. G. C. JOOSTING, Het archief der heerlijkheid Ruinen. Rijksarchief in Drente: Leiden 1907. pp.134. [500.]

Ruislip-Northwood.

CATALOGUE of an exhibition of historical records, ancient documents, maps, prints, photographs and books relating to Ruislip, Northwood and Eastcote. Urban district council: [Northwood 1953]. pp.85. [150.]

Russia.

1. Cartography, 1095.
2. Foreign relations, 1097.
3. History.
   i. Bibliographies, 1101.
   ii. Periodicals, 1102.
   iii. Manuscripts, 1102.
   iv. General, 1104.
   v. Specific periods, 1111.
4. Topography, 1123.

Europe

I. Cartography

FRIEDRICH [VON] ADELUNG, Ueber die älteren ausländischen karten von Russland. Kaiserliche akademie der wissenschaften. Beiträge zur kenntniss des Russischen reiches (vol.iv, no.1): St. Petersburg 1841. pp.[ii].iii.52. [75.]

КАТАЛОГЪ атласовъ, картъ и плановъ архива Гидрографическаго департамента Морскаго министерства. Часть первая. Атласы... Россіи. С.-Петербургъ 1849. pp.[vi].386. [2000.]

КАТАЛОГЪ картъ, плановъ, атласовъ,... составленныхъ... въ военно-топографическомъ депо. Санктпетербургъ 1858. pp.21. [85.]

CATALOGUE des cartes et plans gravés au Dépôt topographique militaire. Saint-Pétersbourg 1862. pp.12. [200.]

[N. BOKACHEV], Географическія карты Россіи xv–xix столѣтій. Каталогъ... библіотеки Н. Бокачева: St. Petersburg 1892. pp.[iv].iii.91.5. [250.]

VASILY [GRIGOREVICH] LYASKORONSKY, Иностранные карты и атласы xvi и xvii вв., относящіеся къ южной Россіи. Кіевъ 1898. pp.22. [75.]

H[EINRICH] MICHOW, Das erste jahrhundert russischer kartographie 1525–1631. Hamburg 1906. pp.[ii].61. [20.]

КАТАЛОГЪ атласовъ, картъ, плановъ, видовъ, албомовъ, флаговъ, руководствъ для плаванія и проч. Министерство морское: Гидрографическій департаментъ: С.-Петербургъ 1911. pp.iv.143. [500.]
— [another edition]. 1912. pp.iv.144. [500.]

V[ERA] F[EDOROVNA] GNUCHEVA, Географический департамент Академии наук XVIII века. Академия наук СССР: Труды архива (vol.6): Москва &c. 1946. pp.446. [1114.]
consists in large part of bibliographies of the maps published by the Academy, and of manuscript maps in its archives.

КАРТЫ и атласы. Каталог. Главное управление геодезии и картографии МВД СССР: Москва 1955. pp.88. [400.]

GENERAL catalog of selected Soviet Union maps. Third edition. Aeronautical chart and information center: St Louis 1961. pp.[ii].53. [696.]*

M. N. MURZANOVA, V. F. POKROVSKAYA and E. I. BOBROVA, Карты, планы, чертежи, рисуки и гравюры собрания Петра I. Академия наук СССР: Библиотека: Исторический очерк и обзор фондов рукописного отдела: Москва &c. 1961. pp.291. [533.]

CATALOG of nautical charts and publications. Region 4. Norway, Baltic and U. S. S. R. Washington 1962. pp.[21]. [250.]

2. *Foreign relations*

SEBASTIANO CIAMPI, Bibliografia critica delle antiche reciproche corrispondenze politiche, ecclesiastiche, scientifiche, letterarie, artistiche dell'Italia colla Russia, colla Polonia ecc. Firenze 1834–1842. pp.[vi].v.366+xii.326+[vi].137. [2500.]

S. DOBROKLONSKY, Указатель трактатовъ и сношеній Россіи съ 1462 по 1826. Москва 1838. pp.xii.118. [400.]

FREDERIK MULLER, Essai d'une bibliographie néerlando-russe. Amsterdam 1859. pp.viii.176. [1243.]
a facsimile was published, Amsterdam 1960.

C[ARL CHRISTIAN GERHARD] SCHIRREN, Nachricht von quellen zur geschichte Russlands, vornehmlich aus schwedischen archiven und bibliotheken. St. Petersburg 1860. pp.80. [large number.]

C. C. UHLENBECK, Verslag aangaande een onderzoek in de archieven van Rusland ten bate der nederlandsche geschiedenis. 's-Gravenhage 1891. pp.279. [large number.]

includes B. Cordt, 'Beiträge zu einer russisch-niederländischen bibliographie'.

LIST of references on the international relations between the United States and Russia. Library of Congress: [Washington] 1915. ff.5. [68.]★

FRANK A. GOLDER, Guide to materials for american history in russian archives. Carnegie institution: Publication (no.239): Washington 1917, 1937. pp.viii.177+[v].55. [10,000.]

LIST of references on the russian policy of the United States. Library of Congress: [Washington] 1920. ff.8. [94.]★
— [another edition]. 1925. ff.9. [110.]★
— — Additions. 1930. ff.10–14. [61.]★

FELIKS LIBERT, Materjały do bibljografji wojny polsko-sowieckiej. Wojskowe biuro historyczne: Warszawa 1935. pp.[ii].xiv.162. [2720.]

HELEN F[IELD] CONOVER, A selected list of references on the diplomatic and trade relations with the Union of Soviet Socialist Republics, 1919–1935. Compiled... under the direction of Florence S[elma] Hellman. Library of Congress: [Washington] 1935. pp.29. [332.]★

A[LLEN] B[ANKS] HINDS, Descriptive list of state papers, foreign: Russia (S. P. 91), 1589–1655. Public record office: 1937. ff.i.12. [250.]*

A[LEKSEI] I[SAEVICH] GUKOVSKY and P. B. ZHIBAREV, Когда и как русский народ бил немецких захватчиков (1242–1918). Указатель литературы. Всесоюзная книжная палата: Москва 1942. pp.24. [500.]

REIDAR ØKSNEVAD, Russland i norsk litteratur. En bibliografi. Oslo 1947. pp.69. [1000].

JANE DEGRAS, Calendar of soviet documents on foreign policy, 1917–1941. Royal institute of international affairs: 1948. pp.viii.248. [5000.]

[ZINAIDA GAVRILOVNA DUDAREVA], Советский народ голосует за мир. Краткий указатель литературы. Государственная ... библиотека СССР имени В. И. Ленина: Москва 1951. pp.36. [250.]

N. M. TRETYAK [*and others*], 300-річчя воз-з'єднання України з Росією (1654–1954). Бібліографічний покажчик. Академія наук Української РСР: Бібліотека: Київ 1953. pp.64. [300.]

I. Z. BOIKO [*and others*], Нерушимая дружба братских народов СССР. К 300-летию воссоединения Украины с Россией. Сборник библиографических и методических материалов для массовых библиотек. Государственная... библиотека СССР имени В. И. Ленина [&c.]: Москва 1954. pp.72. [150.]

A[LEKSANDR] A[LEKSANDROVICH] POPOV Внешняя политика СССР — политика мира. Указатель литературы. Государственная... публичная библиотека имени М. Е. Салтыкова-Щедрина: Ленинград 1956. pp.84. [250.]

V[ERA] V[ASILEVNA] SELCHUK, Что читать о миролюбивой внешней политике СССР. Государственная... библиотека СССР имени В. И. Ленина: Москва 1956. pp.20. [12.]

CO číst o vzájemnych vztazích národů ČSR a SSSR. Okresní lidová knihovna: Kladně 1958. ff.7. [75.]*

ROBERT M[ELVILLE] SLUSSER [*and others*], A calendar of soviet treaties 1917–1957. Stanford university: Hoover institution on war, revolution, and peace: Documentary series (no.4): Stanford 1959. pp.xiii.530. [2500.]

E[VA ABRAMOVNA] GUTERMAN and G[ALINA PAVLOVNA] DEMIDENKO, СССР — знаменосец мира и дружбы народов. Указатель литературы в помощь массовым библиотекам. Государственная публичная историческая библиотека: Москва 1961. pp.40. [250.]

YU[RY] V[ASILEVICH] EGOROV, Мирное сосуществование и борьба за всеобщий мир... Рекомендательный указатель литературы. Государственная... публичная библиотека имени М. Е. Салтыкова–Щедрина: Ленинград 1962. pp.64. [450.]

3. *History*

i. *Bibliographies*

[E. G. VITUKHNOVSKAYA *and others*], Библиография русской библиографии по истории СССР. Аннотированный перечень библиографических указателей, изданных до 1917 года. Государственная публичная историческая библиотека РСФСР: Москва 1957. pp.197. [419.]

E. V. MARKINA and L. I. SHEKHANOVA, Каталог сборников документов, изданных архивными учрежениями СССР. Главное архивное управление: Москва 1961. pp.112. [631.]
limited to the publications of 1917–1960.

ii. *Periodicals*

БИБЛІОГРАФИЧЕСКІЙ каталогъ. Профили редакторовъ и сотрудниковъ. Carouge 1906. pp.202. [5000.]

[L. O. VANKHANEN *and others, edd.*], Большевистская периодическая печать в годы первой русской революции, 1905–1907. Библиографический указатель. Институт марксизма-ленинизма: Москва 1955. pp.64. [140.]

[L. O. VANKHANEN *and others*], Большевистская партийная периодическая печать в период подготовки и проведения Великой Октябрьской социалистической революции (март–ноябрь 1917 г.). Библиографический указатель. Институт марксизма-ленинизма при ЦК КПСС: Москва 1957. pp.72. [107.]

iii. *Manuscripts*

D[MITRY PETROVICH] LEBEDEV, Собраніе историко-юридическихъ актовъ И. Д. Бѣляева [Ivan Dmitrievich Byelyaev]. Московскій публичный и румянцевскій музей: Москва 1881. pp.[iii].95. [2000.]

ALEKSANDR [IVANOVICH] USPENSKY, Записныя книги и бумаги старинныхъ дворцовыхъ приказовъ. Документы XVIII–XIX вв.

вышаго архива Оружейной палата. Москва 1906. pp.v.247.clxv. [2500.]

S. K. BOGOYAVLENSKY, Центральный государственный архив древних актов. Путеводитель. Часть 1. Главное архивное управление НКВД СССР: Москва 1946. pp.364. [large number.]

V[ERA] V[ASILEVNA] SELCHUK, Великие русские революционные демократы: Белинский, Герцен, Чернышевский, Добролюбов. Краткий обзор литературы. Государственная библиотека СССР имени В. И. Ленина: Москва 1954. pp.84. [60.]

S[EMEN] B[ENTSIONOVICH] OKUN, Описание рукописных материалов по истории движения декабристов. Государственная ордена Трудового Красного Знамени публичная библиотека имени М. Е. Салтыкова-Щедрина: Труды Отдела рукописей: Ленинград 1954. pp.79. [400.]

G. A. BELOVA [*and others*], *edd.* Государственные архивы СССР. Краткий справочник. Главное архивное управление: Москва 1956. pp.508. [many million.]

путеводитель по архиву Ленинградского

отделения Института истории. Академия наук СССР: Москва &c. 1958. pp.605. [50,000.]

m[ikhail] n[ikolaevich] tikhomirov, Краткие заметки о летописных произведениях в рукописных собраниях Москвы. Академия наук СССР: Институт истории: Москва 1962. pp.184. [large number.]

личные архивные фонды в Государственных хранилищах СССР. Указатель. Главное архивное управление при Совете министров СССР. Библиотека СССР им. В. И. Ленина and Архив Академии наук СССР: Москва 1962–1963. pp.479+503. [large number.]

iv. *General*

[burchard] adam sellius, Schediasma litterarium de scriptoribus, qui historiam politicoecclesiasticam Rossiae scriptis illustrarunt. Reval 1736.

— Каталогъ писателей, сочиненіями своими объяснявшихъ гражданскую и церковную россійскую исторію. Москва 1815. pp.69. [250.]

каталогъ историческимъ памятникамъ, собраннымъ и изданнымъ Павломъ Мухановымъ [Pavel Aleksandrovich Mukheanov]. Москва 1836. pp.[iv].ii.34. [221.]

[PAVEL MIKHAILOVICH STROEV], Библіотека
Императорскаго общества исторіи и древностей россійскихъ. Москва 1845. pp.vii.355.
[3000.]

[—] — Выпускъ второй. Описаніе рукописей и бумагъ, поступившихъ съ 1846 по
1902 г. вкл. Трудъ Е. И. Соколова. 1905.
pp.viii.935. [6000.]

D[MITRY VASILEVICH] POLENOV, Библіографи-
ческое обозрѣніе русскихъ лѣтописей.
Санктпетербургъ 1850. pp.[ii].148. [600.]

G[RIGORY] N[IKOLAEVICH] GENNADI, Списокъ
книгъ по русской исторіи, вышедшихъ въ
1853 году. [Общество историй и древностей
россійскихъ: Временникъ (vol.xxii, supplement): Moscow 1855]. pp.22. [400.]

G. GENNADI, Указатель историческихъ статей и матеріаловъ, помѣщенныхъ въ губерн-
скихъ вѣдомостяхъ 1853 года. [*s.l.* 1854]. pp.
14. [150.]

—— 1854. [*s.l.* 1855]. pp.20. [225.]
—— 1855. [*s.l.* 1856]. pp.32. [400.]

[PETR PETROVICH LAMBIN and BORIS PETROVICH
LAMBIN], Русская историческая библіогра-
фия Императорская академія наукъ: Санктпетербургъ.

[i]. 1855. 1861. pp.vi.ii.167. [1481.]
[ii]. 1856. 1861. pp.vi.228. [2512.]
iii. 1857. 1865. pp.iv.225. [3126.]
iv. 1858. 1867. pp.iv.239. [3118.]
v. 1859. 1868. pp.iv.vii.300. [4349.]
vi. 1860. 1869. pp.iv.346. [4916.]
vii. 1861. 1870. pp.iv.348. [5066.]
viii. 1862. 1872. pp.iv.358. [4958.]
ix. 1863. 1877. pp.iv.370. [6721.]
x. 1864. 1884. pp.iv.469. [7946.]
[*continued by:*]

V[ladimir] I[zmailovich] Mezhov, Русская историческая библіографія за 1865–1876 включительно. 1882–1890. pp.[ii].xii.436+ [v].458 + [iv].viii.414 + [iv].v.408 + [iv].ix.378 +lviii.451+[iv].iv.433+[iv].440. [66,021.]

v. I. MEZHOV, Литература русской исторіи за 1859–1864 г. вкл... Томъ 1. Санктпетербургъ 1866. pp.xviii.418. [5611.]
no more published.

[KONSTANTIN NIKOLAEVICH] BESTUZHEV-RYUMIN, Русская исторія. Санкт-Петербургъ 1872–1885. pp.[ii].iii.iv.480.ii+[vii].320. [2500.]
—— Geschichte Russlands von Bestushew Rjumin. Uebersetzt von Theodor Schiemann. Mitau [1874[–1876]. pp.[vi].368+[iii].184. [1000.]
no more published.

русская историческая библіографія за
1873–1888. Ревель 1890. pp.113. [1773.]

v[LADIMIR] s[TEPANOVICH] IKONNIKOV, Опытъ
русской исторіографіи. Кіевъ 1891–1908.
pp.[ii].ix.882.cxxii.viii + [v].883–1539.ccxxiii–
ccclxxiii.149.x + [v].x.1056.xxxii.v + [ii].iii.1057–
1955.xxxiii–xlix.76. [40,000.]

E. A. GARNIER, Répertoire méthodique des
ouvrages en langue française relatifs à l'empire
de toutes les Russies qui se trouvent à la Bibliothèque nationale de Paris. Publiée sous la direction de Th. Sabachnikoff [Fedor Vasilevich
Sabashnikov]. Histoire. Premier fascicule. Bibliographie de la Russie: 1892. pp.ix.76. [604.]
   no more published.

v[LADIMIR] I[ZMAILOVICH] MEZHOV, Русская
историческая библіографія. Указатель
книгъ и статей по русской и всеобщей исторіи и вспомогательнымъ наукамъ за 1800–
1854 вкл. С.-Петербургъ 1892–1893. pp.xvi.373
+vii.377+x.514. [34,994.]

A. GIZETTI, Библіографическій указатель
печатаннымъ на русскомъ языкѣ сочине-
ніямъ и статьямъ о военныхъ дѣйствіяхъ
русскихъ войскъ на Кавказѣ. Главный

Штабъ: С.-Петербургъ 1901. pp.[iii].vi.256. [1330.]

CATALOGUS der geschiedenis. Het Russische rijk. Koninklijke bibliotheek: [The Hague] 1904. pp. [v].20. [549.]

N. A. MALINOWSKY, Систематическій указатель книгъ. Выпускъ первый. Всеобщая и русская исторія. Товарищество 'Родной міръ': С.-Петербургъ 1908. pp.45. [Russia: 322.]

УКАЗАТЕЛЬ книгъ по исторіи и общественнымъ вопросамъ. Русское техническое общество: С.-Петербургъ 1909 [*on cover:* 1910]. pp.ix.557.57.7.v. [3000.]

КАТАЛОГЪ книгъ библіотеки Алексѣя Петровича Бахрушина. Императорскій россійскій историческій музей имени императора Александра III: Москва 1911. pp.[iv].190. [4989.]

S[ERGEI] R[UDOLFOVICH] MINTSLOV, Обзоръ записокъ, дневниковъ, воспоминаній, писемъ и путешествій, относящихся къ исторіи Россія и папечатанныхъ на русскомъ языкѣ. Новгородъ 1911–1912. pp.171+198+ 115. [4791.]

BRIEF list of books on russian history and literature. Library of Congress: Washington 1916. ff.2. [16.]*

V[ASILY] YA[KOVLEVICH] ULANOV, Обзоръ популярной литературы по русской исторіи. Русское библіотечное общество: Москва [c.1918]. pp.79. [400.]

VLADIMIR BURTSEV, Russian documents in the British museum. [c.1920]. pp.18. [250.]

DIE GESCHICHTSWISSENSCHAFT in Sowjet-Russland 1917–1927. Bibliographischer katalog. Deutsche gesellschaft zum studium Osteuropas: Berlin &c. 1928. pp.193. [2250.]

ALEXANDRA DUMESNIL and WILFRID LERAT, Catalogue méthodique du fonds russe de la bibliothèque. Société de l'histoire de la guerre: Publications (1st ser.): 1932. pp.iii–xv.734. [6241.]

O[LGA] I[VANOVNA] SHVEDOVA, Историки СССР. Указатель печатных списков их трудов. Под редакцией И. Н. Кобленца [Ioel Naftalevich Koblents]. Москва 1941. pp. 152. [798.]

O[LGA] [IVANOVNA] SHVEDOVA [*and others*], История СССР с древнейших времен до конца xix в. Список рекомендуемой литературы. Москва 1941. pp.112. [1750.]

RUSSIA. A check list preliminary to a basic bibliography of materials in the russian language. Part VII. History of Russia [*on cover:* History, including auxiliary sciences, prior to 1918]. Library of Congress: Reference department: Washington 1944 [*on cover:* 1945]. ff.[i].123. [2014.]*

INTERNAL history of Russia. [University of Cambridge:] Department of slavonic studies: [Cambridge 1919].

    A. 1796–1894[*sic*, 1856]. pp.8. [116.]
    B. 1796[*sic*, 1856]–1917. pp.11. [168.]

CHARLES MORLEY, Guide to research in russian history. [Syracuse, N.Y. 1951]. pp.xiii.227. [840.]

ИСТОРИЯ СССР. Аннотированный указатель литературы для учителей средней школы. Издание 2-е. Под редакцией А. М. Панкратовой. Государственная публичная историческая библиотека: Москва 1952. pp. 400. [2000.]

    — 3-е издание. 1955. pp.408. [2000.]

ХУДОЖЕСТВЕННО-ИСТОРИЧЕСКАЯ литература. Рекомендательный указатель в помощь изучающим историю СССР. Государственная...

библиотека имени В. И. Ленина: Государственная публичная историческая библиотека: Москва 1955. pp.44. [100.]

I. P. DORONIN [*and others*], История СССР. Указатель советской литературы за 1917–1952 гг. Академия наук СССР: Фундаментальная библиотека общественных наук: Москва 1956–1958. pp.726 + 184 + 395 + 132. [29,333.]

I. L. GELLER [*and others*], Что читать по истории СССР. Рекомендательный указатель литературы. Государственная... библиотека СССР имени В. И. Ленина [&c.]: Москва 1961. pp.243. [1000.]

S[ERGEI] S[ERGEEVICH] DMITRIEV, История СССР. Аннотированный указатель литературы для учителей средней школы. 4-е издание. Государственная публичная историческая библиотека: Москва 1962–   . pp. 248+

v. *Specific periods*

–1800

[NIKOLAI NIKOLAEVICH] OBRUCHEV, Обзоръ рукописныхъ и печатныхъ памятниковъ относящихся до исторіи военнаго искуства въ Россіи по 1725 годъ. Санктпетербургъ 1853. pp.151. [1000.]

PAVEL ALEKSANDROVICH MUKHANOV, Каталогъ актовъ XIV, XV, XVI и XVII вѣка, принесенныхъ въ даръ Московскому публичному музею П. А. Мухановымъ. 1865. pp.26. [100.]

МАТЕРИАЛЫ для библиографии по истории народов СССР XVI–XVII вв. Академия наук СССР: Труды историко-археографического института (vol.iv): Ленинград 1933. pp.357. [7500.]

Z. V. ROZENBETSKAYA, Каталог архивных документов по северной войне 1700–1721 гг. Артиллерийский исторический музей: Ленинград 1959. pp.436. [3464.]

ВЫСТАВКА. История русской культуры XI–XVII веков в памятниках письменности. Каталог. Министерство культуры СССР: [Москва 1959]. pp.87. [197.]

R. P. DMITRIEVA, Библиография русского летописания. Академия наук СССР: Институт русской литературы: Ленинград 1962. pp.354. [2194.]

R. P. DMITRIEVA, Библиография русского летописания. Институт русской литературы: Москва &c. 1962. pp.354. [2017.]

[RICHARD HELLIE], Russian history from the end of the 16th century through the middle of the 17th century: a selected bibliography of books and articles in russian. [*s.l.* 1963]. pp.[viii].64. [1500.]*

1801–1900

V[LADIMIR] YA[KOVLEVICH] ADARYUKOV, Библіографическій указатель книгъ, брошюръ и статей къ исторіи 'декабристовъ'. С.-Петербургъ 1903. pp.12.

K. VOENSKY, Отечественная война въ русской журналистикѣ. Библіографическій сборникъ статей, относящихся къ 1812 году. С.-Петербургъ 1096. pp.v.220. [500.]

S. GORYAINOV, 1812. Документы государственнаго и С.-Петербургскаго главнаго архивовъ. Министерство иностранныхъ дѣлъ: С.-Петербургъ 1912 pp.[ii].563.184. [15,171.]

S. VOZNESENSKY, Библиографические материалы для словаря декабристов. Государственная публичная библиотека: Материалы по истории русской науки, литературы и

общественности (серия ii): Ленинград 1926.
pp.152. [3000.]

ДЕЯТЕЛИ революционного движения в
России. Био-библиографический словарь.
Общество политических Каторжан и Ссыль-
но-Поселенцев: Москва.

    i. От предшественников декабристов до
      конца "Народной Воли". Составлен
      А. А. Шиловым и М. Г. Карнауховой.
      1927–1928. pp.xxxiv.coll.222 + pp.xix.
      coll.496. [10,000.]

    ii. Семьдесятые годы. 1929–1932. pp.
      xxiv.coll.406 + pp.[iv].coll.407–836 + pp.
      [iv].coll.837–1384+1385–2156. [35,000.]

    iii. Восемьдесятые годы... Составлен
      М. М. Клевенскии, Е. Н. Кушевой и
      А. А. Шуловым. 1933–1934. pp.xvii.coll.
      690+pp.[iv].coll.691–1580. [15,000.]

    iv. [*not yet published?*]

    v. Социал-демократы 1880–1904. Состав-
      лен Э. А. Корольчук и Ш. М. Леви-
      ным. Под редакцией В. И. Невского.
      1931–1933. pp.xxvi.coll.584 + pp.[iv].
      coll.583–1310+pp.xxii–xxxiv. [15,000.]

I. M. CHENTSOV, Восстание декабристов.
Библиография. Центрархив: Москва &c.
1929. pp.xix.794. [4451.]

DAVID [MICHAEL] SHAPIRO, A select bibliography
of works in english on russian history, 1801–1917.
Oxford 1962. pp.xii.106. [1070.]

[I. L. GELLER], Бессмертный подвиг народа
(Отечественная война 1812 года.) Рекомендательный указатель литературы. Библиотека СССР им. В. И. Ленина: Военный отдел: Москва 1963. pp.32. [120.]

1901–

SELECT list of references on recent russian
history. Library of Congress: Washington 1914.
ff.3. [38.]*

A. A. SHILOVA, Что читать по истории русского революционного движения. Петербург
1922. pp.230. [4000.]

O. I. VLASOV [*and others*], Первомайские про-
кламации. Библиографическое описание.
Ленинград 1924. pp.96. [826.]

V[SEVOLOD NIKOLAEVICH] DURDENEVSKY and
S[EMEN MOISEEVICH] BERTSINSKY, Опыт библиографии общественных наук за революцион-
ено трехлетие (1918–1920). Москва &c. 1925.
pp.vii.271. [5000.]

O. E. VOL'TSENBURG, Библиографический путеводитель по революции 1905 года. Ленинград 1925. pp.253. [962.]

M. DOBRANITSKY, Систематический указатель литературы по истории русской революции. Москва 1926. pp.152. [4000.]

ПЕРВАЯ русская революция. Указатель литературы. Коммунистическая академия: Библиотека: Москва 1930. pp.xix.714. [12,500.] *on the revolution of 1905.*

S. P. POSTNIKOV, Bibliografie ruské revoluce a občanské války (1917–1921) z katalogu knihovny R.z.h. Archivu. Za redakce Jana Slavíka. Ruský zahraniční historický archiv: Praha 1938. pp.xv. 448. [6000.]

V[LADIMIR VASILEVICH] LUCHININ, Русско-японская война, 1904–1905 гг. Библиографический указатель книжной литературы на русском и иностранных языках. Государственная библиотека СССР имени В. И. Ленина: Военный отдел: Москва 1940. pp.144. [1218.]

A[NNA] M[IKHAILOVNA] PANKRATOVA, XXV лет Великой Октябрьской социалистической революции, 1917–1942. Указатель литературы. Москва 1942. pp.200. [400.]

NATALIYA BUSSE, Какво да четем върху великата октомбрийска революция. Препоръчителен списък. Български библиографски институт: Поредица препоръчителни списъци (no.1): София 1949. pp.15. [50.]*

[Z. P. GONCHAROVA and YU. A. GLEZAROVA], Великая октябрьская социалистическая революция. Библиотека СССР имени В. И. Ленина: Москва 1950. pp.28. [15.]

K. I. GOLIKOV, B. B. ZLATOUSTOVSKY and E. V. OLISHEV, Первая буржуазно-демократическая революция в России в 1905–1907 гг. Государственная... библиотека СССР имени В. И. Ленина and Государственная публичная историческая библиотека: Москва 1954. pp.63. [250.]
— — Второе ... издание. Первая русская революция, 1905–1907 гг. Рекомендательный указатель литературы. 1955. pp.80. [400.]

V. P. TITARENKO [and others], Перша російська революція, 1905–1907 рр. Библіографічний покажчик. Академия наук Україн-

ської РСР: Библиотека: Київ 1955. pp.168.
[750.]

z. e. luss, *ed*. Пропаганда литературы о
первой русской революции 1905–1907 гг.
Государственная... библиотека СССР имени
В. И. Ленина: Научно-методический кабинет
библиотековедения: Москва 1955. pp.68.[250.]

s. gelfond and l. likhachova, До 50-річчя
першої російської революції 1905–1907 рр.
Методично-бібліографічні матеріали для бі-
бліотек. Державна наукова библиотека:
Одеса 1955. pp.32. [200.]

[v. g. dubina], К 50-летию первой русской
революции 1905–1907 годов. Методические
и библиографические материалы в помощь
библиотекам. Государственная публичная
библиотека Молдавской ССР имени Н. К.
Крупскоіі: Кишинев 1955. pp.36. [150.]

k. i. golikov, b. v. zlatoustovcky and
e. v. olishev, Первая русская революция
(1905–1907 гг). Краткий указатель литературы. Государственная... библиотека СССР
имени В. И. Ленина and Государственная
публичная историческая библиотека: Москва 1955. pp.60. [300.]

—— Второе:... издание. 1955. pp.80. [500.]

I[VAN AKIMOVICH] PORTYANKIN, Большевистская печать в годы первой русской революции. Москва 1956. pp.128. [70.]

ИСТОРИЯ СССР. Указатель советской литературы за 1917–1952 гг. Академия наук
СССР: Фундаментальная библиотека общественных наук: Москва.

> [i]. История СССР с древнейших времён
> до вступления России в период капи-
> тализма. 1956. pp.726+184. [18,788.]

> [ii]. История СССР в период капита-
> лизма (1861–1917). 1958. pp.394+132.
> [10,508.]

B. I. SHCHEGOLEVA and E. E. TROITSKAYA, *edd.*
К 40-летию Великой октябрьской социалистической революции. Сборник библиографических и методических материалов. Государственная... публичная библиотека СССР
имени В. И. Ленина: Москва 1957. pp.183.
[1500.]

RICHARD SCHÖTZAU and HEINZ GITTIG, Die grosse
sozialistische oktoberrevolution. Auswahlbiblio-
graphie. Schriftenreihe des arbeitskreises der
gesellschaftswissenschaftlichen besatzungsstelle an
den dem Staatssekretariat für hochschulen unter-
stellten wissenschaftlichen bibliotheken (no.5):
Berlin 1957. pp.88. [763.]

M. I. MASENZHIK [*and others*], Да 40-й гадавіны вялікой кастрычніцкай соцыялістычнай рэволюцыі (Зборнік метадычных і бібліяграфічных матэрыялаў). Дзяржаўная бібліятэка БССР: У дапамогу масавым бібліятэкам БССР: Мінск 1957. pp.120. [400.]

E[LENA] D[AVYDOVNA] ZOLOTAREVA and A[SYA] A[BRAMOVNA] KUNINA, В боях за великий октябрь. Произведения советских писателей. Государственная... публичная библиотека СССР имени В. И. Ленина: Москва 1957. pp.116. [300.]

I. S. BELENSKY, P. G. GRANSKAYA and E. A. MILSHTEIN, Подготовка и проведение великой октябрьской социалистической революции. Список литературы. Государственная... публичная библиотека имени М. Е. Салтыкова-Щедрина: Ленинград 1957. pp.29. [250.]★

R[AISA] M[AROVNA] INGLEZI and Z[INAIDA] L[VOVNA] FRADKINA, великая октябрьская социалистическая революция в мемуарной и художественной литературе. Аннотированный указатель. Государственная публичная историческая библиотека РСФСР: Москва 1957. pp.39. [150.]

v. i. MENDELSON, Всемирно-историческое значение великой октябрьской социалистической революции. Краткий указатель литературы. Государственная публичная историческая библиотека: Москва 1957. pp. 36. [150.]

A[LEKSANDRA] S[TEPANOVNA] SMIRNOVA, Великий октябрь. Краткий рекомендательный список литературы. Государственная... публичная библиотека им. М. Е. Салтыкова-Щедрина: В помощь пионерскому активу: Ленинград 1957. pp.20. [50.]

v. z. DROBIZHEV, v. A. DUNAEVSKY and YU. S. KUKUSHKIN, История советского общества в воспоминаниях современников, 1917–1957. Аннотированный указатель мемуарной литературы. Московский... государственный университет имени М. В. Ломоносова and Государственная... библиотека СССР имени В. И. Ленина: Москва 1958. pp.408. [1538.]

N. N. SOLOVEVA, Новые книги о великой октябрьской социалистической революции. Государственная... публичная библиотека СССР имени В. И. Ленина: Москва 1958. pp.63. [200.]

A. N. BAIKOVA [*and others*], Великая октябрьская социалистическая революция... Указатель литературы изданной в 1957–1958 гг. Академия наук СССР: Фундаментальная библиотека [&c.]: Москва 1959. pp. [iii].vi.233 + [v].232–418 + [iii].418–593 + [iii].591–724. [4589.]*

V. A. DUNAEVSKY, Международное значение русской революции 1905–1907 годов. Указатель литературы на русском языке. Государственная ... библиотека СССР имени В. И. Ленина: Отдел справочно-библиографической и информационной работы: Москва 1959. pp.78. [611.]

R. G. EIMONTOVA and A. A. SOLENNIKOV, Движение декабристов. Указатель литературы 1928–1959. Государственная публичная историческая библиотека РСФСР and Всесоюзная государственная библиотека иностранной литературы: Москва 1960. pp.435. [3585.]

ЛИТЕРАТУРА о международном революционном движении. Великая октябрьская социалистическая революция и подъем революционного движения в Болгарии, Вен-

грии, Польше, Румынии и Чехословакии.
Указатель книг и статей, вышедших в свет
в 1951–1958. Академия наук СССР: Фундаментальная библиотека общественных наук:
Москва 1960. pp.192. [1433.]

E. N. GORODETSKY, *ed.* Советская страна в
период гражданской войны 1918–1920. Библиографический указатель документальных
публикаций. Государственная публичная
историческая библиотека: Москва 1961.
pp.576. [3668.]

4. *Topography*

FRIEDRICH VON ADELUNG, Kritisch-literarische
übersicht der reisenden in Russland bis 1700.
St. Petersburg &c. 1846. pp.xxiv.480+[ii].viii.
430. [266.]
   a facsimile reprint was published, Amsterdam 1960.
   — — Критико-литературное обозрѣніе
[&c.]. ...Переводъ... Александра Клевано-
ва. Москва 1864. Часть I. pp.viii.v.264. [400.]
   no more published.

J. CH. STUCKENBERG, Versuch eines quellen-
anzeigers alter und neuer zeit für das studium der
geographie, topographie, ethnographie und sta-

tistik des Russischen reiches. St. Petersburg 1849–
1852. pp.vii.406+v.[ix].688.iv. [20,000.]

L[EONID PAVLOVICH] VESIN, Историческій
обзоръ учебниковъ общей и русской географіи, изданныхъ со времени Петра вели-
каго по 1876 годъ (1710–1876 г.). С.-Петер-
бургъ 1876. pp.[iii].iii.x.674.iv. [232.]

[N. BOKACHEV], Исторія русскихъ земель и
городовъ. Каталогъ... библіотеки Н. Бокачева: St. Petersburg 1896. pp.[iv].387. [1940.]

БИБЛІОГРАФИЧЕСКІЙ обзоръ земской стати-
стической и оцѣночной литературы со времени учрежденія земствъ, 1864–1903 г. Им-
ператорское вольное экономическое общество: С.-Петербургъ 1905 &c.

HELMUT ANGER, Die wichtigste geographische
literatur über das Russische reich seit dem jahre
1914 in russischer sprache. Albertus-universität zu
Königsberg: Geographisches institut: Veröffentlichungen (no.vi): Hamburg 1926. pp.64. [1000.]
the titles are given only in german translation.

[BERTHA KUCHEROV and GISELLA R. LACHMAN],
Soviet geography. [Edited by Nicholas R.
Rodionoff]. Library of Congress: Washington
1951. pp.xx.668. [4421.]

RUDOLF FLECK, Neuere bibliographie zur wirtschaftsgeographie der UdSSR. Kiel 1951. pp. [ii].25. [2000.]*

G. P. BOGOYAVLENSKY, По нашей стране. Краткий указатель литературы по географии СССР. Москва 1954. pp.88. [200.]

G. P. BOGOYAVLENSKY, География СССР. Аннотированный указатель литературы в помощь учителю. Москва 1957. pp.168. [400.]

[E. N. MORACHEVSKAYA], Библиография по районированию и размещению сельского хозяйства СССР (1818–1960). Академия наук СССР: Совет по изучению производительных сил: Сектор сети специальных библиотек: Москва 1961. pp.200. [1600.]

M[ARIYA] I[SAAKOVNA] KOLTUN, Природное (физико-географическое) районирование территории Советского Союза. Указатель литературы изданной в 1917–1960 гг. Государственная . . . библиотека СССР имени В. И. Ленина: Москва 1962. pp.380. [4000.]

CHAUNCY D[ENNISON] HARRIS, Geography, resources and natural conditions in the Soviet Union. An annotated bibliography of selected basic books in russian. University of Chicago:

Department of geography: Chicago 1962. ff.[i].45.
[176.]

Saar.

HELMUT BLEYMEHL, Das geographische schrifttum über das Saarland, von 1946–1952. [Neun-
kirchen 1954]. pp.17. [400.]

Sablé.

P. E. CHEVRIER, Inventaire analytique des
archives de l'hospice de Sablé. Sablé 1877. pp.
v.612. [2300.]

Sachsen–Altenburg.

ERNST CONON LÖBE, Altenburgica. Uebersicht
der literatur zur geschichte des herzogthums
Sachsen–Altenburg. Altenburg 1878. pp.73. [450.]

Sagan.

ERICH GRABER, Die inventare der nichtstaatlichen
archive Schlesiens. Kreis Sagan. Verein für geschichte Schlesiens: Codex diplomaticus Silesiae
(vol.xxxii): Breslau 1927. pp.[v].175. [5000.]

Sahagun, monastery of.

[V. VIGNAU], Índice de los documentos del
monasterio de Sahagun, de la órden de San Benito.

Archivo histórico nacional: Madrid 1874. pp.xi. 691. [2533.]

Saint-Affrique.

G[USTAVE] DESJARDINS and H[ENRI] AFFRE, Inventaire des archives de la commune de Saint-Affrique. Archives de l'Aveyron: Saint-Affrique [printed] 1868. pp.42. [10,000.]

St Albans, diocese of.

[A SURVEY of the ecclesiastical archives of the diocese of St. Albans]. Pilgrim trust: Survey of ecclesiastical archives: [1952]. ff.15. [large number.]*

Saint-Amand.

JULES FINOT and [J.] VERMAERE, Inventaire sommaire des archives communales antérieures à 1790. . . . Ville de Saint-Amand. Lille 1894. pp.xlii.83. [25,000.]

Saint-Amand-Montrond.

HENRI MALLARD and ÉMILE PIVOTEAU, Archives communales et hospitalières de la ville de Saint-Amand-Montrond. Répertoire numérique. Saint-Amand-Montrond 1915. pp.viii.47. [10,000.]

St Anna hofje, Leiden.

P. N. VAN DOORNINCK, Inventaris van het archief van het Sint Anna aalmoeshuis genaamd Sint-Anna-of-Doornincks hofje op de Hooigracht te Leiden. Haarlem 1904. pp.[iii].80. [1000.]

Saint-Bertin, abbey of.

DANIEL HAIGNERÉ [vols.ii–iii: O. BLED], Les chartes de Saint-Bertin, d'après le Grand cartulaire de dom Charles-Joseph Dewitte. Société des antiquaires de la Morinie: Saint-Omer.

    i. 648–1240. 1886. pp.lxvi.471. [867.]

    ii. 1241–1380. [1888–]1891. pp.[iii].532. [1379.]

    iii. 1381–1473. [1892–]1895. pp.[iii].600.[3]. [1428.]

    iv. 1474–1779. [1897–]1899. pp.[iii].543. [1507.]

Saint-Bertrand-de-Comminges.

[A. BAUDOUIN, F. PASQUIER and H. MARTIN], Inventaire sommaire des archives départementales. ... Haute-Garonne. Série E, supplément. Ville de Saint-Bertrand-de-Comminges. Toulouse 1913. pp.xi.800. [large number.]

Europe

Saint-Claude.

G[USTAVE] DUHEM, Inventaire analytique des livres de bourgeoisie de la ville de Saint-Claude. Archives municipales de Saint-Claude: Lons-le-Saunier [printed] 1960. pp.iii–xiii.166. [2000.]

Saint-Denis.

FRÉDÉRIC DUVAL, Inventaire des archives communales. . . . Ville de Saint-Denis. Saint-Denis 1923. pp.12.coll.440. [50,000.]

Saint-Évroult, abbey of.

ALBERT DESVAUX and A[RTHUR] L[OUIS] LETACQ, Essai sur la bibliographie de l'abbaye de Saint-Évroult et du canton de La Ferté-Fresnel. Alençon 1898. pp.81. [175.]

Sainte-Foy-la-Grande.

[GASTON DUCAUNNÈS-DUVAL and JEAN AUGUSTE BRUTAILS], Inventaire sommaire des archives municipales antérieures à 1790.· Ville de Sainte-Foy-la-Grande. Bordeaux 1907. pp.91. [25,000.]

St Gerlach, convent of.

G. D. FRANQUINET, Beredeneerde inventaris der oorkonden en bescheiden van het adelijk klooster

St. Gerlach. Beredeneerde inventaris der oorkonden en bescheiden berustende op het provinciaal archief van Limburg (vol.iv): Maastricht 1877. pp.viii.303. [267.]

Saint-Germain-en-Laye.

[FRÉDÉRIC ALEXANDRE] H[ENRI] STEIN, Les archives de Saint-Germain-en-Laye. Inventaire sommaire. Versailles 1886. pp.24. [large number.]
actually consists in large part of an inventory of the relevant documents in the Archives nationales.

Saint-Jean-d'Angély.

LOUIS CLAUDE SAUDAU, Inventaire sommaire des archives communales antérieures à 1790. Ville de Saint-Jean-d'Angély. La Rochelle 1895. pp.[iii]. 2.91. [15,000.]

Saint-Maixent.

[GUY] A[LFRED] RICHARD, Inventaire-sommaire des archives communales antérieures à 1790 de Saint-Maixent. 1863. pp.vii.vii.3.2.3.2.9.2.6. [5000.]

Saint-Malo.

[   ] PESSEAU, [   ] HAVARD and H[IPPOLYTE] HARVUT, Inventaire-sommaire des archives com-

munales antérieures à 1790. . . . Ville de Saint-Malo. Saint-Malo 1883. pp.[iii].viii.4.7.12.4.10. 40.3.5.[xv]. [20,000.]

H[IPPOLYTE HARVUT, Inventaire-sommaire des archives communales postérieures à 1790. Période révolutionnaire. . . . Ville de Saint-Malo. Saint-Malo 1907. pp.[iii].viii.79. [20,000.]

St Marienhorst.

P. A. A. M. WUBBE, Het archief der abdij St. Marienhorst te Ter Hunnepe. 's-Gravenhage 1931. pp.377. [1307.]

St Marylebone.

ANN [LOREILLE] COX-JOHNSON, Handlist of the Ashbridge collection on the history and topography of St. Marylebone. Public libraries: St. Marylebone 1959. pp.[ii].vi.215. [1500.]*

100 books about St. Marylebone. Public libraries committee: 1963. pp.22. [100.]

Saint-Mihiel, abbey of.

[CARL] L[UDWIG PHILIPP] TROSS, Catalogue des archives de l'abbaye de Saint-Mihiel en Lorraine. 1853. pp.45. [400.]

Saint-Nazaire.

RENÉ [M. M. P. DU COSQUER DE] KERVILER,
Bibliographie saint-nazairienne. Documents pour
servir à l'histoire de Saint-Nazaire (vol.iii): Saint-
Nazaire [printed] 1884. pp.viii.184. [441.]

Saint-Nicholas.

[A. J. V. M.] DE SCHOUTHEETE DE TERVARENT,
Inventaire général analytique des archives de la
ville et de l'église primaire de Saint-Nicolas
(Waes). Bruxelles &c. 1872. pp.[ii].x.356. [750.]

St Oedenrode.

A. R. M. MOMMERS, Inventaris van het oud en
nieuw archief der gemeente St-Oedenrode.
[Veghel] 1928. pp.160.

Saint-Omer.

FÉLIX LE SERGEANT DE MONNECOVE, Inventaire
analytique des registres de l'abbaye de Saint-
Bertin à Saint Omer existant au dépôt des archives
départementales du Pas-de-Calais. Saint-Omer
1874. pp.32. [407.]

A[RTHUR] GIRY, Analyse et extraits d'un registre
des archives municipales de Saint-Omer, 1166–
1778. Saint-Omer 1875. pp.252. [461.]

[BARON CAMILLE DARD], Bibliographie historique de la ville de Saint-Omer. Arras 1880. pp.
[v].84. [568.]
50 copies printed.

[BARON CAMILLE DARD], Bibliographie historique de l'arrondissement de Saint-Omer. Société
des antiquaires de la Morinie: Saint-Omer 1887.
pp.xii.241. [1213.]

HENRI LORIQUET and JULES CHAVANON, Inventaire-sommaire des archives hospitalières antérieures à 1790. . . . Hospices de Saint-Omer. Arras
1902. pp.[iii].iv.139.99.27.28.46.57. [75,000.]

Saintonge.

[VICTOR BUJEAUD], Catalogue des pièces les
plus importantes contenues dans les registres du
parlement de Paris concernant l'Angoumois, la
Saintonge et le Poitou. (Archives de l'empire).
1770–1785. Niort 1865. pp.28. [200.]
100 copies printed.

Saint-Pierre-le-Moûtier.

[HENRI] DE FLAMARE, Inventaire sommaire des
archives départementales. . . . Nièvre. Série B.

Présidial de Saint-Pierre-le-Moûtier. Nevers 1891–1898. pp.467+357. [637.]

Saint-Pons.

J[OSEPH HENRI VICTOR MARIE] SAHUC, Inventaire sommaire des archives communales antérieures à 1790. . . . Ville de Saint-Pons. Montpellier 1895. pp.[iii].iv.153. [2500.]

JOSEPH SAHUC, Inventaire de mes manuscrits, titres, pièces et ouvrages imprimés concernant l'histoire de l'ancien diocèse de Saint-Pons de Thomières. [*s.l.*] 1899. pp.126. [200.]

J. SAHUC, Sources historiques et bibliographie de l'arrondissement actuel et de l'ancien diocèse de Saint-Pons-de-Thomières. Montpellier 1901. pp.88. [638.]

J. SAHUC, Inventaire-sommaire des archives hospitalières antérieures à 1790. . . . Ville de Saint-Pons. Montpellier 1910. pp.81. [10,000.]

Saint-Quentin.

EMMANUEL LEMAIRE, Archives anciennes de la ville de St.-Quentin. Société académique de Saint-Quentin: Publications: Saint-Quentin.

i. 1076–1328. 1888. pp.[iii].cxlvi.562. [500.]

ii. 1328–1400. 1910. pp.[iii].clxxi.456. [350.]
250 copies printed.

VICTOR DESSEIN, Inventaire des archives modernes de la ville de Saint-Quentin, 1789–1898. Saint-
Quentin [printed] 1904. pp.259. [1500.]

Saint-Servan.

JULES HAIZE, Inventaire-sommaire des archives
communales antérieures à 1790. . . . Ville de Saint-
Servan. Saint-Servan 1908. pp.94. [20,000.]

Saint-Trond.

FRANÇOIS STRAVEN, Inventaire analytique et
chronologique des archives de la ville de Saint-
Trond. Saint-Trond.
  i. [1060–1465]. 1886. pp.[iii].488. [1000.]
  ii. [1465–1555]. 1886. pp.471. [1500.]
  iii. [1558–1645]. 1887. pp.509. [2000.]
  iv. [1649–1694]. 1889. pp.496. [2000.]
  v. [1694–1789]. 1892. pp.514. [2500.]
  vi. [1789–1816; supplément et tables]. 1895.
  pp.744. [1500.]

Saint-Vaast, abbey of.

H. LORIQUET [*and others*], Inventaire sommaire
des archives départementales. . . . Pas-de-Calais.

Série H. Abbaye de Saint-Vaast. Arras 1902–1911.
pp.[iii].421+374+[iii].455.8. [large number.]

Salamanca.

J. GONZÁLEZ GONZÁLEZ, Índices del Archivo
histórico de protocolos de Salamanca. Madrid
1942. pp.281. [large number.]

Salford.

J[ACK] LEE, Maps and plans of Manchester and
Salford 1650 to 1843. A handlist. Altrincham
1957. pp.43. [65.]

Salisbury, diocese of.

[A SURVEY of the ecclesiastical archives of the
diocese of Salisbury]. Pilgrim trust: Survey of
ecclesiastical archives: [1952]. ff.23. [large number.]*

Salles-sur-l'Hers.

[JEAN] PAUL LAURENT, Répertoire des archives
communales des cantons de Belpech, Fanjeaux
et Salles-sur-l'Hers antérieures à 1790. Carcassonne
1886. pp.27. [large number.]

Salonika.

INVENTAIRE des correspondances des consuls de France au Levant conservées aux Archives nationales.

> i. Salonique et Cavalla (1686–1792) par N[icolas] G. Svoronos. 1951. pp.155. [large number.]
> *no more published?*

Salzburg.

E. DANNAPPEL, Die literatur der salzburger emigration (1731–35). Verzeichnis der deutschen und in Deutschland gedruckten schriften, welche aus anlass der salzburgischen emigration erschienen sind. Stuttgart 1886. pp.23. [250.]

INVENTAR des Landesregierungsarchivs in Salzburg. Inventare österreichischer staatlicher archive (vol.iii): Wien 1912. pp.88. [large number.]

San Sebastián.

SERAPIO MÚGICA, Índice de los documentos del archivo del excmo. ayuntamiento de la m. n. y m. l. ciudad de San Sebastián. San Sebastián 1898. pp.xv.513.[x]. [5000.]

Santander.

TOMÁS MAZA SOLANO, El archivo del Real consulado de Santander. Santander 1934. pp.80. [500.]

TOMÁS MAZA SOLANO, Catálogo del archivo del antiguo monasterio de Jerónimos de Santa Catalina de Monte Corbán. Centro de estudios montañeses: Fuentes documentales para la historia de la provincia (1st ser., vol.i): Santander 1936. pp.iii–lxiii.446. [1412.]

Santa Verónica, monastery of.

VICENTE MARTÍNEZ MORELLÁ, El monasterio de Santa Verónica (Santa Fez de Alicante). Alicante 1953. pp.43. [197.]
300 copies printed; a list of the documents in the Archivo municipal of Alicante concerning the monastery.

Santiago, monastery of.

AUREA [L.] JAVIERRE MUR and CONSUELO D. DEL ARROYO, Catálogo de los documentos referentes a los conventos de Santiago, Calatrava y Alcántara que se conservan en el archivo secreto del Consejo de la órdenes militares. Archivo histórico nacional: Madrid [1958]. pp.338. [1426.]

Saône, Haute-

INVENTAIRE-sommaire des archives départementales. . . . Haute-Saône. Paris [*afterwards:*
Vesoul] 1865. [very large number.]

    i. Séries A–B. Par Victor Besson. 1865. pp.
       5.33.1.415.

    ii–iii. Série B. Par V. Besson [Jules Finot].
       1874–1884. pp.12.457+xv.450.

    iv. Séries C–F. Par J. Finot, Léonce Lex et
       J. Dunoyer de Segonzac. 1891. pp.xviii.456.

    v. Séries G–H. Par J. Dunoyer de Segonzac
       et A. Eckel. 1901. pp.xii.386.

    Série L. 1942. pp.viii.178.

    Série T. 1912. pp.12.

in progress.

Saône-et-Loire.

INVENTAIRE-sommaire des archives départementales . . . Saône-et-Loire. Paris [*afterwards:*
Mâcon]. [very large number.]

    Séries A–B. Par L. Michon. 1878. pp.iii.6.
       432.

    Série C. Par C. Ragut, L. Michon et L. Lex.
       1924. pp.iv.453.

    Séries D–E. Par L. Michon [A. Bénet et
       Arthur Morgand]. 1877–1933. pp.iii.9.387
       +iii.80.

Série F. Par L. Lex. 1910. pp.xv.394.
Série G. Par L. Michon [*and others*]. 1933. pp[iii].358.
Série H. [1887–]1894. pp.v.496+xvi.188.
in progress.

L[ÉONCE] LEX, Tableau des fonds des archives départementales de Saône-et-Loire. Mâcon [1901]. pp.35. [200.]

L[ÉONCE] LEX, Rapport sur le service des archives . . . de Saône-et-Loire 1888–1889, contenant un tableau des registres d'état-civil ancien des greffes des tribunaux. Mâcon 1889. pp.36. [large number.]

L[ÉONCE] LEX, Inventaire des registres de l'ancienne administration de l'enregistrement et des domaines 1693–1791 déposés aux archives départementales. Département de Saône-et-Loire: Mâcon 1913. pp.15. [150.]

Saragossa.

CARLOS RIBA Y GARCÍA, Lo que se ha escrito sobre los sitios de Zaragoza. Inventario bibliográfico de fuentes é instrumentos de trabajo para el estudio de su historia. Zaragoza 1911. pp.[ii]. 122. [600.]

MANUEL ABIZANDA PROTO, Colección de documentos inéditos del Archivo municipal de Zaragoza desde el reinado de Pedro III al de Juan II. Valencia 1924. pp.29. [125.]

Sarcé.

F[ORTUNÉ] LEGEAY, Inventaire-sommaire des registres de l'état civil antérieurs à 1790 des paroisses d'Aubigné, Coulongé, Lavernat, Sarcé, Vaas et Verneil-le-Chétif. Le Mans 1883. pp.23. [150.]

Sargans.

KARL WEGELIN, Die regesten der Benedictinerabtei Pfävers und der landschaft Sargans. Regesten der archive in der Schweizerischen eidgenossenschaft (vol.i): Chur 1850. pp.[iv].112.xxiii. [916.]

Sarthe.

ÉD[OUARD JEAN MARIE] BILARD, Analyse des documents historiques conservés dans les archives ... de la Sarthe. [Vol.ii edited by Fortuné Legeay]. Le Mans [1854-1862]. pp.[viii].244.

INVENTAIRE-sommaire des archives départementales. ... Sarthe. Le Mans. [very large number.]

Séries A–E. Par A. Bellée et P. Moulard. 1870. pp.5.16.21.8.116.570.

Série B. Par V. Duchemin et J. Dunoyer de Segonzac. 1890–1927. pp.372+282.

Série G. Par A. Bellée. 1876. pp.379.

Série H. Par A. Bellée et V. Duchemin. 1881–1883. pp.422+244.

Série H, supplément. 1952 &c.

Série L. Par J. Dunoyer de Segonzac [*and others*]. 1898–1924. pp.292+98.

in progress.

Saumur.

MARC SACHÉ, Inventaire sommaire des archives départementales antérieures à 1790. Maine-et-Loire. Archives ecclésiastiques, série H, tome II. Abbaye de Saint-Florent de Saumur. Angers 1926. pp.603. [large number.]

CÉLESTIN PORT, MARC SACHÉ and JACQUES LEVRON, Inventaire sommaire des archives départementales antérieures à 1790. Maine-et-Loire. Archives civiles, série E, supplément (suite), tome IV. Arrondissement de Saumur. Angers 1935. pp.ii.382. [very large number.]

JACQUES LEVRON, Inventaire analytique des archives anciennes de la ville de Saumur. Angers.

i. État-civil antérieur à la Révolution. 1953.
pp.vi.159. [large number.]

Savine.

PAUL [PIERRE MARIE] GUILLAUME, Inventaire
sommaire des archives départementales. . . .
Hautes-Alpes. Série E. Mandement et marquisat
de Savine. Gap 1910. pp.xviii.348. [large number.]

Savona.

AGOSTINO BRUNO, Gli archivi del comune di
Savona. Savona 1884. pp.53. [10,000.]

AGOSTINO BRUNO, I registri della Catena. Savona
1888. pp.[iii].28. [500.]

AGOSTINO BRUNO, Gli antichi archivi del comune di Savona. 1890. pp.87. [5000.]

Savoy. [*see also* **Piedmont.**]

ANTONIO MANNO and VINCENZO PROMIS [vols.
ii–ix: A. MANNO; x: MARIO ZUCCHI], Bibliografia storica degli stati della monarchia di Savoia.
Reale deputazione di storia patria: Biblioteca
storica italiana (section iii): Torino 1884–1934.
pp.xxviii.463 + xix.457 + [iv].475 + viii.576 +
[vi].455 + [iv].539 + viii.551 + [v].350 + [ii].536
+xl.501. [42,811.]

INVENTAIRE sommaire des archives départementales. . . . Département de la Savoie. Chambéry. [very large number.]

>Série C. Par [Antoine] Alexis de Jussieu. pp.xi.446+[iii].392.

>Série E, supplément. Par Gabriel Pérouse. 1911. pp.xcix.275.

>Série G. 1915. pp.[iii].53.

>Série H. Par Pierre Bernard. 1932. pp.11.

>Série L. 1925– . pp.xxxiii.coll.318+ .

>Série Q. Par Gabriel Pérouse, Pierre Bernard et Joseph Jannon. 1933. pp.35.

in progress.

DOMINICO CARUTTI, Regesta comitum Sabaudiae Marchionum in Italia ab ultima stirpis origine ad an. MDCCLIII. Reale deputazione di storia patria: Biblioteca storica italiana (vol.v [*sic*, vi]): Augustae Taurinorum 1889. pp.xi.415. [971.]

MAX BRUCHET, Inventaire partiel du trésor des chartes de Chambéry à l'époque d'Amédée VIII. Chambéry 1900. pp.273. [797.]

INVENTAIRE sommaire des archives départementales. . . . Haute-Savoie. Annecy. [very large number.]

>Séries A–C. Par Max Bruchet et G. Letonnelier. 1921. pp.xxiii.412.

Série E. 1904. pp.vi.391.

Série G. Par Claude Faure et Robert Avezov.
   1926–1929. pp.23+25.

Série H. 1932. pp.28.

Série L. 1959. pp.46.

Série N. Par J. Serand. 1913. pp.7.

Série R. 1913. pp.4.

Série V. 1911. pp.4.

Série Y. 1912. pp.4.

in progress.

HENRI FERRAND, Les premières cartes de la Savoie. 1907. pp.27. [50.]

A[LLEN] B[ANKS] HINDS, Descriptive list of state papers, Foreign: Savoy (S.P. 92). Public record office: 1933. ff.i.119. [2500.]*
   covers the period 1579–1660.

[MAX BRUCHET], Répertoire des sources de l'histoire de Savoie. 1935. pp.142. [large number.]

Savoy, London.

[JOSEPH RITSON], A digest of the proceedings of the court leet of the manor and liberty of the Savoy. 1789. pp.[vii].46. [400.]
   reissued in 1794 as part of Ritson's Law-tracts.

Saxe-Meiningen.

CURT FRIESER, Katalog der bibliothek des Vereins für meiningische geschichte und landeskunde. ... Herausgegeben von ... Ludwig Hertel. Verein für sachsen-meiningische geschichte und landeskunde: Schriften (no.32): Hildburghausen 1898. pp.42. [500.]

—— Neu bearbeitet von Hermann Elssmann ... (no.68): 1913. pp.114. [1000.]

Saxony.

GEORG CHRISTOPH KREYSIG, Historische bibliothec von Ober-Sachsen und einigen angrentzenden ländern. Dresden &c. 1732. pp.[xxvi].592.[lii]. [5000.]

—— Neue ... auflage. Theil 1. Leipzig &c. [1749]. pp.[xvi].384. [3000.]
no more published.

BURCARD GOTTHELF STRUVE, Bibliotheca saxonica, scriptores rervm saxonicarvm, missensivm, thvringicarvm et reliqvarvm provinciarvm exhibens. Halae Magdebvrgicæ 1736. pp.[xvi].1178. [lxxxv]. [2500.]

CHRISTIAN SCHÖTTGEN, Inventarium diplomaticum historiæ Saxoniæ superioris ... so viel deren

im öffentlichen druck zu haben. Halle i. M. 1747.
pp.[xxii].coll.818.pp.[xlii]. [10,000.]

CHRISTIAN GOTTLIEB BUDER, Kurze anzeige der
mehresten kayserlichen lehen-briefe auch anwart-
schaften und confirmationen derer privilegien des
chur- und fürstl. hauses Sachsen. Jena 1757. pp.48.
[117.]

POLYCARP GOTTLIEB HEMPEL, Inventarium diplomaticum historiæ Saxoniæ inferioris et omnium
ditionum brunsvico-luneburgicarum. Das ist: verzeichniss derer urkunden . . . in chronologischer
ordnung von 786 bis 1778. Hannover &c. [vol.iv:
Göttingen &c.] 1785-1798. pp.[viii].coll.392+
pp.[viii].coll.466 + pp.[viii].coll.418 + pp.[viii].
coll.520. [17,500.]

BENJAMIN GOTTFRIED WEINART, Versuch einer
litteratur der sächsischen geschichte und staats-
kunde. Dresden &c. 1790-1791. pp.[xvi].776+
xvi.670. [12,500.]
reissued at Leipzig in 1805 as a 'neue auflage'.

JOHANN CHRISTOPH ADELUNG, Kritisches verzeichniss der landkarten und vornehmsten topo-
graphischen blätter des chur- und fürstlich-
Sächsischen landes. Meissen 1796. pp.[x].310.
[2000.]

JOHANN CHRISTOPH ADELUNG, Directorium, d.i. chronologisches verzeichniss der quellen der südsächsischen geschichte sofern selbige aus geschichtschreibern aller art . . . bestehen. Meissen 1802. pp.lviii.250. [890.]

PH[ILIPPE] GUIGNARD, Rapport sur les papiers de s.a.r. le prince Xavier de Saxe, conservés dans les archives du département de l'Aube. Dijon 1853. pp.xi.19. [5000.]

ADOLF ULRICH, Katalog der bibliothek des Historischen vereins für Niedersachsen. Erstes heft. Repertorium der urkunden, akten, handschriften, karten . . . und der gräflich Oeynhausenschen handschriften. Hannover 1888. pp.viii.193. [2250.]

WALTHER SCHULTZE, Die geschichtsquellen der provinz Sachsen im mittelalter und in der reformationszeit. Historische commission der provinz Sachsen: Halle 1893. pp.vii.202. [3000.]

J. J. VERNIER [*and others*], Inventaire sommaire des archives départementales antérieures à 1790. Aube. Série E* (fonds de Saxe). . . . Première partie. Archives particulières du prince Xavier de Saxe. Troyes 1903–   . pp.   +413+328.
in progress.

RUDOLF BEMMANN [vol.iii: and JAKOB JATZ-
WAUK], Bibliographie der sächsischen geschichte.
Königlich sächsische kommission für geschichte:
Leipzig &c.

    i. Landesgeschichte. 1918–1921. pp.xiv.xii.
       521+xviii.614. [25,000.]
    ii. Geschichte der landesteile. 1923. pp.xi.199.
       [2000.]
    iii. Ortsgeschichte. 1928–1932. pp.[v].349+
       [v].371. [15,000.]

GEORG DUTSCHMANN, Literatur zur vor- und
frühgeschichte Sachsens. Mannus-bibliothek (no.
27): Leipzig 1921. pp.[v].32. [650.]

FRIEDRICH BUSCH, Bibliographie der niedersächsischen geschichte für die jahre 1908–1932.
Historische kommission für Hannover, Olden-
burg, Braunschweig, Schaumburg-Lippe und
Bremen: Veröffentlichungen (vol.xvi): Hildes-
heim &c. 1938. pp.xix.749. [10,615.]

[HURST SCHLECHTE and HARALD SCHIECKEL, *edd.*],
Übersicht über die bestände des Sächsischen landeshauptarchivs und seiner landesarchive. Säch-
sisches landeshauptarchiv Dresden: Schriftenreihe
(no.1): Leipzig 1955. pp.295. [very large number.]

GÜNTHER MÖHLMANN and JOSEPH KÖNIG, Geschichte und bestände des Niedersächsischen

staatsarchivs in Aurich. Niedersächsische archivverwaltung: Veröffentlichungen (no.5): Göttingen 1955. pp.282. [very large number.]

HARALD SCHIECKEL, Regesten der urkunden des
Sächsischen landeshauptarchivs Dresden. Berlin.
   i. 948–1300. 1960. pp.579. [2030.]
in progress.

HERMANN KLEINAU, Übersicht über die bestände
des Niedersächsischen staatsarchivs in Wolfen-
büttel. Veröffentlichungen (no.17 &c.): Göttingen
1963 &c.
  in progress.

Scandinavia.

CATALOGUS der geschiedenis. Skandinavië.
Koninklijke bibliotheek: [The Hague] 1904. pp.
[iii].20. [700.]

MATERIALS in the National archives relating to
the scandinavian countries. National archives:
Reference information circular (no.5): [Wash-
ington] 1942. pp.5. [very large number.]*

Scarborough.

[I. H. JEAYES], Description of documents contained in the white vellum book of the Scar-

borough corporation. Scarborough [printed] 1914. pp.99. [500.]

I. H. JEAYES, Catalogue of ancient documents belonging to the corporation of Scarborough. [Scarborough] 1915. pp.[141]. [10,000.]

Schanfigg.

CONRADIN VON MOHR, Die regesten der landschaft Schanfigg im canton Graubünden. Regesten der archive in der Schweizerischen eidgenossenschaft (vol.i, part 3): Chur 1850. pp.45–59.xliv. [100.]

Schaumburg.

FRANZ ENGEL, Die Schaumburg-Lippischen archive und zentralen registraturen. Ihre geschichte und ihr inhalt. Niedersächsische archivverwaltung: Veröffentlichungen (no.4): Göttingen 1955. pp.109. [very large number.]

Scheldt.

INVENTARIS op het Archieffonds van handel en scheepvaart. . . . Aanhangsel. Inventaris op den bundel juridictie op de Schelde. Stadsarchief: Antwerpen 1925. pp.35. [5000.]

Europe

Schiedam.

W. HEERINGA, Het oud-archief der gemeente Schiedam. Schiedam 1908. pp.203.

J. N. M. DRESCH, Inventaris van de oude kerkelijke doop-, trouw- en overlijdensregisters te Schiedam, 1574–1812. Schiedam 1917. pp.21.

Schleswig-Holstein.

JOHAN MOLLER, Introductio in ducatum Cimbricorum, Slesvicensis et Holsatici historiam . . . quadripartita: scripta, quibus illorum topographia, historia, archæologia, & jura 'επιχώρια, vel comprehenduntur, vel illustrantur . . . percensens. Hamburgi 1699. pp.64.[xxxii].292.648. [2000.]

JOHAN MOLLER, Cimbria literata, sive scriptorum ducatus utriusque Slesvicensis et Holsatici, qvibus et alii vicini qvidam accensentur, historia literaria tripartita. Havniæ 1744. pp.[viii].36.752 +[ii].1045+[iv].672.[lvi]. [25,000.]

H. RATJEN, Verzeichniss der handschriften der Kieler universitätsbibliothek, welche die geschichte der herzogthümer Schleswig und Holstein betreffen. Kiel.

    i. Die handschriften zur allgemeinen geschichte. 1847. pp.296. [2000.]

ii. Zur speciellen geschichte und zu dem rechte der herzogthümer. Schleswig-Holstein-Lauenburgische gesellschaft für vaterländische geschichte: Nordalbingische studien, Neues archiv (vol.v, beilage): 1848–1854. pp.xliii.444. [2000.]

EDUARD BALDAMUS, Schleswig-Holstein-literatur. Verzeichniss der in den jahren 1863 und 1864 mit bezug auf die herzogthümer und den deutsch-dänischen krieg erschienenen bücher, karten und pläne. Prag 1865. pp.31. [300.]

EDUARD ALBERTI, Register über die zeitschriften und sammelwerke für schleswig-holstein-lauenburgische geschichte. Kiel 1873. pp.xii.543. [10,000.]

GEORG HILLE, Übersicht über die bestände des K. staatsarchivs zu Schleswig. Mittheilungen der K. preussischen archivverwaltung (no.4): Leipzig 1900. pp.[iii].54. [10,000.]

ERLING STENSGÅRD, Supplément nécessaire de la Bibliographie der neueren deutschen kriegsgeschichte... von Albert Budecke.... Remarques critiques suivies d'une liste de livres sur la deuxième guerre du Slesvig. Samfund Regenburgs minde: Smaaskrifter (no.1): Aarhus 1915. pp.15. [35.]

WILHELM JENSEN, Die kirchenbücher Schleswig-Holsteins, des landesteils Lübeck und der hansestädte. Quellen und forschungen zur familiengeschichte Schleswig-Holsteins (vol.ii): Neumünster 1936. pp.104. [600.]

Schooten.

P. N. VAN DOORNINCK, Inventaris van de oude archieven der gemeenten Schooten en Spaarndam. Haarlem 1894. pp.139. [large number.]

Schuttbourg.

N. VAN WERVEKE, Archives de Betzdorf et de Schuttbourg. Institut grand-ducal de Luxembourg: Section historique: Publications (vol.lv): Luxembourg 1908. pp.[vi].338. [934.]

Scotland.

1. *Cartography*

CATALOGUE of the maps and plans and other

publications of the Ordnance survey of Scotland.
1880. pp.82. [2000.]
— [another edition]. 1892. pp.112. [3000.]

HARRY R. G. INGLIS, JOHN MATHIESON and
C. B. BOOG WATSON, The early maps of Scotland.
Royal scottish geographical society: Edinburgh
1934. pp.120. [1000.]
—— Second edition. By a committee of the
Royal scottish geographical society. 1936. pp.171.
[1500.]

2. *History*

W[ILLIAM] NICOLSON, The scottish historical
library: containing a short view and character of
most of the writers, records, registers, law-books,
&c. which may be serviceable to the undertakers
of a general history of Scotland down to the
Union of the two Kingdoms in K. James the VI.
1702. pp.[ii].4.xl.376. [500.]
*page 241 is followed by pages 241†–256†; sub-
sequent editions form part of Nicholson's* The english
scotch and irish historical libraries, *which is entered
under Great Britain: History, above.*

[SIR JOSEPH AYLOFFE], Calendar of the ancient
charters, &c. and of the welch and scotish rolls,
now remaining in the Tower of London: as also
calendars of all the teaties of peace, &c. entered

into by the kings of England with those of Scotland; and of sundry letters and public instruments relating to that kingdom, now in the Chapterhouse at Westminster. Together with catalogues of the records brought to Berwick from the Royal treasury at Edinburgh; of such as were transmitted to the Exchequer at Westminster, and of those which were removed to different parts of Scotland by order of king Edward I. 1772. pp. [iii].lxx.462.[xxxii]. [5000.]

reissued in 1774 with the author's name.

AN INDEX, drawn up about the year 1629, of many records of charters, granted by the different sovereigns of Scotland between the years 1309 and 1413, most of which records have been long since missing. Published . . . by William Robertson. Edinburgh 1798. pp.liii.196. [3000.]

[JEAN BAPTISTE THÉODORE ALEXANDRE] TEULET, Inventaire chronologique des documents relatifs à l'histoire d'Écosse conservés aux Archives du royaume à Paris, suivi d'une indication sommaire des manuscrits de la Bibliothèque royale. Société d'Abbotsford [Abbotsford club]: Édimbourg 1839. pp.[ix].132. [500.]

covers the period 1249-1666.

MARKHAM JOHN THORPE, Calendar of the state

papers, relating to Scotland, preserved in the state paper department of her majesty's Public record office . . . 1509–1589[–1603]. 1858. pp. xxviii.560+[v].561-1101. [10,000.]

THE RIDDELL papers: a catalogue of the annotated books & manuscripts of the late John Riddell. Edinburgh 1863. pp.xxiv.72. [300.]
50 copies privately printed.

JOSEPH BAIN, Calendar of documents relating to Scotland preserved in her majesty's Public record office, London . . . 1108–1272[–1509]. General register house: Edinburgh 1881–1888. pp.[iii].lxxvii.676 + lxiii.714 + lxxv.610 + xlvii. 679. [8250.]

MILLAR & BRYCE, Hand-book of records in h. m. General register house, Edinburgh. [Edinburgh] 1885. pp.92. [very large number.]

JOSEPH BAIN, The border papers. Calendar of letters and papers relating to the affairs of the borders of England and Scotland preserved in her majesty's Public record office, London . . . 1560–1594[–1603]. General register house: Edinburgh 1894–1896. pp.xlvii.762+xxvii.960. [2232.]

[CYR] ULYSSE [JOSEPH] CHEVALIER, Écosse. Topo-bibliographie. Montbéliard 1895. pp.25. [600.]

CALENDAR of the state papers relating to Scotland and Mary, queen of Scots, 1547–1603, preserved in the Public record office, the British museum, and elsewhere in England. General register house [vols.i–vii, x–xi]: Edinburgh [vol. ix: Glasgow].

> i. 1547–1563. Edited by Joseph Bain. 1898. pp.xliii.806. [1180.]
>
> ii. 1563–1569. 1900. pp.xxxix.842. [1229.]
>
> iii. 1569–1571. Edited by William K. Boyd. 1903. pp.xxxiii.832. [865.]
>
> iv. 1571–1754. 1905. pp.xxxiii.853. [871.]
>
> v. 1574–1581. 1907. pp.xxxv.823. [791.]
>
> vi. 1581–1583. 1910. pp.xxxix.837. [729.]
>
> vii. 1584–1585. 1913. pp.xxxi.736. [667.]
>
> viii. 1585–1586. 1914. pp.xxvii.758. [773.]
>
> ix. 1586–1588. 1915. pp.xvii.785. [605.]
>
> x. 1589–1593. Edited by W. K. Boyd and Henry W. Meikle. 1936. pp.xxxi.1028. [785.]
>
> xi. 1593–1595. Edited by Annie I. Cameron. 1936. pp.xxiv.805. [652.]
>
> xii. 1595–1597. Edited by M. S. Giuseppi. 1952. pp.xvi.658. [454.]

in progress.

CHARLES SANFORD TERRY, The rising of 1745. With a bibliography of jacobite history, 1689–

1788. Scottish history from contemporary writers (no.iii): 1900. pp.xv.322. [750.]
—— New edition. 1903. pp.xv.335. [800.]

M. LIVINGSTONE, A guide to the public records of Scotland deposited in h. m. General register house, Edinburgh. Edinburgh 1905. pp.xxvii.233. [very large number.]

CHARLES SANFORD TERRY, An index to the papers relating to Scotland described or calendared in the Historical mss. commission's reports. Glasgow 1908. pp.62. [large number.]

CHARLES SANFORD TERRY, A catalogue of the publications of scottish historical and kindred clubs and societies and of the volumes relative to scottish history issued by His majesty's stationery office, 1780–1908. Glasgow 1909. pp.xiii.253. [1000.]
—— 1908–1927 . . . by Cyril Matheson. Aberdeen 1928. pp.viii.232. [500.]

[H. W. MEIKLE], A brief bibliography of scottish history for the use of teachers. Historical association: Leaflet (no.21): 1910. pp.8. [150.]
—— [another edition]. Historical association: Pamphlet (no.109): 1937. pp.23. [300.]

ARTHUR R. ANDERSON, A short bibliography on scottish history and literature. Saint Andrew society: Glasgow 1922. pp.43. [450.]

LIST of diplomatic documents, scottish documents and papal bulls. Public record office: Lists and indexes (no.xlix): 1923. pp.[ii].vi.324. [scottish: 500.]

A[NNA] J[EAN] MILL, Inventory of the early manuscript records of the older royal burghs of Scotland. St. Andrews university: Publications (no.xvii): St. Andrews 1923. pp.9. [100.]

SCOTTISH history, general, ecclesiastical, and literary. Revised edition. [National book council]: Bibliography (no.24): 1927. pp.[4]. [125.]

E. R. LINDSAY and A[NNIE] I[SABELLA] CAMERON, Calendar of scottish supplications to Rome, 1418–1422. Scottish history society: Publications (3rd ser., vol.xxiii): Edinburgh 1934. pp.xliii.335. [600.]

OFFICIAL guide to the documents in the historical museum of the Register house. Edinburgh 1952. pp.31. [30.]

JOHN DUNCAN MACKIE, Scottish history. National book league: Reader's guides (2nd ser., no.12): 1956. pp.39. [100.]

REGESTA regum Scotorum. Handlist of the acts of William [&c.]. [University of Edinburgh: Department of scottish history: Edinburgh].*

> 1165–1214. Compiled by G. W. S. Barrow and W. W. Scott. 1958. pp.[iv].47. [541.]
> — Addenda et corrigenda. pp.4.
> 1214–1249. Compiled by James M. Scoular. 1959. pp.[ii].64. [396.]
> 1249–1296. Compiled by Grant G. Simpson. 1960. pp.[ii].69. [423.]
> 1329–1371. Compiled by Bruce Webster. 1962. pp.[iii].121. [812.]

in progress.

3. *Topography*

DETAILED list of the old parochial registers of Scotland. Edinburgh 1872. pp.144. [901.]

SIR ARTHUR MITCHELL and C[ALEB] G[EORGE] CASH, A contribution to the bibliography of scottish topography. Scottish history society: Publications (2nd ser., vols.xiv–xv): 1917. pp.xii. 447+vi.449–706. [20,000.]

— — [supplement]. P[hilip] D[avid] Hancock, A bibliography of works relating to Scotland, 1916–1950. Edinburgh university: Edinburgh [1959–1960]. pp.x.244+viii.370. [12,000.]

INDEX to general register of sasines, 1701–1720. Record office, Scotland: Indexes (no.2): Edinburgh 1917. pp.[ii].iv.882. [25,000.]

INDEX to particular register of sasines for Argyle, Dumbarton, Bute, Arran and Tarbert, 1617–1780. Record office, Scotland: Indexes (no.9): Edinburgh 1926. pp.[iii].911. [27,500.]

READER's guide to books on the face of Scotland. Library association: County libraries section: [Readers' guide (new series, no.3): 1949]. pp.32. [400.]

Seaford.

FRANCIS W[ILLIAM] STEER, Records of the corporation of Seaford. A catalogue. East Sussex county council: Lewes 1959. pp.vi.66. [723.]

Seclin.

JULES FINOT and [J.] VERMAERE, Inventaire sommaire des archives communales antérieures à 1790. . . . Ville de Seclin. Lille 1888. pp.[iii].xii.74. [20,000.]

JULES FINOT and [J.] VERMAERE, Inventaire sommaire des archives hospitalières antérieures à 1790.

. . . Hôpital de Seclin. Lille 1892. pp.[iii].xxx.62. [25,000.]

Segré.

JACQUES LEVRON, Inventaire sommaire des archives départementales antérieures à 1790. Série E. . . . Tome v. Arrondissement de Segré. Angers 1945. pp.[v].336. [large number.]

Seine, department of the.

INVENTAIRE sommaire des archives de la Seine. [very large number.]
> Série D. AZ. Par Marius Barroux. 1935. coll. l.314. pp.[iv].315–351.
> Série V. Par M. Barroux [M. Thorlet]. 1892–1901. pp.[iii].iii.238+xiv.184.

ERN[EST] COYECQUE, Les archives anciennes des domaines de la Seine aux archives départementales. Saint-Denis [printed] 1894. pp.15. [600.]

MARIUS BARROUX, L'accroissement des séries anciennes aux archives de la Seine de 1889 à 1896. État sommaire. Saint-Denis [printed] 1896. pp.38. [2500.]

· LUCIEN LAZARD, Répertoire alphabétique du fonds des domaines. . . . Série des dossiers. Préfecture de la Seine: Archives départementales: 1904–1917. pp.[iii].xx.252+[iii].iii.168. [10,000.]

MARIUS BARROUX and HENRI LEMOINE, État méthodique des documents antérieurs au mois de juin 1871. Archives du département de la Seine et de la ville de Paris: 1925. pp.xiii.coll.110. [3000.]

MARIUS BARROUX and HENRI LEMOINE, État par série des documents antérieurs au mois de juin 1871. Archives du département de la Seine et de la ville de Paris: 1925. pp.xxii.42. [800.]

MONIQUE HÉBERT, JACQUES THIRION and SUZANNE OLIVIER, Catalogue général des cartes, plans et dessins d'architecture. Série N: Paris et le département de la Seine. Direction des archives de France: 1958. pp.xxi.427. [2256.]

Seine-et-Marne.

INVENTAIRE-sommaire des archives départementales. . . . Seine-et-Marne. Paris [*afterwards:* Fontainebleau]. [very large number.]
    Séries A–E. Par [Côme] Lemaire. 1863–1875.
        pp.12.10.45.50.3.292.89.3 + 9.11.313.35.3.
        131.2.
    Série E, supplément – I. 1880. pp.13.437.24.
        36.40.14.3.

Séries G–H. 1864. pp.7.114.219.338.2.

Série·L. Par A. Hugues [S. Canal et Jean Hubert]. 1904–1931. pp.xx.331+223.

[CÔME LEMAIRE], Relevé des documents intéressant le département de Seinte-et-Marne conservés dans les bibliothèques communales de Meaux, Melun et Provins; à la Bibliothèque nationale, à Paris; aux Archives nationales et aux archives des Ministères des finances et des travaux publics. Fontainebleau 1883. pp.[iii].v.335. [10,000.]

Seine-et-Oise.

INVENTAIRE sommaire des archives départementales. . . . Département de Seine-et-Oise. Versailles. [very large number.]

Série A. Par [Charles Marie Henry] Sainte-Marie-Mévil. 1862. pp.118.

Série D. Par E. Coüard. 1904. pp.l.403.

Série E. Par [C. M. H.] Sainte-Marie-Mévil [*and others*]. 1873–1897. pp.445+349+470 +360+lxxxi.431.

Série G. Par E. Coüard. 1895. pp.viii.462.

Série H. Par H[enri] Lemoine. 1944. pp.vii. 180.

Série J. Par H. Lemoine et S. Bouyssié. 1954. pp.32.

Série L. 1911. pp.xlv.499.
Série M. 1936. pp.12.
Série Q. 1950. pp.133.
Série T. 1942. pp.9.
Série V. Par E. Houth. 1942. pp.21.
Série Y. Par Lucien Leroy. 1953. pp.15.
in progress.

[LOUIS REGNIER and J. DEPOIN], Bibliographie historique du Vexin et du département de Seine-et-Oise, pendant les années 1885, 1886 et 1887. Société historique et archéologique de l'arrondissement de Pontoise et du Vexin: Mémoires (vol.xii): 1889. pp.[ii].97. [433.]
the section of mss. is not limited in date.

[ÉMILE] COÜARD[-LUYS] [*and others*], Les sources de l'histoire de Seine-et-Oise. . . . Archives . . . cartulaires . . . épigraphie . . . cartographie . . . monographies communales. Société archéologique de Rambouillet: Versailles 1903. pp.62. [large number.]
also issued, in a slightly different form, by the Société historique et archéologique de Corbeil.

EDGAR MAREUSE, Bibliographie des cartes et documents cartographiques. Conférence des sociétés savantes . . . de Seine-et-Oise: Versailles [printed] 1903. pp.16. [50.]

ANDRÉ LESORT and A. MONIRA, Répertoire numérique de la série C (administrations provinciales). Archives départementales de Seine-et-Oise: Versailles 1912. pp.v.51.

ANDRÉ RHEIN, Bibliographie de l'histoire de Seine-et-Oise. Versailles.

1921. pp.28. [183.]
1922. pp.20. [127.]
1923. pp.20. [107.]
1924. pp.22. [167.]
1925. pp.20. [166.]
1926. pp.20. [189.]

ANDRÉ LESORT, Répertoire critique des anciens inventaires d'archives. Archives départementales de Seine-et-Oise: Versailles [printed] 1936. pp.19. [222.]

[JACQUES LEVRON], Petit guide des archives anciennes de Seine-et-Oise, suivi du catalogue des documents exposés. Archives nationales: 1955. pp.23.

Seine-Inférieure.

INVENTAIRE-sommaire des archives départementales. . . . Seine-Inférieure. Paris [*afterwards:* Rouen] 1864. [very large number.]

Séries C–D. Par Charles de Robillard de Beaurepaire [Jules Vernier]. 1864–1910. pp.18.340.121+300+209.

Série G. Par C. de Robillard de Beaurepaire [et J. Vernier]. 1868– . pp.42.442+xii. 468+482+490 ǀ 488+479+180+198+ viii.102.

Série T. 1908. pp.35.

Série V. 1907. pp.47.

in progress.

PAUL CHEVREUX and JULES VERNIER, Les archives de Normandie et de la Seine-Inférieure. État général des fonds. Rouen 1911. pp.xvi.50. [very large number.]

VICTOR SANSON, Répertoire bibliographique pour la période dite 'révolutionnaire' 1789–1801 en Seine-Inférieure. Rouen [vols.ii–v: Paris] [1911–1912. pp.[ii].278 + [v].279–473 + [iii]. 475–796+797–1090+[ii].1091–1329. [25,000.]

500 copies printed.

Selborne priory.

W[ILLIAM] DUNN MACRAY, Calendar of charters and documents relating to the possessions of Selborne and its priory preserved in the Muniment room of Magdalen college, Oxford. Hampshire

Record Society: 1891–1894. pp.xiv.177+x.122. [6000.]

Sélestat.

[   ] KLEITZ, Inventaire sommaire des archives communales antérieures à 1790. Ville de Sélestat. Strasbourg 1860. pp.8.46. [5000.]

Senlis.

EUG[ÈNE] MULLER, Analyse du cartulaire, des statuts, etc., de Notre-dame de Senlis, 1041–1395. Senlis [c.1875]. pp.ii.230. [401.]

ARMAND RENDU, Exposé du premier volume de l'inventaire-sommaire des archives de l'Oise. Les trois évêchés et chapitres cathédraux de Beauvais, Noyon et Senlis. Beauvais 1880. pp.45. [2500.]

Sens.

MAXIMILIEN QUANTIN, Inventaire-sommaire des archives communales antérieures à 1790. . . . Ville de Sens. Sens 1870. pp.[iii].12.3.2.4.17.7.21.4.3.4.7. [15,000.]

Sévigny-Waleppe.

[CHARLES] HENRI JADART and JULES PRILLIEUX, Les anciens registres paroissiaux de Sévigny-

Waleppe (Ardennes), 1608–1792. Leur dépouillement chronologique. Arcis–sur–Aube 1899. pp.51.
[large number.]

Shavington.

HENRY D. HARROD, The muniments of Shavington, being a catalogue of the deeds and writings
of the Shavington, Cloverly, irish and other
estates of Arthur Pemberton Heywood-Lonsdale.
Shrewsbury [printed] 1891. pp.[ii].v.216. [1750.]

Sheffield, city and diocese of.

W. T. FREEMANTLE, A bibliography of Sheffield
and vicinity. Section 1. To the end of 1700.
Sheffield 1911. pp.xviii.285. [1250.]
no more published.

[E. C.], Short bibliography of the history of
Sheffield. Historical association: Leaflet (no.25):
1911. pp.12. [150.]

T[HOMAS] WALTER HALL, Catalogue of the
charters, deeds and manuscripts in the Public
reference library at Sheffield. Sheffield 1912. pp.
vii.105. [300.]

T[HOMAS] WALTER HALL, Sheffield, 1297 to 1554.
A catalogue of the ancient charters belonging to

the . . . town and parish of Sheffield, . . . with abstracts of all Sheffield wills proved at York prior to 1554. Sheffield 1913. pp.vii.3–148. [200.]

T[HOMAS] WALTER HALL and A. HERMANN THOMAS, Descriptive catalogue of the charters, rolls, deeds, pedigrees, pamphlets, newspapers, monumental inscriptions, maps, and miscellaneous papers, forming the Jackson collection at the Sheffield public reference library. Sheffield 1914. pp.xvi.419. [1000.]

T[HOMAS] WALTER HALL, Sheffield and Rotherham from the 12th to the 18th century. A descriptive catalogue of miscellaneous charters and other documents . . . with abstracts of Sheffield wills proved at York from 1554 to 1560. Sheffield 1916. pp.viii.291. [400.]

T[HOMAS] WALTER HALL, Descriptive catalogue of charters, copy court rolls and deeds forming part of the Wheat collection at the Public reference library, Sheffield, and others from private collections, with abstracts of Sheffield wills proved at York from 1560 to 1566. Sheffield 1920. pp.xv.279. [400.]

T[HOMAS] WALTER HALL, Sheffield and its environs 13th to the 17th century. A descriptive catalogue of land charters & other documents forming the Brooke Taylor collection. Sheffield 1922. pp.vii.28. [16.]

T[HOMAS] WALTER HALL, Worsborough, Eckington and Sheffield. Descriptive catalogue of the Edmunds collection, including charters, court-rolls and estreats. Sheffield 1924. pp.[ix].323. [400.]

T[HOMAS] WALTER HALL, Sheffield, Hallamshire. A descriptive catalogue of Sheffield manorial records. Sheffield 1926–1934. pp.xxxi.237+x.272 +xi.194. [750.]

W. ODOM, A bibliography of Sheffield history. Sheffield 1930. pp.85–98. [300.]

T[HOMAS] WALTER HALL, A descriptive catalogue of ancient charters & instruments relating to lands near Sheffield in the counties of York, Derby, Nottingham & Lincoln. Sheffield 1935. pp.[iii]. v.101. [150.]

A GUIDE to the Fairbank collection of maps, plans and surveyors' books and correspondence in the Reference library. City libraries: Sheffield 1936. pp.[ii].22. [13,636.]

T[HOMAS] WALTER HALL, A descriptive catalogue of charters and manorial records relating to lands in Tankersley, Fanshawe Gate, Dinnington & Longshaw in the neighbourhood of Sheffield. Sheffield 1937. pp.[ii].iv.86. [150.]

т[HOMAS] WALTER HALL, A descriptive catalogue of early charters relating to lands in & near Sheffield. Sheffield [printed] 1938. pp.[iii].46. [60.]

BASIC books on Sheffield history. City libraries: Sheffield 1950. pp.15. [147.]
— [another edition]. 1958. pp.16. [200.]

[A SURVEY of the ecclesiastical archives of the diocese of Sheffield]. Pilgrim trust: Survey of ecclesiastical archives: [1952]. ff.7. [large number.]*

Sherborne.

A CALENDAR of the charters, rolls and other documents . . . contained in the Muniment room at Sherborne house . . . belonging to . . . Sherborne [s.l.] 1900. pp.xiii.276. [1250.]
privately printed.

Shrewsbury.

CALENDAR of the muniments & records of the borough of Shrewsbury. Shrewsbury 1896. pp.[iv].136. [50,000.]

Shropshire.

SHROPSHIRE topographical manuscripts in the British museum. [*s.l.* 1890]. pp.29. [600.]

COMMISSIONERS' awards for inclosing lands, 1773–1891, together with a list of the awards deposited at the Public record office, and of those named in the Interim report of the Clerk and Deputy clerk of the County council. Shropshire county records (no.1): [1901]. pp.19. [2000.]

LANCELOT J. LEE, A full list and partial abstract of the contents of the quarter sessions rolls, 1696–1800. Shropshire county records [no.6]: [*s.l.* 1901]. pp.142. [5000.]

—— 1801–1820 (January). By L. J. Lee and R. G. Venables . . . (no.10): [1905]. pp.viii.143–249. [4000.]

PLANS and documents relating to roads, bridges, railways, canals, water, gas, &c., &c. deposited with the Clerk of the peace for the county of Salop. Shropshire county records [no.8]: Shrewsbury 1902. pp.xii.54. [640.]

GEORGE F. MATTHEWS, Shropshire probates in the Prerogative court of Canterbury, 1700–1749. Camberley, Surrey 1928. pp.68. [1000.]

Europe

A GUIDE to the Shropshire records. Salop county council: Shrewsbury 1952. pp.172. [2000.]

Siena.

[ALESSANDRO LISINI], Inventario delle pergamene conservate nel diplomatico dall'anno 736 all'anno 1250. Parte prima. Reale archivio di stato: Siena 1908. pp.xiv.449. [4000.]

FEDOR [HEINRICH GUSTAV HERMANN] SCHNEIDER, Regestum senense. Regesten der urkunden von Siena. . . . Band I, bis zum frieden von Poggibonsi, 713–30 Juni 1235. Königliches preussisches historisches institut: Istituto storico italiano: Regesta chartarum Italiae: Roma 1911. pp.xcv.460. [1029.]

ALESSANDRO LISINI, Indice di due antichi libri di imbreviature notarili. Commissione senese di storia patria: Siena 1912. pp.xviii.147. [1000.]
also issued as a supplement to vols.xviii–xix (1911–1912) of the Bollettino senese di storia patria.

GUIDA–INVENTARIO dell'archivio di stato . . . di Siena. Ufficio degli archivi di stato: Roma 1951. pp.xxiv.308+[iii].298. [very large number.]

ARCHIVIO del Consiglio generale del comune di Siena. Inventario. Pubblicazioni degli archivi di stato (vol.ix): Roma 1952. pp.xxiii.156. [1000.]

ARCHIVIO del consistoro del comune di Siena. Inventario. Pubblicazioni degli archivi di stato (vol.x): Roma 1952. pp.xxvii.526. [2675.]

ARCHIVIO della Biccherna del comune di Siena. Inventario. Pubblicazioni degli archivi di stato (vol.xii): Roma 1953. pp.xxxi.234. [1500.]

LE SALE della mostra e il museo delle tavolette dipinte. Catalogo. Pubblicazioni degli archivi di stato (vol.xxiii: Archivio di stato di Siena): Roma 1956. pp.xviii.163. [526.]

ARCHIVIO di Balia. Inventario. Pubblicazioni degli archivi di stato (vol.xxvi: Archivio di stato di Siena): Roma 1957. pp.lxxxv.471. [1124.]

ARCHIVIO dell'ospedale di s. Maria della Scala. Inventario. Pubblicazioni degli archivi di stato (vol.xxxvii &c.: Archivio di stato di Siena): Roma 1960 &c.

in progress.

Silesia.

CHRISTIAN RUNGE, Miscellanea literaria, de qvibusdam ineditis historiæ silesiacæ scriptoribus ac operibus. [Specimen I–IV]. Olsnæ [Wratislaviæ] 1712–1717. pp.[viii].24 + [viii].25–48 + [iv].49–761+[viii].77–112. [100.]

CHRISTIAN RUNGE, Notitia historicorvm et historiae gentis silesiacae. Pars I. Vratislaviae 1775. pp.[xxiv].264. [2000.]

no more published.

[G. A. H. STENZEL], Notitia librorum manuscriptorum, historiam silesiacam spectantium, quos servat bibliotheca academica. Universitatis literariae vratislaviensis rector C. A. D. Unterholzner cum senatu auspici novi rectoratus a successore suo ... rite capienda indicit: Vratislaviae [1821]. pp.10. [20.]

[—] — Continuatio. Universitatis literariae vratislaviensis rector H. Steffens [&c.]: [1822]. pp.8. [30.]

CODEX diplomaticus Silesiae. Verein für geschichte und alterthum Schlesiens: Breslau 1857 &c.

in progress.

H[ANS] BELLÉE, Literatur zur schlesischen geschichte für die jahre 1920–1922. Historische kommission für Schlesien: Breslau 1924. pp.[iv].77. [1026.]

SCHLESISCHE bibliographie. Historische kommission für Schlesien: Breslau.

i. Viktor Loewe, Bibliographie der schlesischen geschichte. 1927. pp.xii.587. [7300.]

ii. Ernst Boehlich, Bibliographie der schlesischen vor- und frühgeschichte. 1929. pp. xiv.400. [4750.]

iii. — Bibliographie der schlesischen volkskunde. 1929–1930. pp.xxi.456+[iii].xxxii. 457–877. [10,080.]

BIBLIOGRAFIA historii Śląska. Wrocławskie towarzystwo Milośników historii: Wrocław.

1939–1946. Zestawił Karol Maleczyński. 1954. pp.168. [4215.]

1948–1955. 1961. pp.192. [5402.]
in progress.

Sinigaglia.

ALFREDO MARGUTTI, Bibliografía storica marchigiana. Saggio di bibliografia sinigagliese ossi cenni sulle principali opere risguardanti la città di Sinigaglia. . . . I. Roma 1883. pp.47. [150.]
no more published.

Sinnich, convent of.

G. D. FRANQUINET, Beredeneerde inventaris der oorkonden en bescheiden van de abdij Kloosterrade en van de adellijke vrouwenkloosters

Marienthal en Sinnich. Beredeneerde inventaris der oorkonden en bescheiden berustende op't Provinciaal archief van Limburg (vol.i): Maastricht 1869. pp.viii.311. [Sinnich: 150.]

Sint-Albert.

H. COPPEJANS-DESMEDT, Inventaris van het archief van de heerlijkheid en van de polder van Sint-Albert. Rijksarchief te Gent: Brussel 1960. pp.79. [large number.]

Sittard.

G. D. FRANQUINET, Overzicht der gemeente-archieven en beredeneerde inventaris der oorkonden en bescheiden van de gemeenten Sittard en Venlo. Maastricht 1872. pp.137.

MARTIN JANSEN, Inventaris van het oud archief der gemeente Sittard . . . 1243–1609[–1794]. Sittard [vol.ii: Roermond] [1878–1880]. pp.[iii]. 209+[vi].142. [1000.]

Sixt, abbey of.

A[DRIEN] GAVARD, *ed*. Les archives de l'abbaye de Sixt avant la révolution. Inventaires inédits de 1729 et 1754. Annecy 1911. pp.88. [1000.]

Sleidinge.

J. BUNTINX, Inventarissen. Land van de Woestijne en heerlijkheid Woeste, keure van Sleidinge, Daknam. Rijksarchief te Gent: Brussel 1957. pp. 43. [large number.]

Slovakia.

BIBLIOGRAFIA slovenskej historie. Turč. sv. Martin.

    1939–1941. 1944. pp.56. [500.]
    1942–1944. 1948. pp.122. [1000.]

TEODOR LAMOŠ, Bibliografia k archívom na Slovensku. Slovenský ústredný archív a publikačný ústav poverenictva vnutra: Bratislave 1953. pp.187. [very large number.]

Sodor and Man, diocese of.

[A SURVEY of the ecclesiastical archives of the diocese of Sodor and Man]. Pilgrim trust: Survey of ecclesiastical archives: [1952]. ff.8. [large number.]*

Soignies.

AMÉ DEMEULDRE, Archives des hospices civils de la ville de Soignies, colligées et inventoriées. Soignies [1896]. pp.40. [500.]

Soissons.

AUGUSTE MATTON, Inventaire-sommaire des archives hospitalières de Soissons antérieures à 1790. Laon 1874. pp.[iii].236.36. [50,000.]

Sologne.

ESSAIS bibliographiques pour servir à l'histoire de la Sologne. Romorantin [printed] 1894. pp.32. [450.]

Someren.

J. CUNEN, Inventaris van het archief der gemeente Someren. Someren 1940. pp.216.

Somersetshire.

ARTHUR L. HUMPREYS, Somersetshire parishes. A handbook of historical reference to all places in the county. 1906. pp.xv.384+[iii].385–857. [25,000.]

T[HOMAS] CHUBB, A descriptive list of the printed maps of Somersetshire, 1575–1914. Somersetshire archæological and natural history society: Taunton 1914. pp.xii.232. [500.]

J. E. KING, Inventory of parochial documents in the diocese of Bath and Wells and the county of Somerset. Somerset county council: County records committee (book i): Taunton 1938. pp. xv.400. [large number.]

[A. R. CASS], A handlist of the records of the boards of guardians in the county of Somerset preserved in the Somerset record office. Somerset county council: County records committee: Taunton 1949. pp.129. [very large number.]

SOMERSET in manuscript. Notes on the main archive groups preserved in the Somerset record office, with a description of documents selected for exhibition. Somerset county council: Records committee: [Taunton] 1959. pp.xiv.36. [141.]

Somme.

INVENTAIRE sommaire des archives départementales. . . . Somme. Amiens [very large number.]

> Séries A–B. Par Louis Boca et Armand Rendu. 1883. pp.xiv.440.
> Série B. Deuxième édition. Par Georges Durand. 1920. pp.[iii].444.
> Série C. Par G. Durand. 1888–1897. pp.xxiv. 452+[iii].504+vi.592.
> Série E, supplément. Par G. Durand et Joseph Estienne. 1929. pp.664.

Série G. Par G. Durand. 1902–1910. pp. xiv.632+640.

Série L. Par G. Durand et J. Estienne. 1925. pp.viii.512.

Série O. Par J. Estienne. 1921. pp.144.

Série Q. 1940. coll.102.

Série T. 1950–

in progress.

MARCEL GODET, *ed.* Les brûlements d'archives à Abbeville pendant la révolution. État sommaire des documents disparus. Étude accompagnée de la publication du registre de dépôt des titres féodaux. 1913. pp.162. [1500.]

Soria.

JOSÉ ANTONIO PEREZ-RIOJA, Exposición bibliográfica Soriana (libros, folletos, mapas). Casa de cultura: Soria 1960. pp.36. [487.]

Southampton.

JOHN CORDY JEAFFRESON, List of charters, letters patent, and other muniments of the corporation of Southampton. Borough of Southampton: Southampton 1886. pp.[ii].36. [large number.]

[JOHN CORDY JEAFFRESON], The manuscripts of the corporations of Southampton and King's

Lynn. Eleventh report of the Royal commission on historical manuscripts (appendix iii): 1887. pp.xv.292. [Southampton: 4000.]

PROGRAMME of the charter commemorations. [Catalogue of exhibition of charters, documents, regalia and plate . . . arranged by G. L. Conran . . . and Norman Cook]. Town and county of Southampton: 1947. pp.32. [20.]

Southwark, borough and diocese of.

JOHN GREGORY CRACE, A catalogue of maps, plans and views of London, Westminster & Southwark collected . . . by Frederick Crace. 1878. pp.xxii.696. [1000.]
the collection is now in the British museum.

[A SURVEY of the ecclesiastical archives of the diocese of Southwark]. Pilgrim trust: Survey of ecclesiastical archives: [1952]. ff.7. [large number.]*

Southwell, diocese of.

[A SURVEY of the ecclesiastical archives of the diocese of Southwell]. Pilgrim trust: Survey of ecclesiastical archives: [1952]. ff.15. [large number.]*

Europe

Spaarndam.

P. N. VAN DOORNINCK, Inventaris van de oude archieven der gemeenten Schooten en Spaarndam. Haarlem 1894. pp.139.

Spaarnwoude.

P. N. VAN DOORNINCK, Inventaris van het oud-archief der gemeente Spaarnwoude en Haarlemmerliede. Haarlem 1894. pp.72.

Europe

1. *Cartography*

CATÁLOGO de las obras que se hallan de venta en el mismo. Depósito geográfico e histórico del ejército: Madrid 1929. pp.16. [300.]

2. *Colonies*

RAFAEL ALTAMIRA [ALTAMIRA Y CREVEA], Bibliographie d'histoire coloniale (1900–1930). Espagne. Société de l'histoire des colonies françaises: 1932. pp.3–71. [900.]

3. *Crown*

[JULIÁN PAZ and] AMALIA PRIETO CANTERO, Patronato real, 1834–1851. Edición completa.

Europe

Archivo general de Simancas: Catálogo (no.v): Valladolid 1946–1949. pp.ix.593+754. [7887.]

4. Foreign relations

General

ÍNDICES generales de los tratados, convenios y otros documentos de carácter internacional firmados por España, asi como de las leyes, decretos y reales órdenes que afectan á las relaciones exteriores desde 1801 á 1897 inclusives. Madrid 1900. pp.440. [2500.]

J[OSÉ] LÓPEZ OLIVÁN, Repertorio diplomático español. Índice de los tratados ajustados por España (1125–1935) y de otros documentos internacionales. Consejo superior de investigaciones científicas: Instituto Francisco de Vitoria: Colección de fuentes de derecho internacional: Madrid 1944. pp.671. [2175.]

America

CRISTÓBAL BERMÚDEZ PLATA, Archivo general de Índias. Catálogo de documentos de la sección novena: 'Papeles de estado'. I. Santo Domingo, Cuba, Puerto-Rico, Luisiana y Florida. II. México. Escuela de estudios hispano-americanos: Sevilla 1949. pp.822. [large number.]

Europe

Austria. see Germany

France

[LOUIS PROSPER] GACHARD, Notice sur la collection dite des archives de Simancas, qui est conservée aux Archives de l'empire, à Paris. Bruxelles [1862]. pp.72. [25,000.]

JULIÁN PAZ, Archivo general de Simancas. Catálogo IV. Secretaría de estado. (Capitulaciones con Francia y negociaciones diplomáticas de los embajadores de España en aquelle corte . . .) . . . I. (1265–1714). Junta para ampliación de estudios é investigaciones científicas: Centro de estudios históricos: Madrid 1914. pp.xii.907. [12,500.]
no more published.

[JOSEPH XAVIER ALEXANDRE TAUSSERAT-RADEL], Inventaire sommaire des archives du département des affaires étrangères. Correspondance politique. II. Deuxième partie. Espagne. 1919. pp.[iii].768. [100,000.]

A[LFRED] MOREL-FATIO, Catalogue des manuscrits de m. Morel-Fatio et de H. Léonardon données à la Bibliothèque municipale de Versailles. Bordeaux [1912]. pp.71. [2500.]

JULIÁN PAZ, Catálogo de documentos españoles existentes en el archivo del Ministerio de negocios extranjeros de París. Instituto de Valencia de don Juan: Madrid 1932. pp.iii–xxiii.402. [2000.]

JULIÁN PAZ, Documentos relativos a España existentes en los Archivos nacionales de París . . . 1276 a 1844. Instituto de Valencia de don Juan: Madrid 1934. pp.xi.388. [2000.]

JOSÉ SIMÓN DIAZ, Francia (1501–1600). Instituto nacional del libro español: Departamento de bibliografía: Cien fichas sobre . . . (no.4): Madrid 1959. pp.8. [100.]

this is a list of spanish books of the 16th century bearing on franco-spanish relations; 100 copies printed.

Germany

JULIÁN PAZ, Secretaría de estado. Capitulaciones con la casa de Austria y negociaciones de Alemania, Sajonia, Polonia, Prusia y Hamburgo, 1493–1796. . . . Secunda edición. Consejo superior de investigaciones científicas: Instituto Jerónimo Zurita: Archivo general de Simancas (catálogo ii): Madrid 1942. pp.427. [large number.]

Great Britain

CALENDAR of letters, despatches, and state papers, relating to the negotiations between England and Spain, preserved in the archives at Simancas and elsewhere.

Europe

i. 1485–1509. By G[ustav] A[dolph] Bergen-roth. 1862. pp.[v].cxlvi.472. [605.]

ii. 1509–1525. 1866. pp.ccxix.864. [722.]

— Supplement to volume I. and volume II. 1868. pp.lxxx.468. [104.]

iii. 1525–1529. By Pascual de Gayangos. 1873–1877. pp.[vi].xxxix.1060 + [vi]. xxxvi.1116. [1329.]

iv. 1529–1533. 1879–1882. pp.[vi].xxviii.903 +[vi].xxxii.624+[vi].625–1144. [1189.]

v. 1534–1538. 1886–1888. pp.[vi].xiv.690+ [vi].xx.660. [485.]

vi. 1538–1543. 1890–1895. pp.[iv].xxxii.660 +[iv].li.740. [545.]

vii. [1544]. 1899. pp.[iv].xliii.524. [260.]

viii. 1545–1546. By Martin A. S. Hume. 1904. pp.xlix.642. [483.]

ix. 1547–1549. By M. A. S. Hume and Royall Tyler. 1912. pp.lxiii.603. [400.]

x. 1550–1552. By R. Tyler. 1914. pp.lxi.650. [400.]

xi. 1553. 1916. pp.lvi.513. [400.]

xii. 1554. 1949. pp.xxviii.347. [250.]

xiii. 1554–1558. 1954. pp.xxvii.482. [503.]

MARTIN A. S. HUME, Calendar of letters and state papers relating to english affairs, preserved princi-pally in the archives of Simancas . . . 1558–1567

Europe

[–1603]. 1892–1899. pp.[v].lxiii.708+[iii].742+
[v].lvi.720+lxviii.782. [2401.]

A[LLEN] B[ANKS] HINDS, Descriptive list of state
papers, Foreign: Spain (S.P. 94), 1578–1659. Public record office: 1936. ff.i.219. [5000.]*

RICARDO MAGDALENO REDONDO, Secretario de
estado. Documentos relativos a Inglaterra, 1254–
1834. Consejo superior de investigaciones científicas [&c.]: Archivo general de Simancas: Catálogo
(no.xvii): Madrid 1947. pp.ix.599. [very large
number.]

Italy

ISIDORO CARINI, Gli archivi e le biblioteche di
Spagna in rapporto alla storia d'Italia in generale
e di Sicilia in particolare. Sovraintendenza agli
archivi siciliani: Relazioni, documenti ed allegati:
Palermo 1884[–1897]. pp.viii.547.civ+[iii].607.
[large number.]

ANTONIO ERA, Le raccolte di carte, specialmente
de re aragonesi e spagnoli (1620–1715) esistenti
nell'archivio del comune di Alghero. Sassari 1927.
pp.207. [496.]

RICARDO MAGDALENO REDONDO, Papeles de
estado de la correspondencia y negociación de
Nápoles. Consejo superior de investigaciones

científicas [&c.]: Archivo general de Simancas: Catálogo (no.xvi): Valladolid 1942. pp.xv.413. [large number.]

RICARDO MAGDALENO REDONDO, Papeles de estado. Sicilia. Virreinato español y negociación de Malta. Valladolid 1951. pp.518. [large number.]

EVANDRO PUTZULU, Carte reali aragonesi e spagnole dell'Archivio comunale di Cagliari (1358–1719). Archivio storico sardo (vol.xxvi): Padova 1959. pp.[iii].159. [468.]

Japan

JAMES A[LEXANDER] ROBERTSON, Bibliography of early spanish japanese relations. Compiled from manuscripts and books in the Philippine library, Manila. Asiatic society of Japan: Transactions (vol.xliii, part 1): [Tokyo] 1915. pp.[iv].iv.170. [250.]

Netherlands

JULIÁN PAZ, Archivo general de Simancas. Secretario de estado. Catálogo de los documentos de las negociaciones de Flandes, Holanda y Bruselas, 1506–1795. Paris 1915. pp.185. [5000.]

— — Segunda edición. Consejo superior de investigaciones científicas: Instituto Jerónimo Zurita: Madrid 1946. pp.451. [15,000.]

Europe

Norway

REIDAR [ADOLF PETER KARL] ØKSNEVAD, Spania i norsk litteratur. En bibliografi. Oslo 1947. pp.30. [450.]

Poland. see Germany

Portugal

FRANCISCO MANUEL ALVES, Catálogo dos manuscritos de Simancas respeitantes à história portuguesa. Coimbra 1933. pp.168. [large number.]

Romania

G[EORGE] BAICULESCU, AL. DUTU and DOROTHEA SASSU-TIMERMAN, Echos ibériques et hispano-américains en Roumanie. Bibliographie littéraire sélective. Commission nationale de la République Populaire Roumaine pour l'Unesco: Bucarest 1959. pp.124. [1000.]*

United States

WILLIAM R[OBERT] SHEPHERD, Guide to the materials for history of the United States in spanish archives (Simancas, the Archivo historico nacional, and Seville). Carnegie institution: Publication (no.91): Washington 1907. pp.[ii].107. [very large number.]

Europe

JAMES ALEXANDER ROBERTSON, List of documents in spanish archives relating to the history of the United States, which have been printed or of which transcripts are preserved in american libraries. Carnegie institution: Publication (no. 124): Washington 1910. pp.xv.368. [5332.]

Vatican

ARCHIVO de la embajada de España cerca de la santa sede. Índice analítico de los documentos del siglo XVI [&c.]. Roma.

    i. Siglo XVI. Por Luciano Serrano. 1915. pp. xxxii.138. [50,000.]

    ii. Siglo XVII. Por José M. Pou y Martí. 1917. pp.viii.325. [100,000.]

    iii. Siglo XVIII. 1921. pp.vii.407. [150,000.]

    iv. Primera mitad del siglo XIX. 1935 [1940]. pp.[vii].379. [150,000.]

    — Codices de la biblioteca contigua al archivo. 1925. pp.xii.296. [100,000.]

J[OSÉ] OLARRA GARMENDIA and MARÍA LUISA LARRAMENDI DE OLARRA, Índices de la correspondencia entre la nunciatura en España y la santa sede, durante el reinado de Felipe II. Real academia de la historia: Madrid 1948–1949. pp.iii–xv. 615+[iv].784. [9548.]

Europe

5. History

i. Bibliographies

AGUSTÍN MILLARES CARLO, Notas bibliográficas acerca de archivos municipales, ediciones de libros de acuerdo y colecciones de documentos concejiles. Dirección general de archivos y bibliotecas: Bibliografías de archivos y bibliotecas: Madrid 1952. pp.172. [300.]

ii. Manuscripts

FRANCISCO DÍAZ SÁNCHEZ, Guía de la villa y archivo de Simancas. Madrid 1885. pp.[vi].299. [30,000,000.]

CATÁLOGO de manuscritos españoles [reunidos] por don José Ignacio Miró. Serie primera. Privilegios, cartas, y otras manuscritos pertenecientes a los reinados de varios monarcas de España. Anvers 1886. pp.vii.89. [647.]

G[EORGES] DESDEVISES DU DEZERT, Les archives historiques nationales de Madrid. Historique et inventaire provisoire. Besançon 1901. pp.56. [many million.]

LÉOPOLD MICHELI, Inventaire de la collection Édouard Favre. (Archives de la maison d'Altamira). Bibliothèque publique et universitaire de Genève: Bordeaux &c. 1914. pp.viii.167. [5000.]

FRANCISCO RODRÍGUEZ MARÍN, Guía histórica y descriptiva de los archivos, bibliotecas y museos arqueológicos de España que están a cargo del Cuerpo facultativo del ramo. . . . Sección de archivos. Archivos históricos. Madrid 1916. pp. 828. [many million.]

P. MIGUÉLEZ, Catálogo de los códices españoles de la biblioteca del Escorial. I. Relaciones históricas. Madrid 1917–1925. pp.xlviii.363 + [iii].xi.368. [2308.]

MARIANO ALCOCER [Y MARTÍNEZ], Archivo general de Simancas. Guía del investigador. Valladolid 1923. pp.207. [30,000,000].

JOSÉ [MIGUEL ANDRÉS] TORRE REVELLO, Archivo general central de Alcalá de Henares. Reseña histórica y clasificación de sus fondos. Instituto de investigaciones históricas: Publicaciones (no.xxx): Buenos Aires 1926. pp.34. [very large number.]

FOURTEEN spanish manuscript documents. Hispanic society of America: Hispanic notes & monographs: New York 1926. pp.vii.9. [14.]